With this pathbreaking book Professor Feagin inverts the standard Black History Month narrative. It's not just that African Americans have made valuable contributions to American culture and history. His point is that fundamental aspects of American life simply wouldn't exist were it not for African Americans. This is an exciting reconceptualization of the place of African Americans in American life.

Kirk Johnson, *Sociology, University of Mississippi*

Joe Feagin, the nation's leading civil rights scholar, places African Americans at the heart of America's greatness. Fair, judicious, and exhaustively researched, this book analyzes the many contributions African Americans have made to our country since its inception. Feagin answers those who would have us believe that blacks are a "problem people," a national liability. Through the force of his inimitable scholarship, Feagin documents and discusses the exceptional assets African Americans have delivered to our country—in economics, law, science, culture, and spirituality—and to the global community as well. The great lesson of this book is that the black ethos is an emphatic representation of the American spirit, an ongoing demonstration of the hope and expectation that the poor and downtrodden can stand up against the system and succeed.

Roy L. Brooks, *University of San Diego School of Law*

In this very insightful and powerfully written book, Joe Feagin provides a necessary historical and political corrective. A tour-de-force through US history and its relationship to race and racism, Feagin thoroughly illustrates the positive and consequential contributions of Black Americans from art to entertainment to politics and social science. *How Blacks Built America* is an engaging and must-read text.

Marcus Anthony Hunter, *Sociology, UCLA, and author of* Black Citymakers: How the Philadelphia Negro Changed Urban America

Part history lesson, part sociology of race, and all searing, unflinching analysis. Feagin documents the substantial contributions blacks have made to many segments of US society. This book should put to rest the stereotypes and misconceptions of blacks as lazy, peripheral "takers" and give students a new way to think about the American economy, culture, and political system.

Adia Harvey Wingfield, *Sociology, Georgia State University*

D0141572

How Blacks Built America

How Blacks Built America examines the many positive and dramatic contributions made by African Americans to this country over its long history. Much public and scholarly discussion of African Americans accenting their distinctive societal position, especially discussion outside black communities, has emphasized either stereotypically negative features or the negative socioeconomic conditions that they have long faced because of systemic racism. In contrast, Feagin reveals that African Americans have long been an extraordinarily important asset for this country. Without their essential contributions, indeed, there probably would *not* have been a United States. This is an ideal addition to race and ethnicity courses.

Joe R. Feagin is Ella C. McFadden Professor in sociology at Texas A&M University. Feagin has done research on racism and sexism issues for decades. He has written 67 scholarly books and more than 200 scholarly articles in his research areas, and one of his books (*Ghetto Revolts*) was nominated for a Pulitzer Prize. His numerous Routledge books include *Systemic Racism: A Theory of Oppression* (2006); *Two Faced Racism: Whites in the Backstage and Frontstage* (2007, with L. H. Pica); *White Party, White Government: Race, Class, and U.S. Politics* (2012); *The White Racial Frame* (second edition, 2013); and *Racist America* (third edition, 2014).

Feagin is the 2012 recipient of the Soka Gakkai International-USA Social Justice Award; the 2013 American Association for Affirmative Action's Arthur Fletcher Lifetime Achievement Award; and the 2013 American Sociological Association's W. E. B. Du Bois Career of Distinguished Scholarship Award. He was the 1999–2000 president of the American Sociological Association.

RELATED TITLES FROM ROUTLEDGE

Racist America: Roots, Current Realities, and Future Reparations, Third Edition
Joe R. Feagin

The White Racial Frame: Centuries of Racial Framing and Counter-Framing, Second Edition
Joe R. Feagin

Yes We Can? White Racial Framing and the Obama Presidency, Second Edition
Adia Harvey Wingfield and Joe R. Feagin

White Party, White Government: Race, Class, and U.S. Politics
Joe R. Feagin

Racial Formation in the United States, Third Edition
Michael Omi and Howard Winant

Race, Law, and American Society: 1607–Present, Second Edition
Gloria J. Browne-Marshall

How Blacks Built America
Labor, Culture, Freedom, and Democracy

Joe R. Feagin

Routledge
Taylor & Francis Group

NEW YORK AND LONDON

First published 2016
by Routledge
711 Third Avenue, New York, NY 10017

and by Routledge
2 Park Square, Milton Park, Abingdon, Oxon, OX14 4RN

Routledge is an imprint of the Taylor & Francis Group, an informa business

© 2016 Taylor & Francis

The right of Joe R. Feagin to be identified as author of this work has been asserted by him in accordance with sections 77 and 78 of the Copyright, Designs and Patents Act 1988.

All rights reserved. No part of this book may be reprinted or reproduced or utilised in any form or by any electronic, mechanical, or other means, now known or hereafter invented, including photocopying and recording, or in any information storage or retrieval system, without permission in writing from the publishers.

Trademark notice: Product or corporate names may be trademarks or registered trademarks, and are used only for identification and explanation without intent to infringe.

Library of Congress Cataloging in Publication Data
Feagin, Joe R.
  How Blacks built America : labor, culture, freedom, and democracy / by Joe R. Feagin.
    pages cm
  Includes bibliographical references and index.
  1. African Americans—History. 2. African Americans—Civil rights—History. 3. African Americans—Intellectual life. 4. United States—Race relations. 5. Racism—United States. I. Title.
  E185.F36 2015
  973´.0496073-dc23   2015004282

ISBN: 978-0-415-70328-4 (hbk)
ISBN: 978-0-415-70329-1 (pbk)
ISBN: 978-0-203-79475-3 (ebk)

Typeset in Minion
by HWA Text and Data Management, London

Printed and bound in the United States of America by Publishers Graphics, LLC on sustainably sourced paper.

Contents

Preface   ix

Acknowledgments   xi

1   White Racism, Black Resistance: Seeking Freedom, Justice, and Democracy   1

2   Black Labor: Building the Economy   15

3   Black Genius Shaping U.S. Culture   49

4   Black Counter-Framing: Real Freedom, Justice, and Democracy (1600s–1910s)   93

5   Black Action: Accelerating Freedom, Justice, and Democracy (1700s–1800s)   121

6   Black Counter-Framing and Liberatory Action (1900s–1970s)   143

7   Contemporary Global Impacts: Freedom, Justice, and Democracy   177

Notes   203

Index   229

Preface

In recent years, we have heard many whites, especially conservatives, talk about the need to "take back our country." This comment often references the growing population of color and its increasing political power—dramatically signaled in the election of Barack Obama as the first president of color. This conventional white-racist framing of the country, and thus of African Americans, calls to mind the eloquent reply to white supremacists given by the African American scholar and human rights activist W. E. B. Du Bois at the turn of the twentieth century in *The Souls of Black Folk*:

> Your country? How came it yours? Before the Pilgrims landed we were here. Here we have brought our three gifts and mingled them with yours: a gift of story and song. . .; the gift of sweat and brawn to . . . lay the foundations of this vast economic empire . . . ; the third, a gift of the Spirit.[1]

In his path-breaking 1924 book, *The Gift of Black Folk,* Du Bois elaborated on aspects of these and other gifts of African Americans. Thus, it was black people who

> raised a vision of democracy in America such as neither [white] Americans nor Europeans conceived in the eighteenth century, and such as they have not even accepted in the twentieth century; and yet a conception which every clear sighted man knows is true and inevitable.[2]

Du Bois further assessed some scientific contributions made by African Americans during the slavery era and other important societal contributions made by African Americans then and later.

Over the centuries, many African American activists and interpreters of this country's long trajectory have emphasized similar themes. For instance, in a 1970 *Time* article titled "What America Would Be Like without Blacks," the black novelist Ralph Ellison reflected on this extraordinarily important gift of freedom, as had been seen in the recent civil rights movement:

> [I]t is the black American who puts pressure upon the nation to live up to its ideals. It is he who gives creative tension to our struggle for justice . . . . Without the black American, something irrepressibly hopeful and creative would go out of the American spirit.[3]

More recently, in a 2009 lecture on "Democracy, Social Change, and Civil Engagement," the African American scholar-activist Angela Davis critically examined Barack Obama's first election victory in historical and global perspective:

> But I do want us to relish this victory, to celebrate this moment, this historical conjuncture, to ride for a moment the wave of collective, global emotional solidarities occasioned by this triumph. I want us to relish it, not for what it portends, not for its consequences, but for what it means at this moment in history. For what it means to generations of people of African descent, generations of people of all racial and ethnic backgrounds here and abroad who learned how to place justice, equality, and peace before economic profit, before ideologies of racism. . . . So let us remember enslaved women and men who imagined and struggle for freedom. Let us remember the many activists in the 1930s and 1940s who paved the way for the freedom struggle of the 1950s and 1960s, those who dared to imagine a better place, a better world.[4]

Critical, research-based, and ever insightful African American commentaries like these provided the inspiration for this book. While I examine numerous aspects of what might be called "positive black exceptionalism" over centuries of this country's history, I give most attention to three broad areas of important African American impacts and societal contributions. Thus, I emphasize the centrality of African Americans (1) in providing the massive amounts of labor over centuries that generated much of the past and present development and wealth of this country; (2) in creating many of the cultural innovations, including scientific and technological achievements, that have made this country thrive and become globally influential; and (3) in constantly pressing this country's dominant leadership and institutions forward on issues of *real* liberty, justice, and democracy.

Acknowledgments

I am especially indebted to my talented and hardworking research assistants, Frank Ortega and Rachel Feinstein, and my indefatigable colleague, Kimberley Ducey, for significant library work, insightful suggestions, and copy reading assistance over the course of this long research project. I also thank the following colleagues for their unfailing willingness to discuss ideas and research issues in connection with various versions of this manuscript: Kirk Johnson, Cherise Harris, Ruth Thompson-Miller, Terence Fitzgerald, Joyce Bell, Marcus Hunter, Edna Chun, Glenn Bracey, Noel Cazenave, Aldon Morris, Larry Oliver, Earl Smith, Michael Regan, Sean Elias, José Cobas, Louwanda Evans, Wendy Moore, Candace Hill, Linda Burton, Adia Harvey Wingfield, Jennifer Harvey, Wally Hart, Jennifer Mueller, and Hernán Vera. I also express my gratitude to the dozens of African American students and colleagues—and the hundreds of African American women and men in many field research studies—who have helped me to better understand how systemic racism pervades everyday life and how African Americans have both aggressively resisted that oppression and, at the same time, created vibrant communities and helped to make this country far better, in implementing social justice and democracy ideals, than it otherwise would have been. One day, perhaps, this country can live up to the authentic liberty and justice ideals held so fervently by these remarkable and courageous African Americans.

1

White Racism, Black Resistance
Seeking Freedom, Justice, and Democracy

Today, the dominant mythology of the United States emphasizes the country's early creation and development as mostly being about white courage, hard work, and commitments to freedom. European colonists viewed the new colonies' development as an example for the entire world. In 1630, several ships crossed the Atlantic and brought hundreds of English Puritans to the Massachusetts Bay Colony. On arrival, their leader, the lawyer John Winthrop, gave a sermon insisting that "we must consider that we shall be as a city upon a hill. The eyes of all people are upon us."[1] These ethnocentric Puritans viewed themselves as setting a distinctive spiritual and societal example for "all people." By the time of the 1770s American Revolution and the Declaration of Independence, advocates of this American universalism were rhetorically accenting liberty, justice, and equality as the new country's guiding principles.

A Long Racist History

Clearly, the official mythology about the early founding centuries ignores or downplays the extreme violence and oppression, and thus the immorality, necessary to subordinate those in the way of this European American expansion—initially, the large-scale genocide targeting Native Americans and extensive enslavement of African Americans. It also ignores the role and significance of the large-scale pushback against this subordination coming from these and other Americans of color. From the seventeenth century to the present, European Americans have generated and maintained an array of inegalitarian economic and other social institutions that have unjustly enriched whites and unjustly impoverished Americans of color, institutions so oppressive that they have generated recurring freedom and resistance movements by Native Americans, African Americans, and other Americans of color.

To a substantial degree, many white leaders of the American Revolution revolted against Britain not only to secure greater freedom for themselves but also to protect the country's slavery-based economic system, and thus the enslavement of African Americans, including their own wealth linked directly or indirectly to that system. Certainly, there were other major factors in their revolt, but most white revolutionaries did not revolt to create *real* democracy. Indeed, the expansion of democracy was proceeding faster in Britain than in what became the United States. At the time of the American Revolution, the fifth of the population that was African American (and mostly enslaved) and the substantial population of Native Americans (mostly beyond its borders) facing genocide certainly did not view the emerging United States as a country strongly committed to real liberty, justice, and democracy.

The conventional story about U.S. development after the Revolution is a rosy one about generations of immigrant groups voluntarily creating a socially healthy country reflecting the founding ideals of liberty and justice for all. Yet, Native Americans were already *here* when the numerous Atlantic migrations took place. In addition, one important group, Africans, constituted the only large group forced to come to these shores—often in chains.

Consider the long timeline for white oppression of African Americans, from 1619 to the present day. In 1607, Jamestown became the first permanent English colony in North America. Twelve years later, enslaved Africans were purchased with supplies from a Dutch-flagged ship; they were apparently treated by European colonists as indentured servants. The colonists did not firmly institutionalize slavery until the mid-seventeenth century, yet even in the first decades European-named "negro servants" were treated in very discriminatory ways, as socially and legally inferior.[2] Once the slavery system became economically central and extensively developed by the 1700s, the privilege, status, and wealth that whites in various classes secured generally guaranteed it would be very difficult to move back in time and undo the slavery system. This was demonstrated when an official end to slavery did not come for another century and a half, in 1865, *well past the midpoint* of this country's four-centuries-old history. Even then, after a brief attempt at ending some racial oppression in the Reconstruction era (about 1865–1877), whites established the near-slavery of legal segregation (Jim Crow) for another nine decades (about 1878–1969). Altogether, about three-fourths of this country's history has been grounded in slavery and Jim Crow oppression. Indeed, this country has been officially "free" of extreme racial oppression only since about 1969, when the last major civil rights law went into effect.

Evidently, there is a societal inertia that keeps a social system going over a long period of time and relatively impervious to change unless it is met by a very strong counter force. Established in the seventeenth and eighteenth centuries, this country's system of extreme oppression has indeed been inertial. In making sense of this reality, we need to consider how dominant societal institutions regularly reproduce racial oppression and its racial inequalities. Over nearly four centuries now, an estimated 60 to 70 million African Americans have lived under systemic white racism. Their enslavement, legal segregation, and contemporary oppression have had profound impacts not only on themselves but on many other aspects of this country. As the brilliant African American novelist and essayist Ralph Ellison long ago underscored, without the African American presence, there would be "no slave economy, no Civil War; no violent destruction of the Reconstruction; no KKK and no Jim Crow system."[3]

Covering up Racist History

Opinion surveys have recently shown how few colleges and universities require much in the way of U.S. history courses and how majorities of students know little about white founding figures such as Thomas Jefferson and George Washington. Over the course of their early educations and later lives, most people learn little about this country's two-centuries-plus slavery era or its eight-plus decades of legal (Jim Crow) segregation that followed and only ended about 1969. North American slavery, especially in southern and border states, was an extreme political-economic system that racialized and controlled most major aspects of the lives of enslaved African Americans. The Jim Crow segregation that followed continued this extreme racialized control for most African Americans, again especially in southern and border states. These extraordinarily oppressive realities have frequently been hidden from public view and critical analysis by societal myths. For example, at popular plantation tourist sites, slavery's brutal, torture-filled history is routinely ignored or whitewashed.[4] (One dictionary defines torture as the "practice of inflicting severe pain on someone as a punishment or to force them to do or say something."[5]) Few white Americans, in particular, seem to want critical enlightenment about our history of racial oppression.

The scientist Werner Heisenberg, co-developer of quantum physics theory, commented that, "We have to remember that what we observe is not nature in itself but nature exposed to our method of questioning."[6] Likewise, what we learn about our past and present societal history is substantially shaped by the questions we ask. White Americans, especially elites, have tried from the beginning to the present day to control serious questions probing deeply and publicly into the country's systemic racism. They have frequently covered up or whitewashed the central societal plot of systemic racism, such as by rarely funding research on such a topic or barring educational curricula dealing critically with it. This centuries-old cover-up has made it almost impossible for most white Americans, and many other Americans, to understand that deep-lying historical plot. Nonetheless, this suppressed past dramatically shapes our present.[7]

A remarkable example of hidden history is the fact that for decades Francis Scott Key, who authored our national anthem, the *Star Spangled Banner*, during the U.S. War of 1812 with the British, was a slaveholding lawyer even as he proclaimed a desire for freedom from the British. He wrote several times in that frequently sung song about the "land of the free," yet did *not* mean what he said, for he viewed the new nation as a slaveholding republic of free white men.[8] Significantly, in the anthem's seldom-sung third verse, Key wished death upon formerly enslaved African Americans who, promised their freedom by the British, had fled to British lines, with some fighting courageously with the British for real *liberty*. The slaveholding immorality on which this country was based is clear in these facts about the slaveholder who authored the *Star Spangled Banner*. From the viewpoint of enslaved African Americans, the British were defenders of *real* freedom, and thousands migrated to freedom in the British lines.

Given the massive historical cover-up, what are the contemporary consequences of telling an accurate story of the role of African Americans in U.S. history? Bringing an honest account of white-on-black oppression and black resistance to oppression into the retelling and writing of U.S. history would require a dramatic change in that history's overall presentation and general interpretation. Historical truths are difficult to face when they are as immoral, bloody, and enduring as this country's deepest racial truths. Yet, one can better understand the rage and resistance of African Americans, in the past and the present, if one understands that many critical events in the history of U.S. racial oppression are largely unknown because of a huge cover-up or whitewashing. In addition, over nearly four centuries, a great many Africans and African Americans have battled oppression, but only a little of this history is known outside of black America. From the beginning, enslaved Africans and African Americans fought back. They frequently injured and killed white sailors and other enslavers, fought fiercely against being put on ships, and threw themselves overboard from slave ships. Once inside the U.S. slavery system, they also revolted on a large scale, individually and collectively. Plantation houses and other buildings were burned, crops destroyed, and overseers and slaveowners attacked. At least 300 slave rebellions, including successful revolts and unsuccessful conspiracies to revolt, were recorded during the United States's slavery centuries.[9]

Ignorance of, or misunderstanding, our racialized history means that we cannot act intelligently in regard to many racial matters in the present day. Without understanding our deep societal plot of racial oppression, we cannot understand the urgent need for meaningful reparative actions for Americans targeted by oppression, including a large-scale makeover of this society. Unsurprisingly, few whites today have the ability to comprehend, even moderately, the realities of systemic white racism from a black point of view. Ralph Ellison underscored how different this experience is:

> In our society it is not unusual for a Negro to experience a sensation that he does not exist in the real world at all. He seems rather to exist in the nightmarish fantasy of the white American mind as a phantom that the white mind seeks unceasingly, by means both crude and subtle, to lay to rest.[10]

Systemic Racism and its White Frame

Let us pause to consider a few dimensions of the systemic racism that is central to the deep racial plot of the United States. Systemic racism is a material, social, and ideological reality that is well embedded in all major institutions. Over the long history of white oppression of Americans of color, racism has been systemic and foundational and has included: (1) the many exploitative and discriminatory practices of whites; (2) the significant resources, privileges, and power unjustly gained by whites and institutionalized in a dominant racial hierarchy; (3) the maintenance of substantial racial inequalities by well-institutionalized social reproduction mechanisms; and (4) the many racial prejudices, stereotypes, images, ideologies, emotions, interpretations, and narratives that constitute the dominant white racial frame (worldview) that rationalizes and implements everyday racial oppression.[11]

Very important in reproducing this systemic racism over the centuries has been the transmission from one white generation to the next not only of unjustly gained material resources but of a strong *white racial framing* of this society. A long-term historical creation, this still-dominant racial frame, this racial worldview, and its important pro-white and anti-others sub-frames are reproduced moment to moment within social networks that contextualize whites' everyday lives. An individual's understandings, images, and knowledge about racial matters hang together because they draw important elements from the larger white racial framing, which is stored and reproduced in that individual's social networks.[12] Whites routinely operate out of this dominant white racial frame—for example, in discriminating against Americans of color—and often with little awareness of its existence.

In addition, the dominant white racial frame is opposed by the anti-oppression counter-frames of African Americans and other Americans of color and by the traditional home-culture frames that the latter draw on for their everyday lives and in developing resistance counter-frames. Living in this systemically racist society has required the development of a major black counter-frame to the dominant white frame, one that assists in survival and individual and collective resistance (for detail on racial frames, see Chapter 3). In interview studies involving hundreds of black respondents, my colleagues and I have found that black Americans in all walks of life are usually very aware of, and sensitive to, the multifaceted reality of everyday racism for themselves, their families, and other Americans of color. They are, on average, much more conscious of the reality and importance of the country's highly racialized past and present than are white Americans.

Still, the country's major white-controlled institutions, such as the public schools and mainstream media, constantly press the all-pervasive white racial frame on the minds of all Americans, including all Americans of color. Most of the latter are influenced by that omnipresent and dominant frame. For example, research using the white and black photos of the Implicit Association Test has found that nearly half of black respondents revealed a subtle pro-white or anti-black bias in responses to the photos. (The overwhelming majority of whites show this serious bias.) Because of societal pressures, virtually all black Americans must operate to some degree out of it to make their way in white-dominated institutions, and some have indeed operated very aggressively out of it. This contemporary situation of constantly competing interpretive frames confronting black Americans—the pervasive white racial frame versus the resistance-linked black counter-frame—signals just how powerful systemic white racism still is.[13]

Of course, many whites have been able to see at least a few of the problematical aspects of the dominant white frame, and a few have been able to assess it critically and operate frequently out of deeper understandings of racism gained from paying serious attention to the black counter-frame. In later chapters, we assess some white examples, such as John Brown and Albion Tourgée (see Chapter 5). There we observe that major progress in the anti-racist direction has required much equal-status contact with black Americans—and extensive and willing white learning from them about racism's realities.

In addition, the collective memory of whites that protects and communicates the white racial frame is essential to perpetuating racial oppression across the generations. Also important for white perpetuation of systemic racism is the sustained collective forgetting of society's harsh racist realities. Perpetuating racial oppression over the long term requires much collective forgetting and selective remembering. Recent research on the Jim Crow era demonstrates that most such forgetting and misremembering abandons white responsibilities for past oppression or glorifies white achievements, all in line with whites' racial-group interests.[14] This white repression of history and trained ignorance of oppression have been critical to living comfortably as a white person in a still-racist society to the present day.

The principal architects, builders, and maintainers of this society's racial oppression, including its rationalizing frame, have long been white men, especially elite men. For the most part, they have made the most critical decisions and substantially developed the more important U.S. structures and institutions and the dominant white framing from which the white public and scholars alike have typically viewed U.S. racial matters. It is striking, too, that they are almost never called out and fully assessed for what they have done as elite, white, and male Americans in regard to establishing and maintaining systemic racism over nearly four centuries.

Positive Black Exceptionalism

Thanks to the dominance and pervasiveness of the white racial frame, when considering black Americans, most whites and many other nonblack Americans very frequently think in negatively framed terms that greatly emphasize pathologies. Well into the twenty-first century and assisted by the mass media and popular culture, this negative framing has commonly exaggerated and racialized notions of gang members, thugs, lazy workers, or welfare recipients. This white pattern has been true for many decades. For example, in a famous 1940s book critical of Jim Crow segregation, *An American Dilemma*, Gunnar Myrdal nonetheless emphasized a negative list of alleged black deficiencies:

> The instability of the Negro family, . . . the emotionalism in the Negro church, the insufficiency and unwholesomeness of Negro recreational activity, the plethora of Negro sociable organizations, the narrowness of interests of the average Negro, the provincialism of his political speculation, the high Negro crime rate, the cultivation of the arts to the neglect of other fields, superstition, personality difficulties.[15]

Significantly, this is the framing of a white liberal social scientist. Writing decades later, sociologist Joyce Ladner noted that

> Traditional sociological analyses have failed to explore the unique experiences and culture of Blacks. . . . Historically, sociologists have portrayed Blacks as disorganized, pathological, and an aberrant group. The myths of 'cultural deprivation,' 'innate inferiority,' 'social disadvantagement,' and 'tangle of pathology' characterize the writings of many sociologists up to the present time.[16]

While there certainly are individual and social pathologies with which black Americans must regularly grapple—and many of these reflect long-term efforts of racial oppression—a great many white media analysts, scholars, and politicians have highly exaggerated these pathologies and ignored or downplayed the many positive realities and impacts of black Americans on this society. In addition, these analysts of black America usually avoid discussing the great array of social pathologies generated by white America, including centuries of racial oppression.

Today, the regular use of the phrase "black exceptionalism" remains negative in discussions in popular and scholarly literatures.[17] Recently, I searched but could not find *anyone* in trillions of Internet Web sites who used "positive black exceptionalism" or "positive African American exceptionalism" for the experiences or impact of African Americans, in the past or the present. I found just eight brief discussions with the phrase "positive impact" used in connection with black or African Americans— mostly in regard to Black History Month.

I show in much detail throughout this book that there is an extraordinarily important and *positive* black exceptionalism that is constantly revealed in the centuries-long history of this society. Outside of black America itself, recognition of these extraordinarily important black inputs into the shaping of U.S. culture and society is mostly missing. Significant aspects of this positive exceptionalism include the large-scale and dramatic impacts that African Americans have had (1) in building up the country's infrastructure, wealth, and long-lived economic prosperity; (2) in shaping the country's culture in regard to music, literature, religion, and language; and (3) perhaps most important, in creating or greatly shaping the expansion of authentic liberty, justice, equality, and democracy over the centuries since this country's official establishment by its mostly white-racist, anti-democratic "founding fathers."

Historian William Piersen has underscored how hard it is for whites and nonblack people of color to take this African heritage seriously,

> for it is not often . . . that *Africans and African Americans are presented as cultural founding fathers and mothers* with life-building agendas of their own. We have no trouble assuming the influence of Europe and Europeans on our history and culture, but until recently we have tended to reject the idea that the cultures of Africa could also have had significant effect.[18]

Consider brief examples, discussed in detail later. Some incontrovertible impacts of African Americans are obvious, such as their centuries-old impact on distinctive music genres (for example, jazz, blues, rock, country, hip hop), while others are almost unknown to the general public. As we will see in Chapter 2, over three-and-a-half centuries African Americans did massive amounts of uncompensated and backbreaking work as enslaved workers and poorly compensated work as Jim-Crowed workers to build up this country's great infrastructure, wealth, and international power. For this country's first two-plus centuries, African Americans constituted the principal group of workers of color who supplied very profitable labor for white employers—slave plantation owners, other farmers, and manufacturing and other urban employers. Not only were huge and durable profits made off this labor, but its extensive use allowed many whites to work beyond the hardest drudge labor, including supervisory jobs as plantation overseers, skilled blue-collar workers, urban white-collar employees, and government officials. Without this highly exploited African American labor creating great white wealth over many generations, there might not have been a United States—and certainly not at the time that it was officially constituted.

Consider, too, little-known facts about the black role in the expansion of liberty, justice, and democracy. For those people whose historical education about African American efforts in this regard is deficient, the 1960s civil rights movement seems to be the main, usually vague, memory of black contributions to matters of social justice in the United States. However, as we will see later, over nearly four centuries, the black liberation movements targeting systemic racism have been at the center of our long history of group struggles for social justice and expanded democracy. There have been many hundreds of such movements, small and large. These have included hundreds of attempted slave uprisings, the activist organizations of early black freedom writers and advocates, the "underground railroad" organization of black abolitionists before the Civil War, the Union military units with hundreds of thousands of black volunteers during that war, and the last century of black civil rights and black power movements. Du Bois wrote that much white accounting of slavery and Reconstruction leaves "no room for the real plot of the story"—the "hurt and struggle of degraded black millions in their fight for freedom and their attempt to enter democracy."[19] Significantly, too, from the historical records of the late seventeenth and early eighteenth centuries, we see enslaved, formerly enslaved, and free blacks regularly insisting upon and acting on a *real* liberty-and-justice framing of the entire society, indeed well before whites celebrated liberty and justice rhetorically in the founding documents of the late eighteenth century.

Over our first centuries, African Americans were the *first American group to develop a vigorous liberation and anti-oppression counter-framing of this society* in thousands of pamphlets, books, and speeches, and at numerous national conventions. Assisted by nonblack Americans on occasion, the black freedom movements have been a major reason for much of the progress—albeit only partial progress—that this country has made on issues of liberty, justice, and democracy. Still, African Americans rarely get appropriate credit, outside of their communities, for these remarkable efforts and consequent societal changes—for taking us, finally in 1969, beyond our three-plus centuries of slavery and Jim Crow oppression in regard to African Americans. Indeed, this country's extensive and systemic racism has not been static but has periodically shifted in a more just and democratic direction—and often in response to the assertive organization of African Americans acting as agents of freedom.

Centrality of Black Americans: White Oppression and Obsession

Some analysts have raised the question of why, in detailed assessments of U.S. racism, African Americans often take central place. The major reason is that whites, especially elites, have *positioned* those whom they define as "black" as the central racialized "other" in this society's institutions and in the white framing of those institutions, from the seventeenth century to the present. To create a mighty nation, powerful whites have greatly exploited black labor and other black resources on a huge scale for much of our history, usually to generate wealth and build up a country with white-controlled institutions. They have built a country with hundreds of millions of hours of uncompensated African American labor. African Americans' time of experience with white oppression is the longest for any North American group except Native Americans. Native Americans have suffered great oppression for at least as long, but they have not been as central to whites' negative racial framing and to large-scale labor exploitation *within* this white-dominated society. The often declared "father" of the U.S. Constitution, James Madison, famously made their centrality quite clear early on, insisting that "the case of the black race *within our bosom* . . . is the problem *most* baffling to the policy of our country."

For centuries now, whites in all classes have been obsessed with black Americans, a point made well by the savvy black abolitionist Frederick Douglass in a nineteenth-century speech:

> He is alike present in the study of the learned and thoughtful, and in the play house of the gay and thoughtless. We see him pictured at our street corners, and hear him in the songs of our market places. The low and the vulgar curse him, the snob and the flunky affect to despise him, the mean and the cowardly assault him, because they know . . . that they can abuse him with impunity. . . . Of the books, pamphlets, and speeches concerning him, there is literally, no end. He is the one inexhaustible topic of conversation at our firesides and in our public halls.[20]

Douglass is a towering figure in U.S. history, a premier activist for liberty and justice and a scholarly genius in assessing the dimensions of U.S. racism.

Over the centuries, African Americans have been especially central to the white *sense of self*. As African American essayist James Baldwin put it, the "black man has functioned in the white man's world as a fixed star . . . and as he moves out of his place, heaven and earth are shaken to the foundations."[21] Ralph Ellison made a similar point about white identity. As he saw it, whites have long struggled to define themselves collectively. One way "that has been used to simplify the answer has been to seize upon the presence of black Americans and use them as a marker, a symbol of limits, a metaphor for the 'outsider.'"[22] For most of this country's history, whites have most often defined who *they* are over against the marker of black Americans as premier racial "outsiders." Until the 1950s, defamation-of-character laws permitted whites to claim in court that they were badly defamed when labeled "black." In contrast, a black person could not sue for being labeled "white."[23]

In addition, over the centuries, no other U.S. racial group has seen as much written about its supposed racial inferiority and problems such as allegedly pathological families and culture. Sadly, in the past and present, this white obsession can be seen in hundreds of thousands of white articles, books, pamphlets, and movies focusing on issues of black inferiority and white superiority. Nobel-prize-winning novelist Toni Morrison has pointed out that black Americans are regularly present

> in the construction of a free and public school system; the balancing of representation in legislative bodies; jurisprudence and legal definitions of justice. It is there in theological discourse; the memoranda of banking houses; the concept of manifest destiny and the preeminent narrative that accompanies . . . the initiation of every immigrant into the community of American citizens. The presence of black people is inherent, along with gender and family ties, in the earliest lesson every child is taught regarding his or her distinctiveness.[24]

Community Making by Black Americans: Endurance and Impact

Let us understand, too, that in their centuries-old struggle for freedom and justice, African Americans *themselves*, individually and collectively, have created the group called African Americans. They thereby became fully *American*. This statement seems obvious, yet much white framing and discriminatory treatment of African Americans signals that they are *not* seen by many whites as authentic Americans. (Many whites, for example, have not viewed even President Barack Obama as a "real American" and questioned his U.S. birthplace.) In addition, some research indicates that the mainstream media and major political commentators regularly assert that "Americans" think a certain way when they actually mean "white Americans."[25]

One remarkable, profound, and lasting achievement—over more than two centuries—of enslaved Africans from different societies and their descendants was to actively create an African *American* group that has had a great positive impact on U.S. development. In 1827, Richard Allen, a free black minister, underscored the point that the new United States was *theirs*: "This land which we have watered with our tears and our blood is now our mother country."[26] While whites did create "black" and "white" people as categories in their racist hierarchy, African American efforts are the principal reason for the reality of a cohesive, creative, and accomplished African American people. Little mainstream scholarly and popular discussion deals substantially with the normal lives and folkways that African Americans have created over the centuries within the extraordinarily difficult contexts of this systemic racism. Sociologist Glenn Bracey has summarized this dramatic reality: "Our existence as African Americans is perhaps our greatest accomplishment. Out of the ashes of white denigration, we gave birth to ourselves."[27]

How have African Americans managed not only to endure but often to thrive in the face of extreme oppression? With much blood, sweat, and tears! Consider how extraordinary it is that African Americans have survived, and resisted, centuries of economic exploitation and uncounted white violent attacks under slavery, Jim Crow, and contemporary discrimination. White-racist framing notwithstanding, African Americans have long had strong family networks that assisted greatly in this endurance and survival. They have endured by generally including all those oppressed, of whatever their skin shade and background, as part of black communities. They have endured by laboring together under extremely oppressive everyday conditions, by constant community creation and interpersonal support, by great empathy and sustenance for those resisting racism, by creating strong spiritual and other cultural innovations, and by framing white racism critically for what it is and resisting it in individual and collective ways. Strikingly, too, most African Americans have in key ways lived by a *more moral* value system than most whites, for a majority of the latter have been committed for centuries to an immoral and unjust racist system and to a mythology of white virtuousness and superiority rationalizing racial oppression.

Thinking about this strong black morality and human sensitivity today, I have noticed several examples in recent media accounts. For instance, African Americans have been much more critical of, and much less supportive of, numerous routine operations of our criminal justice system, such as the retaliatory punishment of the death penalty. Not long ago, one mainstream media report discussed death-penalty issues and the controversial execution of Troy Davis, a black man convicted of killing a white off-duty police officer. The latter's white family strongly sought the death penalty. Opinion surveys indicate that most whites support the death penalty, while a significant majority of black Americans are opposed.[28] One reason for this attitudinal divergence is likely that African American families have frequently had much negative experience with the criminal justice system and do not trust white officials therein to be consistently fair, such as in the application of the death penalty. (Given comparable crimes, black men are much more likely to suffer the death penalty than whites.) Even in horrific hate crime murders of black men by whites, black families of the victims have often not sought the death penalty. Again we observe the values of black Americans in seeking a more just and fair society, for they know about how harsh legal punishments have frequently been used in racially unjust ways.[29]

Thus, as agents and activists regularly shaping their own freedom-and-justice successes, African Americans have knowingly contributed much to larger human rights developments in the evolving societal creation called "the United States." Most of the white leaders of the American Revolution did *not* revolt for real democracy but to protect the economic and political institutions of a slavery-based society generating much white wealth and prosperity. Indeed, most were fearful of significant "democracy." In his major book, *Notes on the State of Virginia*, the most famous of the revolutionaries on issues of equality and justice and principal author of the Declaration of Independence, Thomas Jefferson, does not even discuss the issues of equality, justice, and democracy accented in that Declaration. He does occasionally discuss "freedom" but not in reference to the least free, the enslaved Americans. A major slaveholder throughout his long life, Jefferson was, like many others in the founding white elite, heavily invested in the slavery system and for the most part only good at rhetorical commitments to these great ideals. As historian Gerald Horne has noted, it is far from sufficient to counter this complicity in extreme racial oppression with the notion, asserted by many, that the 1776 Revolution did create "a template for the subsequent extensions of liberty to those who were initially excluded." This dubious crediting is like "giving the jailers of apartheid credit for the enfranchisement of Nelson Mandela," instead of giving the revolts of those oppressed principal credit for major societal changes that did eventually come.[30]

Conclusion

To a substantial degree, centuries of anti-oppression revolts and liberation protests by African Americans saved this country from the determined intent of elite and ordinary whites to maintain first the slavery system, then the Jim Crow system of near-slavery, and now persisting racial discrimination. Over nearly four centuries now, this African American resistance has forced the country's white leaders in the direction of a more *democratic* country, thereby making meaningful the democratic ideal most whites have rhetorically asserted to be the country's core ideal.

W. E. B. Du Bois wrote a path-breaking revisionist history of Reconstruction that eventually revolutionized the writing of U.S. history. In his conclusion to this book, he eloquently summed up the impact of Africans and African Americans on this country:

> The most magnificent drama in the last thousand years of human history is the transportation of ten million human beings out of the dark beauty of their mother continent into the new-found Eldorado of the West. They descended into Hell; and in the third century they arose from the dead, in the finest effort to achieve democracy for the working millions which this world had ever seen. It was . . . an upheaval of humanity like the Reformation and the French Revolution.[31]

2
Black Labor
Building the Economy

At Barack Obama's first presidential inauguration in 2009, a provocative poem presented by Elizabeth Alexander, the African American poet for the inauguration, cited the long history of African American workers who had made possible much U.S. economic and other social progress and, thus, Obama's election. Alexander put it this way: "Sing the names of the dead who brought us here, who laid the train tracks, raised the bridges, picked the cotton and the lettuce, built brick by brick the glittering edifices they would then keep clean and work inside of."[1]

In *The Wealth of Nations*, the prominent eighteenth-century economist, Adam Smith, emphasized that the true wealth of any country lies substantially in the labor of its people. Significantly, over long centuries, much of the critical profit-generating labor that built up this country came from many millions of African American workers, virtually all of them enslaved workers, Jim-Crow-segregated workers, or current workers still suffering racial discrimination. Important to this country's economic system since the late seventeenth century, African Americans have likely been more at the essential labor core of this white-dominated society for a longer period of time than any other racially oppressed group. Indeed, Americans of European descent made extensive use of brutally enslaved black labor for much of this country's history. In an autobiographical account published after he escaped enslavement, the abolitionist Frederick Douglass reported on recurringly cruel labor forced on enslaved workers by his slaveowner's employee:

> We were worked in all weathers. It was never too hot or too cold; it could never rain, blow, hail, or snow, too hard for us to work in the field. Work, work, work, was scarcely more the order of the day than of the night. The longest days were too short for him, and the shortest nights too long for him.[2]

This white-on-black oppression originated mainly as labor exploitation in the seventeenth century and has long been the archetype of well-institutionalized racial oppression.

Historically, as well as in recent decades, white Americans have generally ignored this long labor history and commonly portrayed African American workers and their families as "lazy" and not hardworking. However, as Claud Anderson has underscored, over several centuries up to the 1960s, African American workers were actually the national model "for doing the hardest, dirtiest, most dangerous and backbreaking work" in this country. Reflecting on the slavery era, he adds, if nonblacks had been the better workers,

> why would supposedly bright [white] businessmen spend 250 years traveling half way around the world to kidnap [many] . . . innocent, but lazy blacks, then knowingly bring them to America to do work that other ethnic groups could do better?[3]

Centrality of Black Laborers: The Long Slavery Era

Over several centuries, a brutal Atlantic slave trade was inaugurated and controlled by Europeans and European Americans. This human trafficking involved hundreds of North American and European ships in thousands of voyages that involved shipping millions of Africans across the Atlantic. One scholarly estimate is that 10 million to 11 million Africans survived the harsh middle passage of the Atlantic slave trade on their way to the Americas.

With profits in mind, armed European and European American traders and enslavers arrived in Africa and began a massive cross-Atlantic trade in human beings. They raided or traded with African societies whose economies typically were not centered in profit making from slavery. They played off one African society's leaders against others, constructed hundreds of slave ports, and fought many battles. Some Africans were taken directly, but most were captured under authority of African leaders who were under European pressure or seeking European weaponry or other goods. Oftentimes, African leaders began by trading African goods for those of Europeans, but when they no longer had goods Europeans wanted, they turned to trading people they held in servitude, often from African intergroup conflicts. Most of those brought by Europeans in their slave ships came from Africa's Atlantic coast, from areas that are now the Congo, Angola, Sierra Leone, Guinea, and Senegal.[4] In the North American enslavement crucible, African peoples with diverse cultural backgrounds, often culturally advanced in significant ways compared to Europeans (for example, agricultural technologies), became "blacks"—an unfamiliar name applied by their enslavers.

The European-origin enslavers and their supporting cast of European Americans created an enslavement system whose massive legacies have shaped this country to the present and soon named themselves "whites" as part of an already dominant white racial frame in this new society. Recall that the white frame is a broad worldview—including racial stereotypes, images, narratives, and much more—that whites generated to rationalize their ever-expanding system of oppression. This legitimating framing was essential to the expansion of the white-generated capitalism that brought great wealth to whites as a group and great impoverishment to blacks as a group. We observe evidence of its effectiveness, and contemporary relevance, throughout this book.

Most African Americans today are descendants of African workers shipped to and enslaved in North America by white Americans between the 1600s and the mid-1800s. Their ancestors were central to building up what became the United States. Barely a century into the British-American slave-trading and plantation-creating operations, in the 1740s, a business pamphleteer fully noted the centrality of African workers to Great Britain's great prosperity and wealth:

> It is also allowed on all Hands, that the trade to Africa is the Branch which renders our American Colonies and Plantations so advantageous to Great Britain: that Traffic only affording our Planters a constant supply of Negro Servants for the Culture of their Lands in the Produce of Sugars, Tobacco, Rice, Rum, Cotton, Fustick, Pimento, and all other our Plantation Produce . . . . The Negroe-Trade therefore, and the natural consequences resulting from it, may be justly esteemed an inexhaustible Fund of Wealth and Naval Power to this Nation.[5]

Unmistakably, this white pamphleteer suggests that there is a general white consensus that the enslaved African and African American workers have provided an "inexhaustible fund of wealth" for whites both in Britain and in its American colonies. Note, too, the white racial frame that is already in operation—in the name given to those enslaved ("Negro") and the euphemistic description of their work ("Servants") and the white-centered orientation of the writer.

Many in the Western capitalistic elite and other classes of white Europeans, including those settling in the Americas and Africa, became well-off in this expanding trade in enslaved workers and slave-produced agricultural products from slave farms and plantations. Under this country's slave labor system, from the mid-seventeenth century to the mid-nineteenth century, African American workers were a major, if not the major, group of workers who supplied the most profitable labor for white employers of many kinds—plantation owners, other substantial farmers, transportation corporations, and urban-industrial employers. The extent and importance of this enslaved labor is hard to overestimate. For more than three centuries, many millions of highly exploited black workers laboring during slavery and the near-slavery of Jim Crow segregation were substantially and disproportionately responsible for building up the country's wealth and prosperity.

White slaveholders were very aware of the importance of the labor of black men, women, and children to their prosperity and the country's economic development. While they spoke publicly of black Americans as lazy and inferior, in their own management theorizing and practice, of which they were proud, they frequently portrayed enslaved black workers as superior to white laborers, especially in productivity.[6] For much of this country's history, black men, women, and children labored long and hard for white slaveowners. Black men, not white men, did much of the hardest labor in southern fields and processing facilities. Black women often became the backbone of slavemaster's homes. Wearing his historian's hat, W. E. B. Du Bois sharply put it,

> [S]he played her part in the uplift of the South. She was an embodied sorrow, an anomaly crucified on the cross of her own neglected children for the sake of the children of masters who bought and sold her as they bought and sold cattle. Whatever she had . . . she surrendered it to those who lived to lynch her sons and ravish her daughters.

Ironically, he adds, from her "breast walked forth governors and judges, ladies of wealth and fashions, merchants and scoundrels who lead the South."[7]

George Fitzhugh, a leading southern social scientist and apologist for slave labor, frequently accented its great importance in this country:

> Our slaves till the land, do the coarse and hard labor on our roads and canals, sweep our streets, cook our food, brush our boots, wait on our tables, hold our horses, do all hard work, and fill all menial offices.[8]

Whites actually coined a racist phrase—which they have used since the 1830s—accenting this hard, dangerous, and backbreaking work. Historian David Roediger notes that, "Not only was nigger work synonymous with hard, drudging labor but to nigger it meant 'to do hard work,' or 'to slave.'"[9] By the mid-nineteenth century, according to the *Oxford English Dictionary*, this racist verb had come to mean working like a black person and doing very hard work. Significantly, southern apologists such as Fitzhugh spent much effort in their writings defending southern slaveholders against northern critics who, often accurately, charged white slaveholders with chronic "idleness." For centuries, these white slavemasters were described as "idlers" because of their dependence on enslaved labor for most hard labor on their plantations and other farms.

By the eighteenth century, white plantation owners and large farmers, together with other slaveholders, owned not only much human capital in the form of enslaved workers but much of the country's productive agricultural land and a large proportion of the agricultural products, livestock, plantation buildings, and processing mills. Because of the labor of enslaved African Americans, the southern region of this country was the most economically prosperous and politically powerful from the mid-eighteenth century to the mid-nineteenth century. Often forced to work in an unfamiliar land, mostly in southern areas, enslaved African and African American workers produced massive amounts of sugar, coffee, tobacco, rice, and cotton. Much of this agricultural production was marketed directly to consumers or processed in manufacturing plants to create other products, such as textiles, in North America and Europe. Products created directly or indirectly by enslaved workers became a substantial part of the relatively prosperous, even luxurious, lifestyle of the upper classes and growing middle classes here and in numerous European countries.[10]

Enslaved Laborers and the Slaveholding Elite

One of the great ironies of this "democratic" country's history is that enslaved African American workers made possible the societal reality we call, usually with no critical reflection, "the founding fathers." These were elite white men, such as the slaveholding presidents George Washington, Thomas Jefferson, and James Madison, who would almost certainly not have been so wealthy and influential without the huge amount of enslaved labor, and the indigenous lands, that they "owned." Consider George Washington, celebrated today in the name of the United States' capital city and its tall monument there. At one point in the 1780s, this brutal slaveholder and his wife held a huge number of these "founding workers," about 216 African Americans, in bondage. His plantation records reveal that he usually viewed them as economic investments much like his farm animals and landed plantations. One scholar has described the great wealth and luxury provided by hundreds of these workers at his plantations:

> Slaves washed his linens, sewed his shirts, polished his boots, saddled his horse, chopped the wood for his fireplaces, powdered his wig, drove his carriage, cooked his meals, served his table, poured his wine, posted his letters, lit the lamps, swept the porch, looked after the guests, planted the flowers in his gardens, trimmed the hedges, dusted

the furniture, cleaned the windows, made the beds, and performed the myriad domestic chores.[11]

Washington's overseers used torture, such as flogging, and he vigorously pursued enslaved runaways. Similarly, the principal author of the "Declaration of Independence," Thomas Jefferson, lived in luxury because he held hundreds in bloody and barbarous bondage over his lifetime. Both men did occasionally express criticisms and reservations about slavery, but neither freed more than a few of those they enslaved during their own lifetimes. When they held powerful government positions, including the U.S. presidency, they did little to end the enslavement system from which elite whites profited. Moreover, like some of Washington's close relatives, Jefferson was the father of numerous children with an enslaved woman he economically exploited and long coerced into sexual relations with him.[12]

Ironically, enslaved labor created the possibility and reality of a significant group of powerful whites who, by the mid-eighteenth century, had the economic wherewithal to successfully revolt for their freedom from the British government. By the time of the 1770s colonial rebellion against Great Britain, with its equality-asserting "Declaration of Independence," slavery-centered agricultural production in Virginia made it the wealthiest of the colonies and home of leading slaveholders.[13]

White Wealth Holders, Rebellious Black Labor

This centuries-long pattern of black wealth creation for most white social classes continued over ensuing decades. At the time that the United States was entering a bloody Civil War in 1861, one-fourth of white families in southern and border areas held nearly 4 million black Americans in bondage. These white families, especially those enslaving large numbers, were powerful not only in the southern economy but in the national economy and in southern and national politics. So great was southern economic capital in enslaved workers and their families that it exceeded that of all capital invested in manufacturing and other industrial assets in the northern states.[14] Indeed, up to the beginning of the Civil War, the South was so economically prosperous and politically powerful that military experts thought the southern Confederacy would win an intersectional war. This view about the clout of Confederate states was correct in accenting white wealth and political power but overlooked one crucial aspect: this wealth being built on the backs of millions of enslaved people with desires and agency of their own.

One way that we know African American labor was central and crucial for the white South's great economic prosperity and development was that the withdrawal of much of that labor guaranteed the eventual demise of the slavery-centered Confederacy. During the Civil War, large numbers of African American laborers played a critical role in the Confederacy's defeat. Abandoning fields and processing facilities, many escaped to the North. Some 200,000-plus African Americans, most formerly enslaved, joined military units and fought to end slavery. Other formerly enslaved workers provided most of the 300,000 or so black support troops for the Union military. At least as important, many who were unable to flee southern oppression participated in a type of "general strike"—that is, they cut back on work efforts for slavemasters. Some engaged in sabotage and espionage benefitting the Union cause. As Abraham Lincoln admitted late in the war, courageous African American soldiers and support troops were critical to the Union victory and, thus, to ending the slavery system—and to some meaningful implementation of the liberty-and-justice rhetoric long articulated by the country's white leadership.[15]

Over the centuries during which the slave labor system was central to this country's economy, enslaved workers likely received the least in return for being employed in hard labor of all large groups of workers in that era—or, probably, ever since. Whites, in turn, benefitted hugely from slave labor. A typical slaveholder spent an average of about $19 a year (about $500 in today's dollars) on upkeep of an enslaved worker.[16] Given such low expenses (and paying no wages) in return for many hundreds of hours of work annually, much profit was often made. Enslaved workers generated between 1790 and 1860 at least $1.6 billion and as much as $94 billion (in current dollars) in lost income that went to slaveholders, depending on one's assumptions about the U.S. economy. Slaveholders and other white employers gained this income as significant profits, which in turn usually became family wealth passed along over generations of descendants, to the present day. Some scholars have calculated what this stolen wealth—plus lost interest generated by it over generations—might likely be today. In current (2013) dollars, estimates range between $4.9 trillion and $11 trillion. Even these huge estimates do not include significant wealth generated from enslaved black labor before 1790.[17] If we consider the current value of all wealth generated for slaveholding interests from the time of slavery's development in the seventeenth century to its ending in the 1860s, plus interest and calculated in current-year dollars, that total lost wealth for African Americans would be far greater than $11 trillion.[18]

A white slaveholder holding one enslaved black worker had significant economic power, a point overlooked by most analysts of our slavery states. Williamson and Cain measure economic power as the "value of something as a percent of total GDP between then and now." The percent-GDP value for one average enslaved person in the 1850s is about $2.6 million today. While this number is large, the wealth "in slaves was a large proportion of the total wealth [GDP] of the nation." Moreover, this economic power commonly meant greater political power than for those without such "capital."[19]

Significantly, the foundations of the wealth of many white elite and middle-class families in the present, were laid in the centuries-long slavery era. White slaveholders were landed capitalists, and a great many transmitted significant assets to later white descendants, many of whom became professionals, politicians, and entrepreneurs in various economic areas. The latter "built factories, chartered banks, incorporated canal and railroad enterprises, invested in government securities, and speculated in new financial instruments."[20] Indeed, the generations of transmitted wealth from the extensive slave labor system have been essential to the growth and expansion of modern capitalism, indeed to the present day.

Other White Beneficiaries of Black Labor

Slaveholders were not the only beneficiaries of this economic and political system. Enslaved workers generated profits for many other white employers in rural and urban settings. These employers often hired enslaved workers from their slavemasters. Such employers often mixed free white labor with this hired black labor—with the latter being easier to hire and fire and not having the rights of white laborers.[21]

Not surprisingly, a majority of other whites in the South, and a great many in the North, benefitted from employment that was directly or indirectly related to this slave labor system—in such occupational tasks as policing enslaved workers, growing foodstuffs for plantations, handling transport and trading of those enslaved and their agricultural products, engaging in skilled trades necessary for plantations, and running local governments and financial institutions, among many other tasks.[22] Furthermore, extensive use of African American labor allowed many thousands of whites to move beyond manual drudgery and into supervisory jobs and jobs as white-collar employees in businesses and government agencies.[23] Even the most aggressive nineteenth-century white defenders of slavery periodically underscored how much whites depended on enslaved workers, as in this commentary of George Fitzhugh:

> The doctor, the lawyer, the mechanic, the dentist, the merchant, the overseer, every trade and profession, in fact, live from the proceeds of slave labor at the South. They divide the profits with the owner of the slaves. He has nothing to pay them except what his slaves make.[24]

Unmistakably, a little-noted impact of centuries of enslaved black labor is how it assisted greatly in the movement of many white workers and their families into greater prosperity, and over the generations, into the country's established middle class.

Additionally, Fitzhugh was insistent on how much whites in the North and Europe depended on labor of enslaved workers for their prosperity:

> But you Yankees and Englishmen . . . make more money from our cotton, and tobacco, and sugar, and indigo, and wheat, and corn, and rice, than we make ourselves. You live by slave labor—would perish without it. . . . You live by our slave labor. It elevates your whites as well as ours, by confining them, in a great degree, to skillful, well-paying, light and intellectual employments—and it feeds and clothes them. Abolish slavery, and you will suffer vastly more than we. . . .[25]

One common misunderstanding of this country's slavery system is that it mainly affected southern areas. However, substantial profits and capital from the trade in slave-produced products facilitated northern manufacturing and helped to increase demand for manufactured products across the globe. For instance, the slave plantations, slave trade, and associated commercial activities were the foundation of much of New England's economy. Some 160 slaveholding families were prominent in that northern area. Their family businesses and many other northern businesses were directly or indirectly dependent on the system of enslaved labor. These included major businesses in sugar, molasses, and rum. Other northern capitalists built slave ships, and yet others marketed and shipped slave-produced products such as cotton and also goods derived from cotton and other agricultural production. Using cotton produced by enslaved workers, mostly in the South, nineteenth-century textile mills in New England became the first major U.S. industry and a major employer of white workers. Enslaved black workers elsewhere had thereby made possible a successful textile industry, one generating wealth for northern white entrepreneurs and income for northern white workers.[26]

Beyond New England, white trading in enslaved Africans and their products played a significant role in making New York City a major city—and one soon to be at the heart of the growing economy. Indeed, the world-famous Wall Street area began as a major arena of slave buying, selling, and hiring out. There and elsewhere in the North, profits generated by the grueling labor of those enslaved, usually farther south, were recirculated through banking institutions and became investments in commercial, shipping, insurance, railroad, and industrial companies during and after the slavery era. Northern bankers and investors made large profits off the backs of distant enslaved workers. Major banks such as the Bank of Philadelphia and J.P. Morgan-Chase provided capital for southern banks that directly funded the enslavement of African Americans, and more than 15 major U.S. companies such as Aetna and Lehman Brothers got their start in selling goods to, making loans to, or insuring slaveholders.[27] It seems likely a great many powerful capitalists who have arisen since the nineteenth century have had a substantial portion of their fortunes developed out of inherited or loaned capital that had its ultimate origin in enslaved African American labor.

The Internal Trade: Enslaved People as "Investments"

The expansion of the cotton economy, together with the economies of other important agricultural products, stimulated many slaveholders' desires for yet more enslaved workers. A key part of U.S. economic development in the nineteenth century involved a massive, unprecedented internal slave trade. While the external slave trade was officially abolished in 1808, it continued for decades but increasingly alongside this more important internal trade in human beings. Enslaved black workers were a major commodity as brutal slave traders criss-crossed southern and border states, buying and selling workers from one area to another. As new white-owned farms and plantations opened in areas west of Georgia, enslaved workers were bought by whites from East Coast agricultural areas. Like other parts of the slavery system, this brutal and bloody internal trade was also financed and facilitated by numerous white lawyers, insurance agents, and bankers and many ordinary whites doing work such as that of the infamous slave patrols.[28]

A little-known fact about the U.S. enslavement system is that these enslaved African American workers were valuable not just for their immediate labor for their white owners but as embodied capital and, thus, accumulating wealth. They were very valuable as human commodities in a variety of regional capitalistic markets and as human "collateral" that a white slaveowner could borrow against. Historian Seth Rockman has summarized this horrific U.S. reality:

> Even in locations where wage labor was more productive, slavery could remain vital because owners held on to slaves as commodities rather than as workers. So long as someone somewhere was willing to pay for that commodity, slaves retained a value that enhanced their owners' estates, provided collateral for loans, and served as the dowries and inheritances that predicated generations of white prosperity on the ownership of generations of black families. In this regard, the perpetuation of slavery in a place like Baltimore owed less to the actual labor compelled from enslaved workers and more to the fact that plantation purchasers in Charleston, Augusta, New Orleans, and throughout the South were willing to pay hundreds of dollars for Baltimore slaves.[29]

Not surprisingly, the expansion of new agricultural economies in territories and states to the west stimulated slaveholders' taking, often by violence, of yet more lands of indigenous peoples, including areas that became the slave states of Mississippi and Alabama. The bloody system of African American enslavement regularly linked southern, northern, and western regions—and many of their leading capitalists—together into an ever-expanding and greatly profitable national market in indigenous lands, enslaved workers, and the products from the latter's hard labor.

Enslaved Labor: Foundation of the Industrial World

Without both the national and the international trade in enslaved African American workers and in the massive number of products they produced on slave farms and plantations, and in other enterprises, various regions in the North American colonies—and, later, the United States—would almost certainly not have had the dramatic economic developments experienced during the eighteenth and nineteenth centuries. Slavery was central to the economic prosperity and wealth not only of Britain and its North American colonies but of countries such as Spain, France, and Brazil—and especially to elite whites and enterprises invested in slavery.

Profit making in slavery-based commercial and agricultural developments greatly fostered the burgeoning industrial revolution in the United States and Europe. The development of inventions and innovations critical to industrial development—such as inventor James Watt's improved steam engine—were often funded by banking institutions whose loans had their ultimate origins from profits from slavery and/or were first developed for use in slavery-linked industries.[30]

During the two-plus centuries of American slavery, the extensive trade in African American workers and their products between Europe, Africa, and the Americas created the foundation for the modern economic world. From the early eighteenth century to the mid-nineteenth century, the impact of the North American slave trade and labor system extended well beyond wealth enhancement for individuals there. The slavery system linking Africa to both American continents played a major role in the development of the world's dominant economic system—modern capitalism.

Writing in the nineteenth century, the astute economist and activist Karl Marx recognized that slavery systems created by European imperialism had generated much of the original economic assets (capital) that became the very foundation for the modern industrialized capitalistic system:

> Direct slavery is as much the pivot upon which our present-day industrialism turns as are machinery, credit, etc. Without slavery there would be no cotton, without cotton there would be no modern industry. It is slavery which has given value to the colonies, it is the colonies which have created world trade, and world trade is the

necessary condition for large-scale machine industry. . . . [W]ipe North America off the map and you will get anarchy, the complete decay of trade and modern civilization. But to do away with slavery would be to wipe America off the map.[31]

Similarly, Du Bois noted that on the "bent and broken backs" of enslaved black workers and other workers of color were laid "the founding stones of modern industry."[32] Clearly, white-run agricultural and commercial enterprises using enslaved laborers generated much profit and wealth in colonial and U.S. development, and much of this capital played a very central role in the later and great expansion of agricultural, commercial, and industrial capitalism across the United States and the globe. To reiterate Marx, "to do away with slavery would wipe America off the map" economically and politically.

Without this enormous enslaved labor force, modern capitalism would likely not have arisen, at least when it did arise, and expanded so dramatically. Unmistakably too, modern capitalism emerged as a fully developed and systemic racism. That systemic racial oppression has long been at the core of modern capitalism.

Building Infrastructure: Education, Government, Transportation

Beyond their work in agriculture, enslaved workers did much of the work over two centuries that built up the country's educational, government, and transportation infrastructure, although most of this work is ignored in mainstream history books and mainstream media. To take a dramatic example, the labor of enslaved African Americans directly or indirectly played a very important role in the construction of early colonial colleges and universities—which were often developed to facilitate and legitimate the expansion of a slavery-centered economic system. The first four colonial colleges—Harvard (1636), William and Mary (1693), Yale (1701), and New Jersey (1746)—were private and depended heavily on funding coming from well-off slaveholders. The great profits made off enslaved black laborers and the products they produced were the source of many contributions and endowments that helped to build these colleges. In addition, college officials frequently used enslaved workers to construct and maintain campus buildings and to provide food and other services for white students. College trustees and presidents were often slaveholders, and other trustees, administrators, faculty members, and students were connected with white slaveholding families. These colleges and universities included William and Mary, the University of Virginia, Brown University, Rutgers University, Williams College, the University of Alabama, the University of South Carolina, and the University of North Carolina. Indeed, slave-constructed buildings on numerous college campuses are still used, and many buildings there are still named after slaveholders. We might note, too, that some of these colleges also produced a few white graduates who became abolitionists.[33]

Young white men, many from plantations and other farms of the slaveholding South, were able to attend these colleges because their ancestors gained wealth off the backs of enslaved laborers. Many did not have to become farmers (a likely result without slavery) and instead became ministers, teachers, lawyers, merchants, bankers, physicians, and government officials in the South and North. Not surprisingly, as Craig Wilder underscores, numerous such colleges and universities were designed to be "instruments of Christian expansionism, weapons for the conquest of indigenous peoples, and major beneficiaries of the African slave trade and slavery." They were central to European imperialism in North America and sought to "convert indigenous peoples and soften cultural resistance, and extend European rule over foreign nations."[34] From their establishment in the seventeenth and eighteenth centuries to the end of slavery in the mid-1860s, a major purpose was to generate and perpetuate key elements of the dominant white racial framing of a slavery-centered society. Key ideas in this white racial frame included the necessary dominance of white civilization and the "right" of whites to take lands of indigenous peoples. The racial categorizations of "white" superiority and "black" inferiority were taught there and were central to an early white framing that rationalized the country's established racial hierarchy.[35]

The labor of enslaved African Americans directly or indirectly funded much early development of the physical sciences in these colleges and universities. That arduous labor enabled some whites to have the time and assets to become doctors and scientists—whose later work then was also often funded by slaveholders, land and slave speculators, and related merchants and bankers.[36] The new "scientific racism" generated by many of these scientists aggressively asserted notions of distinctive human "races" with different physical characteristics that were viewed as inherited and part of a natural racial hierarchy. Scientists at leading colleges and universities such as Harvard and Yale developed or reinforced a pseudo-scientific view of African Americans as biologically and innately inferior and thus deserving of comprehensive subordination.[37]

Colleges and universities were not the only institutions linked directly to the labor of enslaved African Americans. Indeed, it is hard to exaggerate the extent that enslaved (and later Jim-Crowed) labor was used to build up significant aspects of this country's extensive physical infrastructure, including major public and private buildings throughout the southern and border states. Enslaved workers built many of the great mansions, including the lavish plantation houses of Thomas Jefferson (Monticello),

George Washington (Mount Vernon), and James Madison (Montpelier). The highly exploited labor of African Americans indirectly funded or directly built many white churches, hospitals, state houses, city halls, and other important public and private institutions' facilities during the slavery and Jim Crow eras, many of which still dominate the country's rural and urban landscapes. From the late eighteenth century to the mid-nineteenth century, state government buildings in the South and federal buildings in Washington, DC, including the White House and the Capitol, were constructed, expanded, or rebuilt substantially by enslaved black laborers in both unskilled and skilled construction workforces.[38]

In the case of the U.S. Capitol, enslaved black workers cut the stones and brought them from quarries to build the walls, floors, and majestic columns of that building. Ironically, skilled black workers also cast and put a Statue of Freedom (a woman figure apparently in Native American garb) on the top of the Capitol dome. Significantly, too, not until 2012 did the U.S. Congress decide to recognize publicly this substantial African American labor but only with a modest "Slave Labor Commemorative Marker" in the Capitol visitors' center.[39] Few industrialized countries have had important buildings constructed by enslaved laborers.

In addition, significant portions of the country's early transportation and other industrial infrastructure were built, in whole or part, by enslaved workers doing the difficult, usually manual work. Theodore Kornweibel has noted that in the decades before the Civil War, railroads in almost every southern and border state used enslaved workers:

> First, slaves along with modest numbers of white workers constructed most if not all southern railroads . . . . Second, probably all southern railroads (and some in the border states) were operated and maintained by a mixed labor force of whites, enslaved African Americans, and small numbers of free Blacks.[40]

By the mid-1850s, the number of enslaved railroad workers reached about 10,000 annually, perhaps the largest number working in southern industries. Most white southerners left the hard unskilled industrial work in the South to enslaved and free black workers. Even after slavery, during the Jim Crow era, black workers were essential for southern and border state railroad companies. Significantly, recent reparations lawsuits brought by descendants of these highly exploited laborers have named some large railroad companies as defendants because of the significant facilities built by enslaved workers working for earlier companies they have absorbed over the years since slavery.[41]

Most of white America, and some of the rest of the nonblack population, is still a long way from coming to an honest engagement with the impact and significance of this country's long slave-labor history. A serious engagement should include a clear recognition and understanding of the huge contributions that many millions of highly exploited black workers have made in generating this country's massive infrastructure, economic growth, and enormous wealth. Indeed, most past and present accounts of slavery by mainstream analysts of various kinds have ignored or tried to sanitize critical aspects of black labor and other oppressive experiences in the slavery era. Euphemisms are one way in which this is still done. Those enslaved become "servants" or their poor housing becomes "servant quarters," including at old plantation sites that are major tourist attractions. The passive tense is often used. "Africans were brought to this area," instead of "whites enslaved Africans." In addition, ill-informed conservative analysts today have insisted that enslaved Africans badly needed the supposedly "civilizing" enslavement process and that slavery was "good" for those enslaved.[42]

Fetishizing Private Property: Slavery's Legacy

The slave labor system lasted for more than two centuries and had many systemic effects on this society, effects going beyond creating assets and other wealth for millions of whites. One reason that substantial racial change has been difficult over this country's history is that slaveholding elites played a central and determinative role in the creation of intentionally undemocratic economic, legal, and political institutions—to a substantial degree to protect their unjust impoverishment of hardworking enslaved (and free) African Americans. The slave labor system they controlled was not an anomaly marginal to these economic and political institutions, but was central from the seventeenth century to its demise in the 1860s.

In many ways, racialized slavery's impacts are still revealed throughout this country's economic and political institutions. To take a very important example, the slave labor era permanently shaped many aspects of the legal system that still buttresses all U.S. institutions. As Robin Einhorn has shown, that slave labor system played a critical role in the development of our distinctive private property ideas and laws. For instance, the Supreme Court's famous Dred Scott decision (1857) bluntly decreed that black Americans had "no rights which the white man is bound to respect." However, it did more than celebrate the dehumanization of African Americans. The court's all-white majority decreed that an act of Congress that

> deprives a [white] citizen of the United States of his liberty or [slave] property, merely because he came himself or brought his property into a particular Territory of the United States could hardly be dignified with the name of due process of law.[43]

This infamous ruling on enslaved human "property" set in place, influential to the present day, a sacred status for private property that does not exist in most other Western countries. To a significant degree, the U.S. celebration of private property persists today because powerful slaveholders and slave traders once worried greatly that their "people property," enslaved black workers, might flee and affect their profits. Over time, this distinctive and intensive emphasis on private property rights affected U.S. workers of all racial-ethnic backgrounds by making capitalistic companies stronger and workers' unions and the "welfare state" much weaker than in most European countries.[44]

In addition, the wealth generated by enslaved black workers gave white slaveholders much greater political power in the U.S. system than they otherwise would have had. The U.S. Constitution set up political institutions to protect the extensive holding and exploitation of African Americans as enslaved property—including a House of Representatives and an electoral college shaped by the extra representation given to white (mostly southern) slaveholders by the Constitution's three-fifths clause (the "federal ratio"). Because they held so many African Americans in bondage, slaveholders had very disproportionate control over the presidency and the Congress for most of the country's history before the Civil War. In the beginning, our often anti-democratic constitutional system was substantially created to protect the economic and political interests of white slaveholders and their merchant and other allies, especially including their interest in protecting the enslavement of human "property."[45]

The slavery system also set in place an especially authoritarian policing system, one that privileged whites, including in classes below that of the powerful white elite. Wide-ranging efforts to control black Americans and prevent them from gaining their freedom included an early development of "slave patrols," armed policing organizations mostly composed of ordinary whites. Especially in the South, these slave patrols often evolved into police departments that enforced Jim Crow segregation. The slave patrols were among the first government-funded policing units and were motivated by widespread white fears of blacks trying to free themselves from oppression, either individually or by organizing collective uprisings.[46] Note, also, that in recent decades, we have seen how contemporary white-run police departments too often continue this very old policing tradition of fearful racial profiling and other racialized, inegalitarian policing.

The Reconstruction Era: Black Savings, White Wealth

The enslavement era is not the only era that is still relatively unknown to most Americans. Most also lack knowledge of "Reconstruction," which lasted for a decade or so after the Civil War. At the end of that war, Congress passed a law setting up the Freedmen's Bank (1865–1874). Before that time, most African Americans, enslaved or free, had no savings, and those who did were mostly excluded from white-run banks. Because the Freedmen's Bank seemed to be buttressed by the U.S. government, many newly freed (and other) black Americans put their usually small savings in the thirty-four branches of the bank. By 1874, the total amount of deposits was large for that era, totaling about $7 million ($1.38 billion in 2013 dollars). That part of this bank's story is better known, although it is often connected to usually false accusations of "black corruption" during Reconstruction. The part of the history that is relatively unknown is that numerous branches of the Freedmen's Bank used these savings of black workers and their families to make loans and mortgages mostly to affluent whites. In addition, their mostly white bank directors and managers frequently were corrupt or poor administrators and often, directly or indirectly, embezzled money or otherwise made illicit personal profits off the bank branches. As Frederick Douglass, called in toward the end to head up the failing bank, put it, it was "The black man's cow, but the white man's milk." In 1874, Congress liquidated the bank, and a great many black depositors never got their savings back. As sociologist Marcus Hunter has noted, "Not only were black depositors not being repaid, their money was given to mostly well-to-do whites, and mainstream [white-owned] banks continued to exclude them."[47]

Many historians and other commentators have noted the "40 acres and a mule" promises made to those formerly enslaved by progressive Republican members of Congress and other white leaders in the 1860s. However, most newly freed blacks did not receive any land or other assets such as those promised. In some ways, this "40 acres" argument is still a distraction from the harsh societal reality imposed by whites in various classes on African Americans after the Civil War. The reason is that it may suggest to many whites and other nonblacks that African Americans then were not significant agents of their own improvement after slavery but were only waiting for government "handouts." In contrast, the Freedmen's Bank's substantial deposits reveal how very hardworking the newly freed black workers and their families were. The Freedmen's Bank example reveals that, without any government provision of significant assets to compensate for centuries of barbarous state-backed enslavement, modest-income black workers were Horatio Alger models of thrift; by the 1870s they had managed to save up the equivalent of $1.38 billion today just in branches of this Freedmen's Bank. They did this within a decade after many were freed from one of the world's worst slave systems. Yet, in subsequent white-created bank crises, black depositors lost a huge proportion of what they had saved in the Freedmen's Bank and in other white-run banks that went bankrupt in the "bank panics" of the 1870s.[48]

The current value of these assets, most of them lost because of financial decisions of white men who frequently made substantial wealth off their involvement, totals far more than just the current value of the deposits lost. To get a full estimate of the significance of these lost resources, one needs to add in an estimate of the substantial interest lost over the intervening 140 years—that is, the economic enhancement that would have been created if those assets had been available to that generation of depositors and the numerous generations that have lived since that time. Average U.S. Treasury Bond rates have been 4.9 percent since 1900. If we use that conservative economic enhancement rate and figure just the compound interest on a conservative estimate of $4 million lost to black depositors in the Freedmen's Bank collapse, one gets a figure of about $241 billion (in current dollars) lost to generations of African Americans, mostly because of corrupt and incompetent actions of whites who generally controlled that bank and frequently generated white wealth from their involvement.

Jim Crow Segregation: Semi-Slave Labor

After official slavery ended in the 1860s, yet more undeserved white profits and wealth were generated by thousands of white agricultural and other employers who extensively exploited millions of extremely underpaid African American workers. In the decades after Reconstruction, black southerners faced an expanding and barbarous form of Jim Crow oppression, in numerous ways much like slavery. As Frederick Douglass sagely noted, in this shift to official segregation, African Americans had moved from white individual's control to white group control:

> In nearly every department of American life [black people] are confronted by this insidious influence. It fills the air. It meets them at the workshop and factory, when they apply for work. It meets them at the church, at the hotel, at the ballotbox, and worst of all, it meets them in the jurybox. . . . [The black American] has ceased to be a slave of an individual, but has in some sense become the slave of society.[49]

Much continuing exploitation of the labor of African Americans took the form of sharecropping and tenant farming, a type of farming often forced on them to expand white incomes and assets. Economist Gerald Jaynes has described the "long pay" that black tenant farmers, sharecroppers, and other laborers got in this exceedingly exploitative system—that is, they got compensated for their hard work only at the end of a harvest season and then only after paying off debts for supplies that were owed to the white farmer they labored for or to his associates. Frequently, they were unable to pay off these debts and became in effect "chained" to that white farmer and a specific geographical area.[50] In an 1888 speech on the anniversary of black emancipation from slavery in Washington, DC, the savvy Douglass denounced the "so-called emancipation as a stupendous fraud." Back from a visit to southern states, Douglass concluded that the condition of the African American there was extraordinarily impoverished and oppressed because under tenancy and shareholding conditions,

> he is systematically and universally cheated out of his hard earnings. The same [white] class that once extorted his labor under the lash now gets his labor by a mean, sneaking, and fraudulent device. That device is a trucking [company store] system which never permits him to see or to save a dollar of his hard earnings. . . . The highest wages paid him is eight dollars a month, and this he receives only in orders on the store, which, in many cases, is owned by his employer. . . . He can charge the poor fellow what he pleases and give what kind of goods he pleases, and he does both. . . . [This system also] puts it out of the power of the Negro to save anything of what he earns.[51]

Douglass then underscored the point that this extreme white exploitation and extortionist profit making

> is not the only evil involved in this satanic arrangement. It promotes dishonesty. The Negro sees himself paid but limited wages—far too limited to support himself and family, and that in worthless scrip—and he is tempted to fight the devil with fire. Finding himself systematically robbed he goes to stealing and as a result finds his liberty—such as it is—taken from him, and himself put to work for a master in a chain gang, and he comes out, if he ever gets out, a ruined man.[52]

"Crimes" against a near-slavery system are not, in broader moral perspective, immoral or criminal acts but are absolutely necessary for human survival. Still, black reactions to this extraordinary oppression created problems for black communities and fed the white-racist image of blacks as "criminals"— as they still do today.

Douglass then made clear that this new slavery was assisted and guaranteed by white-run governments. Consider a black southerner's

> relation to the national government and we shall find him a deserted, a defrauded, a swindled, and an outcast man—in law free, in fact a slave; in law a citizen, in fact an alien; in law a voter, in fact, a disfranchised man. In law, his color is no crime; in fact, his color exposes him to be treated as a criminal.[53]

In effect, African Americans faced a "totalitarian" society in which state-backed oppression could be found in most of its nooks and crannies. The pioneering activist-scholar Ida B. Wells-Barnett accented how Jim Crow oppression was grounded in the material reality of white economic exploitation and protected by pervasive violent controls, such as lynchings, of black men and women.[54]

During the legal segregation era, millions of workers were utilized in many different ways to generate yet more profits and wealth for white employers, large and small. Their exploitation took place in an array of work settings, not just in agriculture. As one white man put it in Greensboro, North Carolina, black southerners should not be provided constitutional rights because their segregated labor is necessary to build up white wealth: "He tills our farms, clears away our woods, builds our railroad beds, generally is a necessary factor of industrial [and] agricultural life in our section...."[55] To take one key example, much extraction of important mineral resources, such as coal, was done by highly exploited black laborers. This coal was essential to U.S. industrialization, as it fueled the iron and steel plants that supplied much of the fabrication of materials for that expanding industrialization.[56]

In this era of blatant, often savage discrimination black workers were usually paid substantially lower wages—either directly or indirectly through the method of job channeling and stratification—than white workers. Black women workers had to endure the greatest wage exploitation.[57] In hard times, such as the 1930s Great Depression, black workers were usually first to be laid off and the last to be rehired. During this Depression, to make things worse, federal relief programs typically provided black workers with lower pay and oftentimes hired black workers only after unemployed whites had been hired.[58]

In addition, some workers in the Jim Crow era suffered even more extreme economic exploitation. One large group was composed of convict laborers who were forced to work in coalfields and other settings. From just after the Civil War until about 1930, many black men in numerous states, mainly in the South, were imprisoned for an array of often minor or trumped-up crimes, such as vagrancy ("no job") and then leased out by white-controlled government agencies and forced into workplace conditions much like slavery. In this convict-leasing system, tens of thousands were farmed out to white employers involved in coal mining, quarrying, agriculture, railroad and road construction, and lumber operations.[59] Yet again, white employers often made significant profits off this forced labor, thereby providing capital for other investments or for enhancing the economic opportunities of later white generations. Note, too, that white-run local and state governments usually secured significant revenue from these employers of convict labor.

Northern Workplaces: De Facto Segregation

In the early twentieth century, as industrialization expanded dramatically, especially in the northern states, African American workers were sought out for new industrial jobs. In 1918, for instance, Dwight Thompson Farnham, an influential white engineer, published an advocacy article on "Negroes as a Source of Industrial Labor." In this Jim Crow segregation era, northern labor experts such as Farnham often accented the importance of southern black workers as a major new source for industrial workers, a source that was necessary to use if the industrializing economy was to continue to expand.[60]

However, this new manufacturing employment for African Americans did not mean an end of socially enforced segregation, just a new form. In northern states, much segregation was informally enforced by discrimination and often threats of white violence. Northern oppression took the form of de facto rather than legal segregation of southern states. There was extensive job segregation in workplaces and much white use of racist framing in controlling black workers. In the 1910s, Detroit area employers such as the expanding Ford Motor Company hired black workers fleeing from southern Jim Crow areas and immigrant workers from southern and eastern Europe. Contrary to white notions of black laziness, these black workers were desperate for work and usually took any job that they could find. Ford's and other manufacturing companies' white managers frequently pitted the European immigrant workers against African American workers so as to maintain a more compliant labor force. Indeed, white managers and owners communicated their highly racist framing of black Americans to new white immigrants to create racial barriers among workers and reduce the chances of racially integrated union organizations.[61]

Researchers Elizabeth Esch and David Roediger have documented how the "scientific management" experts involved in northern industrialization actively sought to understand and "develop 'the races' not only for the purpose of accumulating capital but also for the organization of modern production."[62] Moreover, the idea of the "white race" being wise in its management of workers of color was regularly involved in corporate management of black and other industrial workers. Decades earlier, one might recall, white slaveholders had also prided themselves on their black labor management skills ("We know our blacks" thinking). Indeed, to the present day, capitalistic management has periodically used some white racial framing to divide or otherwise manage labor in numerous companies.[63]

More Jim Crow: Black Military Service

From the 1940s to the 1960s, the white government officials running U.S. military operations during World War II, the Korean War, and the

Vietnam War actively recruited African American workers and soldiers to ensure the country's success in war efforts, even as the latter suffered wide-ranging discrimination in these situations. For instance, African Americans were utilized as essential support troops and, occasionally, as frontline troops in World War II, a war officially fought for "liberty and freedom" against German Nazi operations in Europe. In spite of rigid Jim Crow segregation in the U.S. military, some 93,000 African Americans served in the Quartermaster Corps, with thousands serving as courageous drivers in the truck convoying system called the "Red Ball Express" that supplied U.S. military advances in 1944. Almost three-fourths of the drivers were African Americans, and their efforts, according to the Department of Defense, "played a major role in the Nazis' defeat."[64] Another group of segregated black military units, called the Tuskegee Airmen ("Red Tails"), were African American aviators and their support troops. Nearly 1,000 African Americans were trained as pilots, flew 1,500 missions in World War II, and won a great many military honors. Many other African Americans served as support troops and bomber crew members in these units.[65]

About a million black Americans served in World War II, yet they were rigidly segregated. Most were given racially segregated, typically menial and manual support jobs and kept in low ranks at meager pay. Rarely covered well in U.S. history books, only in March 2007 were they finally recognized with the Congressional Gold Medal. As one Tuskegee Airman, Herbert Carter, has explained, "You grow up feeling a love for your country in spite of its imperfections. You're happy and proud to be an American who just happens to have a different pigmentation, a different skin color."[66] Moreover, returning home, they often found there that they, even in uniform, had little real "freedom" from racial oppression. Indeed, some were beaten up or lynched in the South for insisting on their freedom in the United States.[67] In later U.S. wars, including the Korean and Vietnam wars, African Americans were over-represented among the U.S. troops, with persisting discrimination within the military ranks a recurring problem. Paul Murray sums up the long years of the draft, from 1917 to 1970: "Although the official policies of the Selective Service System have always benefited white registrants, only recently has the Army abandoned its theories of black inferiority. Now both institutions are cooperating to draft as many blacks as possible."[68]

Exploiting Labor, Destroying Businesses

Writing about the Jim Crow South in the 1940s, African American social scientist Oliver Cox emphasized how powerful whites had greatly exploited the labor of non-Europeans in North America. He underscored the point that this exploitation was not about "an abstract, natural, immemorial feeling of mutual antipathy between groups, but rather a practical exploitative relationship with its socio-attitudinal facilitation."[69] A century earlier, the economist Karl Marx had analyzed the exploitation of subordinated workers by capitalistic employers, who secured profits by taking part of the value of workers' labor for their own purposes—thus not paying workers for the full value of their work. In the slavery system, black workers had been coerced into giving their efforts for far less than its economic value. Similarly, under Jim Crow situations, white employers generally had the power, because of state-backed and institutionally facilitated discrimination, to extort additional value from the labor of black employees as compared with that of white employees. Under legal segregation, millions continued to be super-exploited in an expanding racist-capitalistic society. Yet again, from profits off this exploited black labor, many white men and their families prospered economically, as have many of their inheriting descendants to the present day.

Calculating the total positive impact of black Americans in building up this country during the Jim Crow era is not possible, nor is it possible to calculate the total losses for black Americans from such massive discrimination. Clearly, huge amounts of uncompensated black labor again built up white prosperity and wealth in this Jim Crow era. We have previously estimated the economic productivity of, and thus losses to, enslaved black Americans and their families from centuries of highly coercive labor, as perhaps about $11 trillion in contemporary dollars. After slavery, the economic losses for black Americans continued to be high under the blatantly discriminatory Jim Crow conditions that most faced until the 1960s. Just for the Jim Crow years 1929 to 1969, researchers have estimated these particular losses for African Americans to be about $5.4 trillion (in 2013 dollars).[70]

Moreover, in the Jim Crow era, many African Americans built up businesses in communities across the South and Southwest, and significant family assets were created. However, numerous businesses were intentionally destroyed by violent whites, such as in the large-scale massacres of black people and major destruction of businesses in the black communities of Wilmington (North Carolina) and Tulsa (Oklahoma). In the latter city during the summer of 1921, white rioters destroyed "forty-one grocers and meat markets, thirty restaurants, fifteen physicians, five hotels, two theaters, and two newspapers." They burned churches, schools, and "eighteen thousand homes and enterprises," and killed hundreds of black residents.[71] In this manner, whites destroyed not only businesses but established communities. Even where there was not such collective violence and terrorism, the majority of black Americans were blocked from receiving equitable home and other loans, adequate public educations, and fair access to many business opportunities outside their communities. Large-scale white discrimination also meant that whites generally faced considerably less job, home loan, and business competition and thus had much greater access to economic opportunities and much greater ability to pass along their unjustly gained assets to latter generations.

Nonetheless, in spite of these long decades of extreme Jim Crow oppression, the prodigious work and great sacrifices of African Americans again built up thousands of viable and supportive communities. They thereby contributed very courageously and significantly to general American prosperity and progress.

Jim Crow Unwilling to Die: Contemporary Labor Exploitation

African American workers continue to play a very significant role in the U.S. economy. Writing in the 1990s, the prominent African American law professor, Derrick Bell, underscored the point that workplace discrimination has long been designed "to facilitate the exploitation of black labor, to deny us access to benefits and opportunities that otherwise would be available, and to blame all the manifestations of exclusion-bred despair on the asserted inferiority of the victims."[72] As in the past, today's workplace discrimination is exploitative in that white employers often take more of the economic value of the still substantial labor of black workers than that of comparable white workers. Some are just paid less, but others are intentionally steered into segregated or quasi-segregated job categories for which they are often overqualified but that ensure they get paid less. Indeed, in the contemporary economy, a majority of black male workers are employed in unskilled, semi-skilled, service, or other relatively low-paid blue-collar jobs, in professional and managerial positions disproportionately serving black consumers, or in part-time positions that do not pay enough to live on. Others are disproportionately unemployed or underemployed. Black female workers also face substantial workplace discrimination in white-dominated institutions, no matter what their educational level and employment category may be.[73]

Underemployment and De-industrialization

Not surprisingly, given persisting and systemic racism, when the U.S. economy worsens, as it regularly does, black workers usually fare worse than white workers. For many decades to the present, black workers have been kept as an important "reserve army" of unemployed and underemployed workers, often in the growing prison-industrial complex, until they are needed when the economy again expands. Prominent politicians frequently describe the economy as "improving" or "very good" when that assessment is focused on white workers. Even then, a much larger proportion of black workers than white workers remain underpaid, unemployed, or underemployed in low-wage or part-time jobs.

Moreover, as more and more jobs have been shipped out of the country to lower-wage factories and other facilities ever more aggressively since 1960, black blue-collar workers in many areas have become less essential for capitalistic production and profitability. Indeed, as this formerly essential labor became less necessary in the 1960s, many whites in the economic elite were finally accepting of government efforts to abolish coercive legal segregation, including that in employment settings. Many of these employers no longer sought the large numbers of black workers on whom they had previously depended for manufacturing enterprises. By the 1960s and 1970s, numerous white-controlled industries that had been built up substantially by African American workers were abandoning many of them to a life of greater poverty, unemployment, and underemployment.[74]

Numerous northern cities, such as Detroit, and their large populations of black workers were being abandoned by white employers and related capitalists as they moved to southern and overseas areas with weak or no unions and fewer environmental regulations. Thus, in research on Detroit's decline as a major industrial city, Thomas Sugrue has underscored how black workers in the 1930s–1950s era had migrated in large numbers from the Jim Crow South to take many jobs in the expanding auto industry and defense-related industries, yet were usually discriminated against and kept in lower-wage positions with less chance of skilled training and advancement. The corporate executives' discriminatory decisions were frequently implemented by white-controlled unions. Once in place, this workplace discrimination had immediate and long-term effects on the health and wealth of black workers, their families, and descendants. When manufacturing plants were closed by Detroit's corporate decision makers, as has been the case in many cities during the decades-long process of urban decline, these black workers had less job protection and were among the first to be demoted or terminated. Well-institutionalized white racism extended beyond Detroit's workplaces to local housing, public services, and schools. Upwardly mobile white workers often worked hard to keep black families out of their more advantaged, increasingly middle-class neighborhoods— and, thus, away from important public services, including quality police protection and better schools that could assist them in upward mobility.[75] Again and again, ordinary whites were assisted in this racialized barrier creation by local and national white political and economic elites.

African Americans have long fought to secure the same community services as those of white Americans. Yet they have faced chronic and everyday discrimination in all regions of the country in the era of U.S. industrialization, and later de-industrialization. Thus, this highly discriminatory process intentionally limiting black education and economic advancement took place not only in Detroit but in numerous other cities in the Midwest and Northeast, such as Baltimore, Chicago, Milwaukee, New York, and Philadelphia. Repeatedly, African American workers who helped greatly to build up the country's major industries were abandoned first when such blue-collar workers were no longer needed.[76] Not surprisingly, no longer did white decision makers make the necessary public investments previously made in urban schools and other social support programs that had facilitated the growth of these urban industries and the country's white middle class. Once patterns of urban racial discrimination in employment, housing, and school patterns are put firmly into place, their effects can last for many decades.

Super-Exploitation of Prison Workers

The highly discriminatory pattern of excluding black workers from advancement into skilled and better-paid jobs and the maintenance of large numbers as a "reserve army" of the unemployed and underemployed, have been central features in the development of the economy since the nineteenth century. This persists to the present day. We have noted the importance of convict labor, a type of reserve army, to white employers in the Jim Crow era and the collusion of government officials. New versions of this exceedingly discriminatory system have persisted into the present, a "new Jim Crow" reality. In recent decades, some in the country's political-economic elite have intentionally created a huge prison population that is very disproportionately black (and Latino). One likely reason for this elite action is to further "control" the large black, especially male, working class—and, not incidentally, to increase the supply of very low-wage manufacturing workers in prisons. Unquestionably, we now have an extensive prison-industrial system that generates significant profits for an array of corporations, including those that build and maintain private prisons and those that make significant use of prison labor.

The scale and importance of this prison-industrial complex were dramatically expanded under the conservative Ronald Reagan administration in the 1980s. That administration significantly expanded the U.S. "war on drugs," even though in opinion polls then Americans revealed little concern about drug issues. Legal scholar Michelle Alexander notes that this elite "war" was not really about "public concern about drugs" but more about white "concern about race." That is, there is continuing fear among whites, and especially in much of the white elite, about black rebellion against growing unemployment and underemployment that developed in the 1970s and 1980s after the civil rights era. The reelection of the reactionary Reagan, followed by the election of his conservative vice president, George H. W. Bush, showed that ordinary white voters were also unconcerned with the substantial racial discrimination involved in the expanding drug-war arrests and were also "willing to forego economic and structural reform" that would benefit themselves "in exchange for an apparent effort to put blacks back 'in their place.'"[77] Not surprisingly, surveys of whites found that their racist attitudes, and not actual crime rates, were the more important factors shaping their support of the newly aggressive anti-crime measures.[78]

Between 1981, the beginning of the Reagan administration, and 2008, the number of incarcerated Americans more than quadrupled, from half a million to about 2.3 million. Only 12 percent of the population, African Americans are now imprisoned at nearly six times the rate of whites and make up about 40 percent of this massive imprisoned population. Much of this racial inequality in imprisonment comes from various forms of discrimination in the criminal justice system. For instance, in the country as a whole, black youths account for 26 percent of juvenile arrests, yet they make up 58 percent of those sent to state prisons. Roughly equal percentages of whites and blacks admit to using illegal drugs, yet blacks are far more likely to be arrested and sent to prison. Overall, blacks make up about 12 percent of drug users but are 38 percent of those arrested and 58 percent of those imprisoned in state prisons for drug offenses. Even more relevant to the prison labor issue is that blacks with drug offenses are also kept in prisons longer than whites for similar offenses.[79] This massive imprisonment of black Americans signals once again that white Americans, and most importantly the white elite, are unconcerned with the severely damaging impact of high unemployment on black families and communities—much of that damage the legacy of the Jim Crow era—and much more concerned with maintaining the existing racial hierarchy and its unjust economic inequalities benefitting whites. Gradually, however, as we move on into the twenty-first century, the high cost of this imprisonment for this society generally is beginning to dawn on some in the white population.

As with convict labor in the Jim Crow era, black prisoners are today processed and used by the prison system in intentionally discriminatory and exploitative ways. In U.S. prisons, black and other prison workers are usually paid far less ($1–$10 a day) than the wages of comparable workers outside prisons. A large array of local, national, and international companies have thereby exploited these black workers and often made substantial profits from them. These include electronics and computer companies such as Nortel, Hewlett-Packard, Intel, Honeywell, Texas Instruments, Compaq, Microsoft, and IBM; airplane manufacturers such as Boeing; and retailers of consumer goods such as Nordstrom, Revlon, Target, Pierre Cardin, Victoria's Secret and many other U.S. firms.[80]

Even more strikingly, a little-known, billion-dollar U.S. government corporation (UNICOR) exploits this slave-like labor to make goods and provide services for government agencies. This is a federally created government corporation with 110 factories at 79 federal prisons, and its highly exploited prison workers manufacture most of the military's "helmets, ID tags, bullet-proof vests, canteens, night-vision goggles, ammunition belts, tents, shirts, bags, and pants."[81] The prison-industrial complex thus helps sustain the military-industrial complex, including its often racialized adventures overseas. Many other products are made for the private sector. Legal scholar Noah Zatz has estimated that as many as 1 million inmates are working for corporations and government agencies:

> Perhaps some of them built your desk chair: office furniture, especially in state universities and the federal government, is a major prison labor product. Inmates also take hotel reservations at corporate call centers, make body armor for the U.S. military, and manufacture prison chic fashion accessories, in addition to the iconic task of stamping license plates.[82]

Sociologist Terence Fitzgerald summarizes the situation thus:

> The oppressive acts of slavery are still occurring—not in the cotton or sugar fields but within the walls of the prisons' industrial complex. And in the process, primarily Black and Brown males are being exploited for the benefit of the White racial frame.[83]

The conditions for imprisoned black (and Latino) workers again suggest a type of neo-slavery, with few worker's rights, benefits, and protections; and they often work for very long work days and weeks. The mostly white employers secure yet other advantages. These black workers' jobs are strictly controlled and do not require sick leave or vacation days—that is, they are major profit-generating workers from a corporate viewpoint. Significant coercion, reminiscent of earlier white "labor management" of "their blacks," is involved because black and other prison workers lose privileges and "good time" if they do not engage in these low-wage jobs. Indeed, inmates are sometimes physically punished if they do not work.[84] Once again, super-exploited black labor dramatically contributes to the build-up of white wealth and prosperity, this time in the contemporary era.

Contemporary Discrimination: More White Gains

Previously, I have drawn on various sources to estimate losses to African Americans for extensive work they did as the enslaved and to Jim-Crowed workers who built up so much of this society's economy and public and private infrastructure. Given that blatant and subtle racial discrimination has continued in many employment sectors, we can also roughly estimate more contemporary losses to African American workers and their families. Calculating the more recent losses stemming from continuing discrimination in the job market after 1969, the end of official segregation, one can build on an estimate for the year 1979 of economic losses to black workers of about $395 billion (in 2013 dollars).[85] Additionally, calculating these losses for the years since 1969, one might reasonably conclude that African American workers have again lost several trillion dollars in income and wealth just from contemporary racial discrimination by whites in various U.S. labor markets.

Moreover, the size of the current economic value of the black labor productivity stolen by whites through all the institutional mechanisms of slavery, Jim Crow segregation, and contemporary discrimination totals many trillions of dollars. In addition, there are the huge monetary losses that African Americans suffered because of the loss of lands and other property that was stolen or destroyed by whites during the slavery and Jim Crow centuries. Over much of the nineteenth and twentieth centuries, white families benefitted greatly from anti-black discrimination in the distribution of lands under federal homestead acts. After the Civil War, up to the 1930s, the U.S. government provided about 246 million acres of land to about 1.5 million farm homesteads. These were overwhelmingly white, because the large numbers of black families in these areas were excluded by discriminatory actions, including racial violence. Many white families built up substantial wealth from these homestead land assets over several generations—and in southern areas often with the labor of black workers and tenants. One researcher has estimated from data projections that as many as 46 million whites are contemporary descendants and beneficiaries of these often unjustly enriched white homesteaders.[86]

Not only have black families been excluded by blatant discrimination from many such wealth-generating assets, but the land they have secured by diligent work efforts has often been stolen from them or made difficult to develop over decades of Jim Crow and contemporary discrimination. To take one major example, over the last eight decades, subtle and overt loan discrimination in the banking industry and subtle and overt discrimination against black farmers in agricultural markets and programs have played an important role in sharply reducing the number of black farms and farmers. Black-owned farmland declined from about 15 million acres in the early twentieth century to about 2.3 million acres in the early twenty-first century. Eventually, black farmers brought a lawsuit against the Department of Agriculture for compensation for racial discrimination in federal farm programs; thousands of claims had been settled by the early twenty-first century for more than $641 million.[87] For many decades, discrimination by white officials in control of important private and government agricultural programs put major racial barriers in the way of African American farmers, contributing to their unjust impoverishment and that of their descendants. The consequences of such discrimination once again included greater white prosperity. During the same period, white farmers had racially privileged access (e.g., less competition for loans and farm programs) that contributed greatly to their unjust enrichment and that of their descendants.

For many decades, too, black families have also lost access to housing loans—and thus much likely wealth in the form of housing equities—from white lending officials' discriminatory lending practices. During the Jim Crow era, there was much home loan discrimination, and in the contemporary era, this loan discrimination has persisted. One egregious example took place in the "Great Recession" of 2008–2010. In that period, black homeowners were frequently channeled into risky subprime (high-interest) home loans by mostly white lenders. However, a majority of these families had credit scores that should have enabled them to get loans with more favorable interest rates and conditions. Federal government reports indicate that black homebuyers were more than twice as likely as comparable white homebuyers to receive these high-interest loans, even when loan amounts and incomes were comparable.[88]

As happened with the Freedmen's Bank in the nineteenth century, banking officials made billions of dollars off African American borrowers in this discriminatory process. The latter lost an estimated $71 billion to $92 billion, one of the greatest losses of potentially inheritable wealth for African Americans in the contemporary era. Yet again, black wealth built up from long years of work and saving efforts was lost because of the discriminatory and unethical actions of mostly white-controlled banking institutions. In addition, this loss of family wealth was accompanied in many cases with a loss of homes through bank foreclosures, which in turn had very negative effects on the daily lives of black families and of entire neighborhoods. One United for a Fair Economy report concluded that the racist framing of borrowers of color led white-dominated

> banks and brokers to deliberately and coldly seek to boost their profits by targeting minority subjects with faulty loan products. . . questionable measures that in previous decades would have been roundly condemned as predatory . . . began to look more and more attractive to an industry worried about its future profits.[89]

Once again, billions in increased white wealth were made off the hard work and steady savings of African Americans.

Continuing Social Reproduction of Inequality

The total economic value of the hundreds of millions of unpaid hours of work that African Americans did to build up this country over nearly twenty generations is enormous, no matter how calculated. Economic losses to African Americans from white oppression over the centuries, direct and indirect, are likely to be much more than the current U.S. gross national product (about $17 trillion). In addition, there are the nonmonetary costs involved for African Americans. These have included the huge physical and psychological costs from the great pain, suffering, and death associated with all aspects of systemic racism for centuries. There is the incalculable cost of millions of lives cut short by long centuries of slavery and by the Jim Crow discrimination in segregated workplaces, hospitals, and other institutions lasting into the late 1960s. Discussing intelligence, a prominent Harvard biologist once put it this way: "I am, somehow, less interested in the weight and convolutions of Einstein's brain than in the near certainty that people of equal talent have lived and died in cotton fields and sweatshops."[90]

Most economic losses for African Americans as a group over centuries have meant significant gains, directly or indirectly, for a great many white Americans and their descendants. Much of middle-class white America might not exist without those centuries of racial exploitation. In innumerable ways, the all-encompassing subordination and exploitation of black Americans has contributed significantly to the creation, growth, and maintenance of the advantages of most people in the white middle class. Stolen black labor and property frequently became income, profits, and wealth for whites as individuals and as owners of farms and other enterprises—and then became economic assets and wealth passed along over many family generations. White workers as a group have had far more good economic opportunities and gained far more assets and wealth than have the black workers in the same eras who were racially subordinated, segregated, and excluded. Low-wage black labor has also increased whites' economic prosperity in yet other ways, including the low-paid service labor provided by black domestic workers, food workers, and other manual workers, that has lessened the cost of desirable goods and services secured by middle-class white Americans in their quest for comfort and prosperity.

Quite central to how this inegalitarian society has routinely operated are the mostly hidden social inheritance mechanisms that ensure that most people in each new generation of whites inherit some asset-generating racial privileges and socioeconomic resources and assets. In the recent past and the present, a majority of whites have inherited significant economic resources, such as a house equity or family savings, and/or social capital such as access to a good education and good job networks. Pioneering research by sociologist Jennifer Mueller on white families and families of color has dramatically demonstrated the large scale of the socioeconomic and government resources passed along the generations. Mueller found huge racial differences in the acquisition and intergenerational transfer of economic assets over several generations to the present day. White families averaged

> more than six times as many transfers of monetary assets across generations in these families histories—216 transfers of monetary assets reported in the 105 white families' histories, compared to a paltry 13 such transfers reported among 39 families of color.[91]

Transfers of land, property, and businesses were also much more common for white families than for families of color. If this were not enough advantage, this intergenerational reproduction of significant assets across white generations was well buttressed by an array of pro-white government programs. (For example, officials implementing federal homestead land acts from the 1860s to 1930s and the GI Bill after World War II excluded or otherwise discriminated against black applicants.). Over several generations Mueller's white families had received five times as many instances of these government-assisted assets as the families of color.

Conclusion

This chapter documents the extensive contributions of black labor over nearly four centuries of this country's dramatic development. This reality has meant great contributions to the economy by black workers and their families, contributions so massive that there would perhaps be no United States without them. Much of this massive labor history is unknown to most people or is marginalized in contemporary discussions of racial matters. It needs now to be aggressively foregrounded in almost all educational and other informational settings.

Undeniably, too, one of the immense contributions of African Americans to this society goes well beyond their physical labor to include their penetrating insights into the deep realities and operations of our foundational and systemic racism, in the past and present. In the discussions of the astute analyses of Jim Crow by Frederick Douglass, Ida B. Wells-Barnett, and Oliver Cox, we observed their clear recognition of the extensive material exploitation of African American lives and labor that has long been central in the black counter-framing response to this country's systemic racism. More recently, in the 1960s, black activist Kwame Ture and black historian Charles Hamilton critiqued limiting notions about individual racism and wrote in detail about the material realities of more contemporary oppression, what they termed perceptively the "institutional racism" in various sectors of this society.[92] Furthermore, in the 1970s, Angela Davis and Philomena Essed extended this perspective and underscored the distinctive material realities of oppression that took place because of the intersections of racism and sexism in the oppressed lives of African American women. They accentuated how women of color regularly produced community-imbedded knowledge to counter the concrete expressions of gendered racism.[93]

This extraordinary counter-framing and community-imbedded knowledge—at the core about real liberty and justice for all—constitute yet another major gift to this country as a whole, albeit one rarely recognized outside African American communities.

3

Black Genius Shaping U.S. Culture

One of the great ironies of U.S. history is that most Americans, especially most whites, are unaware of the huge positive and shaping impacts that African Americans have had on important aspects of this society's mainstream culture. In a certain sense, we are *all African Americans* in terms of certain cultural practices whose origin has mostly been lost or forgotten. African- and African American–influenced cultural and societal realities include not only those in the areas of music, literature, religion, and sports but also those in regard to important technological advances and even to how U.S. English developed and is still spoken. Indeed, one can argue it is the African and African American inputs into U.S. culture that often make it quite distinctive from the cultures of European countries.

In spite of these profoundly significant influences on the mainstream culture, from the first decades of intergroup contact, a great many white analysts have framed and attacked the culture of Africans and African Americans in white-racist terms. For example, in his 1785 book, *Notes on the State of Virginia*, the major intellectual and founding figure, Thomas Jefferson, laid out a vigorously racist framing of black Americans as highly inferior to whites, including in their cultural characteristics. He alleged they were much less intelligent, irrational in reasoning, musically and religiously unsophisticated, and without significant cultural advances that should be respected by whites. From the seventeenth century to well past the middle of the twentieth century, most influential whites overtly and aggressively agreed with Jefferson.[1] Indeed, the early colleges and universities mentioned in the last chapter were centers for the academic development of such anti-black ideologies, including the aggressive "scientific racism" of the nineteenth century.

Well into the middle of the twentieth century era, the racialized attack on African American culture could be found in important social science analyses of U.S. racial matters. Recall from Chapter 1 the famous social science book, *An American Dilemma*, authored by Gunnar Myrdal. There, this liberal social scientist argued that "Negro culture" is "a pathological condition, of the general American culture." Major features of this highly exaggerated pathological culture included family instability, religious emotionalism, and high crime rates. This often negative and racist framing of black America has persisted in many areas of white America to the present.[2]

Co-Workers in the Kingdom of Culture

While their actions are less well known than those who assert this white supremacist perspective, many African American analysts have for centuries forthrightly pushed back against it, in the process revealing much insight into how this racist society operates. Responding to prominent analysts such as Myrdal, the great U.S. novelist, Ralph Ellison, argued that people who have survived centuries of oppression do more than just react:

> Are American Negroes simply the creation of white men, or have they at least helped to create themselves out of what they found around them? . . . Myrdal sees Negro culture and personality simply as the product of a "social pathology." Thus he assumes that "it is to the advantage of American Negroes as individuals and as a group to become assimilated into American culture, to acquire the traits held in esteem by the dominant white Americans." ... Which, aside from implying that Negro culture is not also American, assumes that Negroes should desire nothing better than what whites consider highest. But in the "pragmatic sense" lynching and Hollywood, fadism and radio advertising are products of the "higher" culture, and the Negro might ask, "Why, if my culture is pathological, must I exchange it for these?" It does not occur to Myrdal that many of the Negro cultural manifestations which he considers merely reflective might also embody a rejection of what he considers "higher values."[3]

In this perceptive counter-framed view, Ellison underscores *pathological* elements in the dominant culture, which are easily observed by those subordinated. While Ellison recognizes negative features of black culture, he adds that there is much "of great value and richness, which, because it has been secreted by living and has made their lives more meaningful, Negroes will not willingly disregard."[4]

In recent years, no one has fully detailed the important black impacts on key aspects of U.S. sociocultural realities, but there have been many, including those with profound national and global significance. As one expert lately put it, various aspects of the contemporary culture of African Americans—including "clothing, dance, hairstyling, music, song, speech, and worship"—have spread to many corners of the globe.[5]

Indeed, more than a century ago, the ever-prescient W. E. B. Du Bois accented the important cultural interactions and mutual influences already long underway between white and black Americans. The general objective of the black American was *not* to

> bleach his Negro soul in a flood of white Americanism, for he knows that Negro blood has a message for the world. . . . This, then, is the end of his striving: to be a co-worker in the kingdom of culture, . . . to husband and use his best powers and his latent genius. These powers of body and mind have in the past been strangely wasted, dispersed, or forgotten.[6]

One aspect of this kingdom-of-culture reality is that African American cultural creations should not be viewed as just appendages tacked onto the dominant culture but as co-equal cultural efforts.

Akinyele Umoja has underscored the African cultural heritage those enslaved brought with them, which became an element in this "kingdom of North American culture." Enslaved Africans negotiated difficult environments and designed "their own New African cultural matrix borrowing on West and West-Central African institutions . . . [which became] a significant and foundational factor in the identity, social life, and political culture, including insurgent resistance."[7] Many of these Africans had been members of important organizations, including African secret societies. They often recreated, as much as they could under bondage, African organizations. They came "equipped with a model of community organization in the absence of legal authority and social power." Their commitment to such organizations was frequently ideological, which "insured that Africans entering the Americas did not simply stop being African."[8] One substantial group among those enslaved were Muslims, who were often literate and maintained key elements of their faith, including "dietary laws, dress codes, spiritual routines, and even producing and smuggling copies of the Koran—all in the hostile cultural environment of the . . . United States."[9]

Consequently, we must keep in mind that much in the way of African American cultural development has from the beginning been most significant *within* and *for* African American families and communities. It has accented communalism and cooperation. Within enslaved and free black communities, such creations and innovations have been important for cultural survival and cultural thriving. Much of this home and community development is certainly "American culture." To be African American is *to be American*.[10] Moreover, whether they are appropriated fairly or unfairly by the dominant culture, black cultural creations have been significant independent efforts and constantly generative and supportive of lasting black communities. Accordingly, Patricia Hill Collins suggests that the important values of a racial group "have concrete, material expression: they will be present in social institutions like church and family, in creative expression of art, music, and dance, and, if unsuppressed, in patterns of economic and political activity."[11]

A society's dominant culture often changes, usually gradually, as new groups move into the society and new cultural elements are added and some older elements are marginalized or discarded. Central elements of this country's white-dominated mainstream culture—such as those having to do with the capitalistic economy, legal institutions, and constitutional polity —have stayed relatively stable and/or Anglocentric over long periods, while other aspects have long been shaped or reshaped by new groups coming into the society. In this latter case, the mainstream culture has evolved from time to time with shifting conditions of everyday life as these are affected or shaped by newcomers. In most discussions of this society, the cultures of particular racial and ethnic groups are conceptualized as involving "integrated patterns of human behavior that include the language, thoughts, communications, actions, customs, beliefs, values, and institutions."[12] However, such discussions of cultural patterns frequently leave out the racial-power hierarchy that controls *which* cultural aspects come to dominate and *how* they are incorporated or expressed. White Americans, especially those in the elite, have long determined just how Americans of color are institutionally oppressed and often whether or how their cultural creations affect the mainstream culture and larger society.

Not surprisingly, European-origin and European-influenced cultural elements have typically been dominant in many areas and thus often problematical for non-European Americans. In all walks of life, African Americans have long been, or hoped to be, jointly working for real racial desegregation and associated sociocultural pluralism in a society founded on white supremacy. Even now, however, few whites have even thought about the cultural and societal importance of the recurring resistance by African Americans to racial oppression—and thus the importance of their adding cultural commitments to making this country much freer than it otherwise would have been.

More generally, few whites have been willing to fully accept the importance of black labor in the U.S. "kingdom of culture" demonstrated in this chapter. Recall from Chapter 1 Piersen's point that "Taking the African heritage seriously can be disorienting [for nonblacks], for it is not often (or at least not often enough) that Africans and African Americans are presented as cultural founding fathers and mothers with life-building agendas of their own."[13] In this chapter, I analyze just a few of the substantial creative and progressive influences that African Americans have had on important sociocultural aspects of this society generally, even as they have regularly been prevented from using their best "powers of body and mind."

Black Creativity and Impact: Centuries of Music

Belatedly, in summer 2000, the U.S. House passed a resolution officially recognizing "the importance of the contributions of African-American music to global culture and the positive impact of African-American music on global commerce" and calling "on the people of the United States to take the opportunity to study, reflect on, and celebrate the majesty, vitality, and importance of African-American music."[14]

In a number of ways, this country's first distinctive and lasting homegrown music was that of African Americans. This was first a matter of black home and community life. As Cornel West puts it, "music has really been the fundamental means by which Black people have been able to preserve sanity and dignity and, at our best, integrity."[15] Over four centuries, nonetheless, the great musical genius and innovations of African Americans, developed within and important to black communities, have had scores of effects on the larger U.S. musical culture. Numerous scholarly and popular analysts have demonstrated the important impact on the historically white-controlled music mainstream of an array of historically black musical genres, including spirituals, blues, cakewalks, ragtime, jazz, gospel music, rhythm and blues, and rock and roll. These musical innovations generally began as part of the distinctive cultural realities of black communities.

There is a deep historical background to this musical narrative. As Howard Dodson notes, the West African societies from which most enslaved Africans were taken in the eighteenth and nineteenth centuries were not the mythical backward societies of the white-racist framing of that time or now, but

> had dynamic, vibrant, expressive cultures. The languages spoken were unusually animated, by most European standards. Peppered with proverbs, they were sources of moral and ethical training as well as simple vehicles of communication. . . . Indigenous musics, which were extremely complex, permeated all aspects of traditional African social life. They were used to establish and maintain the rhythms of work. No festival or life-cycle celebration was complete without the presence of music, the moving rhythmic center of traditional African social and cultural life.[16]

These African musical styles, rhythms, and linguistic talents are evident in much African American music. Indeed, the highly rhythmic "Ring Shout" singing and counter-clockwise circle dancing brought from African societies had great impact not only on the development of black religious patterns but on the associated development of spirituals ("sorrow songs") and other musical genres. The Ring Shout involved much call-and-response singing, and in Africa and the United States, it has been closely associated with African American religious rituals and rituals of respect for ancestors. As historian Sterling Stuckey puts it, the use of Ring Shout circles "for religious purposes in slavery was so consistent and profound that it . . . gave form and meaning to black religion and art."[17] Ring Shout rituals also provided opportunities in enslaved communities for cultural sharing that enabled enslaved Africans from different areas of Africa to effectively create *one* African American group.

Again, through recurring cooperative efforts and respect for diverse African-origin groups, these African Americans created not only an integrated people but their own important family, religious, and other sociocultural traditions and institutions. Black music—spirituals, blues, ragtime, jazz, rock, rap, and other genres—have had a spoken or instrumental call-and-response pattern, musical interaction, and improvisation. Black male and female performers have been maestros "of sound, movement, timing, the spoken word."[18] These collective traditions and sociocultural institutions have long provided a foundation for black resistance to white oppression, but they are far more than reactions to whites. They are cultural essentials in the positive realities and textures of everyday life for African Americans as a group.

Blackface Minstrelsy: White Racism and Musical Theft

From at least the 1700s onward, enslaved African Americans were often encouraged or forced by slaveholders to sing, dance, and be musical. In many a white enslaver's mind, singing by enslaved workers in the fields reduced the threat of open rebellion. Moreover, with great regularity, whites have borrowed heavily from black musical styles and patterns, most often without overt attribution. One of the first conspicuous examples of substantial white theft of black music, musicality, and dance is that of the white minstrels, whose "blackface" shows provided popular entertainment for millions of whites from the 1820s to the late 1800s. Minstrel shows were the first distinctively American theatrical performances, and most early minstrel companies were all-white.[19] In front of crowds of mostly white men, whites in blackface performed an array of musical numbers and comedy skits, often comically portraying plantation-like settings. The minstrel music and dancing drew from the music and dance of enslaved (sometimes free) African Americans with whom these whites had contacts. Early leaders of minstrel troupes, such as E. P. Christy, learned about African Americans' musical artistry from observing enslaved workers who sang while working and from their evening dances and singing. Repeatedly, ever since, white America "has shown its love for black culture—especially black music—but most often when presented *by white artists*."[20]

Early white pilfering of black music, dance, and folk stories was aggressively shaped by a racist framing of black Americans. White performances of black-sourced musical and dance elements typically involved racialized distortion, corruption, and degradation. William Piersen summarizes the key elements in this process thus:

> Minstrels pandered the folk style of plantation slaves into a popular art form that kept much of the sound and humor of black music but demeaned and prostituted the source. The upbeat melodies remained, but the biting satire directed against whites was reversed. . . . The minstrelsy had become a way for whites to imitate and enjoy African-American musical traditions without acknowledging African-American artistic excellence in a way that would have endangered institutions of racial oppression and exploitation that were built on myths of black inferiority.[21]

Racist caricaturing and mimicking of black Americans were centerpieces of minstrel shows, which featured anti-black epithets, a mocking of black English dialects, and portrayals of white-racist fantasies, such as those about oversexed black women.

This distinctive blackface minstrelsy provides an excellent example of the centuries-old white *obsession* with black Americans that I underscored in the first chapter. As Eric Lott has documented, to a substantial degree white minstrelsy involved a pathological fascination with black bodies that "underlies white racial dread to our own day," even as "it ruthlessly disavowed its fleshly investments through ridicule and racist lampoon." Minstrelsy also routinely functioned to disguise slavery's extreme oppression, which was hidden in the minstrels' "pretending that slavery was amusing, right, and natural."[22] Moreover, by presenting enslaved (later, Jim-Crowed) African Americans in highly racist terms, the supposed virtuousness of whites and "white civilization," central to the long-dominant white framing of society, were repeatedly highlighted. The minstrel performances relentlessly signaled that whites were the smart, courageous, and civilized "race," while blacks were the dumb, cowardly, oversexed, and uncivilized "race." Note, too, that these "nigger shows," as most whites termed them, were popular with all classes of whites—from ordinary white workers to U.S. presidents, including John Tyler, James Polk, Millard Fillmore, Franklin Pierce, and Abraham Lincoln. Literary celebrities, including the "liberal" Mark Twain, also celebrated them under this highly offensive name.[23] Whites of various classes were enticed by, obsessed with, and desirous of an array of such black musical tunes, styles, and practices.

The widespread performances by blackfaced whites did have a complex relationship to black America. On the one hand, the racist minstrel shows, songs, and other paraphernalia were important in producing or propagating over the decades a broadly racist framing of black Americans—for elite and ordinary whites, and especially in regions with few black residents. On the other hand, the minstrel shows did introduce much black music, musicality, dance, and folklore to millions of whites, often for the first time, and thus represented the first widespread white recognition of the importance of black-generated cultural innovations. Over time, the new musical melodies, rhythms, and styles taken from black America were blended into, and thus shaped, the U.S. musical mainstream in major ways. In this fashion, U.S. musical traditions became rather distinctive from those in Europe. Many features of this black musical infusion have long been seen in appreciative terms as valuable by Americans of various racial and ethnic backgrounds.[24]

The minstrel troupes helped to introduce new musical instruments. They made significant use of instruments like the banjo and tambourine that had African and African American origins. Among the important African importations into the North American music scene were early versions of what became the American banjo, which was mainly crafted by early African American musicians. White and other nonblack musicians, including minstrels and their musical descendants, have used the banjo for generations at home and in public performances. Unfortunately and significantly, the banjo's African and African American ancestry has been lost in the white public's mind, and most now view the banjo as just an "American" creation. Still, its sounds and rhythms have African and African American roots.

Another complexity in the history of minstrelsy and similar public entertainment involves the position of early black musicians and other black performers. The minstrel shows, and subsequent racialized show business and movie settings controlled by whites, gave them opportunities to perform and develop much larger audiences. Yet, at the same time, they were usually forced into caricatured minstrel-type performances to please white audiences. Later on, these performers included numerous African American musicians, dancers, and other show business performers who would become prominent and influential, such as Bessie Smith, W. C. Handy, and Ethel Waters. In a largely white-controlled national entertainment system, their stereotyped performances were the main avenue open to them in developing their entertainment talents for broader and national audiences. Eventually, they moved on to develop their own styles that were more independent from white pressures and racial framing.[25]

Blackface minstrelsy's many impacts have persisted over nearly two centuries now, in recurring presentations of black characters, dialogue, and folk themes in various white-controlled cultural productions. Whites have long produced an array of variations on blackfaced routines and musicality for their own fun *and profit*. Thus, during the mid- to late-nineteenth century, numerous white musicians and composers, including the famous Stephen Foster (1826–1864), drew heavily on the music of enslaved (later, Jim-Crowed) African Americans, sometimes from the minstrel show versions of African American music and sometimes more directly. Some white songwriters wrote popular "Ethiopian songs," often with blackface-minstrel distortions of black English dialects, for the minstrel companies and for the white public to sing at home.[26] Considering the broader effects of more than a century of blackface minstrelsy, Eric Lott notes that from Stephen Foster's world-famous "Oh! Susanna" in the nineteenth century to rock-and-roll legends such as Elvis Presley in the twentieth century and "from circus clowns to Saturday morning cartoons, blackface acts and words have figured significantly in the white Imaginary of the United States."[27]

Indeed, this white imaginary—or, more precisely, this white-racist framing—can be seen in the performances of blackfaced actors in the most famous of early silent movies, *The Birth of a Nation* (1915), a mainstream Hollywood movie celebrating the white supremacist Ku Klux Klan. Minstrelsy's effects on the racialized characters and other racist imagery can also be observed in major nineteenth century novels sympathetic to the conditions faced by black Americans, such as *Uncle Tom's Cabin* (1852) and *The Adventures of Huckleberry Finn* (1885). Moreover, into the decades of the twentieth century, the minstrel show legacy provided a major stimulus for the extensive use of blackface and related minstrel-type routines in pioneering "talkie" movies such as *The Jazz Singer* (1927). Whites have continued to appear in various blackface roles, including in *Watermelon Man* (1970), *Trading Places* (1983), *Soul Man* (1986), and *Tropic Thunder* (2008), and in numerous television series. Not surprisingly, given the white obsession with black Americans, the blackfaced minstrel-type shows were openly performed into the 1960s, and today blackface performances are still offered at white fraternity and other college parties, as well as in the Halloween and holiday settings of ordinary white Americans and in media performances by a lengthy list of celebrities.[28]

Spirituals: Music of Life and Respect

Since the nineteenth century, the African American music that has had perhaps the greatest spiritual impact on Americans of diverse backgrounds has been that of the spirituals, the creative "sorrow songs" set long ago by talented enslaved Americans to often poignant melodies. Du Bois put this sharply: The African American "folk-song—the rhythmic cry of the slave— stands today not simply as the sole American music, but as the most beautiful expression of human experience born this side the seas." Furthermore, he insists that this music remains the "singular spiritual heritage of the nation and the greatest gift of the Negro people."[29]

The spirituals had a different meaning for African Americans, whether enslaved or free, than they had for most whites. They expressed the deep pain and emotions stemming from the severe tortures of enslavement and were usually distinctive in how little they directly referenced white slaveholders and slavery. Indeed, the pain and hope expressed in the spirituals often were set in, as Lawrence Levine puts it, a social reference group of *only* African American relatives and fellow religionists. Those enslaved thus created significant musical and spiritual distance from their oppressors— once again, creating authentic and independent *African American* selves. The powerfully expressive spirituals and associated religious practices were much more than coping mechanisms, for they constituted the everyday "instruments of life, of sanity, of health, and of self-respect."[30] They signaled the great ability of African Americans to take on horrific conditions and make something beautiful within them—that is, to "make something out of nothing." Moreover, deeply spiritual music like this, as Herbert Marcuse put it, "lies in its power to break the monopoly of established reality (i.e., of those who established it) to define what is *real*."[31] Such brilliant creativity and resilience is one of the great and persisting character traits of African Americans, now over centuries.

Over time, the distinctive texts and melodies of these powerful folk songs were appropriated and utilized in various ways by whites. Some songs, such as "Swing Low, Sweet Chariot," were just copied straight into the beloved hymn books of white churches, while many became the basis for white popular and classical music compositions.[32] A surprising example is the still frequently sung hymn, the famous "Battle Hymn of the Republic." This hymn's melody is from an African American camp-meeting spiritual, which in turn had deep African musical roots. Unmistakably, the black spirituals' style, rhythms, and spirituality have had lasting impacts on the religious and secular music of white Americans and that of many other people across the globe. For instance, in the 1890s, the influential European classical composer Antonin Dvořák, who came to the United States to head a music conservatory and was attracted to the originality of African American music, stated strongly in newspaper articles that the *artistic future* of U.S. music lay in African American melodies and rhythms, such as those of the spirituals and ragtime pieces. Like African American analysts such as Du Bois and James Weldon Johnson writing a few years later, Dvořák expressed the view that

These beautiful and varied themes are the product of the soil. They are *American*. They are the folk songs of America, and your composers must turn to them. In the Negro melodies of America, I discover all that is needed for a great and noble school of music.[33]

Significantly, too, Dvořák's still widely performed "New World" symphony was greatly influenced by the spirituals' melodies and rhythms that he admired.

Unsurprisingly, there was an intense reaction to Dvořák's assertively expressed view of the path-breaking importance of African American music, and strongly negative and positive opinions were expressed in the media by prominent whites in the United States and Europe, including many in the white music world. Moreover, over the next few decades, numerous white classical composers in the United States—such as the pioneering Roy Harris, Aaron Copland, and Leonard Bernstein—were greatly influenced by the melodies and rhythms of the spirituals and other African American musical genres.[34]

Blues: The Central Role of Black Women

As Sterling Stuckey underscores, those enslaved courageously if often subtly attacked the slavery system in their bluesy spirituals generations before the "blues" were named as a distinctive genre.[35] Many contained repeated blue notes and antiphonal call-and-response singing like that of Ring Shout ceremonies brought from African cultures. One record of another type of "blues" singing is in the 1840s autobiography of Frederick Douglass. When an enslaved youngster, he listened to the voices of those enslaved as they walked on errands:

> While on their way, they would make the dense old woods, for miles around, reverberate with their wild songs, revealing at once the highest joy and the deepest sadness. . . . They told a tale of woe which was then altogether beyond my feeble comprehension; they were tones loud, long, and deep; they breathed the prayer and complaint of souls boiling over with the bitterest anguish. Every tone was a testimony against slavery, and a prayer to God for deliverance from chains. The hearing of those wild notes always depressed my spirit, and filled me with ineffable sadness, I have frequently found myself in tears while hearing them. . . . Slaves sing most when they are most unhappy. The songs of the slave represent the sorrows of his heart.

After destroying the myth of "happy slaves," Douglass adds his personal testimony: "I have often sung *to drown my sorrow*, but seldom to express my happiness."[36] Clearly, the workaday bluesy songs of individuals were kin to the sorrowful spirituals. There is depth to the African American music tradition that can be considered pessimism, yet is actually what scholar Derrick Bell called "racial realism," that is, an old African American approach to dealing sanely with oppressive conditions. Similarly, reflecting on art in totalitarian states such as Nazi Germany, Jewish philosopher Herbert Marcuse pointed out that the pessimism of resistant art is "not counterrevolutionary. It serves to warn against the 'happy consciousness' of radical praxis."[37] Such realism has an honesty and liberating power that can facilitate targeted resistance.

Jim Crow segregation replaced slavery with slavery-like economic and political conditions, but as the scholar Angela Davis has noted, most people gained more personal freedom in travel, securing education, developing family relationships, and exploring sexuality in relationships of their choosing.[38] Together with the harsh Jim Crow experiences, these life experiences provided sources of commentary in the musical innovations of blues, blues-based gospel, and jazz. Indeed, black female blues singers were the first to make important recordings in the 1920s, although later on male blues singers came to dominate the genre. (Women such as Sister Rosetta Tharpe pioneered in blues-based gospel music in the late 1930s.) Daphne Duval Harrison has summarized the role of black women who in the 1920s pioneered in blues singing. Her research

> provides the reader with an opportunity to see these women as pivotal figures in the assertion of black women's ideas and ideals from the standpoint of the working class and the poor. It reveals their dynamic role as spokespersons and interpreters of the dreams, harsh realities, and tragicomedies of the black experience in the first three decades of this century; their role in the continuation and development of black music in America. . . . Further, it expands the base of knowledge about the role of black women in the creation and development of American popular culture.[39]

These outspoken women not only sang about harsh life conditions from a working-class viewpoint but articulated what came to be called feminist (womanist) perspectives.

The black feminism theme has been developed further by Angela Davis in her examination of three exceptional singers of the 1920–1940s Jim Crow era—Gertrude "Ma" Rainey, Bessie Smith, and Billie Holiday. In their often path-breaking songs, these blues singers tended to be more radical on some matters than jazz musicians, as in the anti-lynching song, "Strange Fruit," made famous by the great Billie Holiday. Davis anticipated a "strong consciousness of race," but found that "The more I listened to their recorded performances ... the more I realized that their music could serve as a rich terrain for examining a historical feminist consciousness that reflected the lives of working-class black communities."[40]

Like the music of other musicians oriented to the black working class, much blues and jazz music was frowned on by some black and many white intellectuals, those who prized conventionally prestigious art, such as painting and literature, as defined by the dominant culture. Yet, it is the black popular music that is deeply rooted and most impactful. Cornel West has recently argued that there is a constant need to wed radical analyses of U.S. racism and imperialism by black intellectuals and activists with popular black female and male "cultural expressions of genius and talent—be it in music, be it in dance, be it among the younger generation or older generation." A creative interplay between this anti-racist, anti-imperial radicalism and the "antiphonal forms of call and response, the syncopation, the rhythm, the rhyme, the tempo, the tone that you get in the best of Black cultural forms" is necessary to sustain the dignity, sanity, and savvy resistance to oppression of African Americans as a group.[41] The black freedom movement often made these connections between popular music and musicians and demonstrations against Jim Crow oppression.

Especially when sung and played within black communities, much popular music has long provided important *spaces* away from the dominant culture, spaces in which black humanity, agency, and creativity are central and where women, men, and children can safely critique a racist society. Historically and now, popular music such as blues, jazz, and rap involves resistance to oppression by keeping vibrant the old "ideals of humanity, ideals of equality, ideals of humility, ideals of resistance and endurance."[42]

Early Twentieth Century Impacts on Dominant Culture

Since the early twentieth century, African American music—especially spirituals, blues songs, ragtime, jazz—has had recurring and extensive impacts on the popular and classical music of the larger society and on societies across the globe. As the literary scholar, James Weldon Johnson, noted about this innovative music in the 1920s,

> This power of the Negro to suck up the national spirit from the soil and create something artistic and original, which, at the same time, possesses the note of universal appeal, is due to a remarkable racial gift of adaptability; it is more than adaptability, it is a transfusive quality.[43]

Johnson further emphasized that African American music was noteworthy for creative rhythms, emotions, and melodies: "In the riotous rhythms of Ragtime the Negro expressed his irrepressible buoyancy, his keen response to the sheer joy of living; in the 'spirituals' he voiced his sense of beauty and his deep religious feeling."[44] Once again, we see that black music was music of the home culture, designed for and by local community musicians.

Not surprisingly, too, white composers and other musicians have long been influenced by the melodies of African American music and by the innovative rhythms and lyrical styles developed within black communities. Hundreds of white musical compositions and arrangements were taken directly from, or inspired by, this extraordinarily creative music of black communities. Like the nineteenth century white songwriter Stephen Foster, many popular white songwriters in the twentieth century—for example, Jerome Kern ("Ol' Man River") and George and Ira Gershwin (the operetta *Porgy and Bess*)—openly borrowed rhythmic and melodic innovations from African American spirituals, ragtime, and jazz.[45]

One very important reason for this broad and increasing black impact on U.S. musical culture lay in what is called the *great migration* out of the South, which I examine in detail in Chapter 6. Between World War I and the 1970s, some 6 million to 7 million black southerners escaped the oppression of the Jim Crow South by courageously pulling up stakes and moving to the North. They brought innovative African American music. Blues, jazz, and other distinctive African American music, and African American musicians, that had origins mainly in the South would not likely have greatly influenced the mainstream musical culture without this great northern migration.[46] The great migration created new urban social contexts quite unlike those of the South, settings where black newcomers, including entrepreneurs and artists, interacted with many other black Americans of diverse backgrounds and with more receptive whites to reshape not only black culture but eventually the "inner workings of mainstream culture industries."[47] Indeed, over the decades before and after World War II, the large numbers of black musicians and other artists stimulated much diversity in the dress, language, and sexual expression of nonblack Americans across the country, effects persisting to the present day. The image of numerous northern cities changed in the decades before World War II, as they became part of what was termed the "Jazz Age," a dramatic reflection of the impact of African Americans on popular culture.[48]

White Denial: Black Musical Influence

From the 1910s to the 1940s, thus, the increase in integrated musical settings, such as nightclubs in New York and other major cities, spurred an increasing use of black music and musicality by white performers and composers. Nonetheless, apparently fearful of an honest recognition of their debt to black communities and musical innovations, many white songwriters, musicians, and producers, then and now, have pushed back against the suggestion that they have imitated or stolen black musical material, themes, and styles. Instead, many have openly rejected this debt or claimed that they have only drawn "a little" from black music traditions to make their original musical compositions. We will observe other examples of recurring white denial of positive black exceptionalism and white cultural debts later on. This denial seems to be an integral part of the white racial frame, evidently reflecting its central dimension accenting white virtuousness.

Consider country music, often considered an especially white musical genre because most fans are now white. As one review notes, today white country music spokespersons and fans often "intentionally marginalize black historical contributions, tend to view African-American successes with country songs as aberrations, and persist in the belief that whiteness within the country genre is both fixed and natural." [49] Indeed, since the 1920s, white record executives and their copywriters, bowing to pressures of white conservatives disturbed at "immoral" jazz and other modern music have "tried to present hillbilly music as a wholesome, white Anglo-Saxon alternative to the growing sensuality and crudeness that seemed to define the nation's mass culture."[50] Yet again, the white frame's assumption of white virtuousness arrogates to whites much cultural invention and superior morality.

Actually, however, dozens of southern black musicians were playing innovative "hillbilly" music prior to the early 1930s, a number recording in mixed black and white groups. Moreover, numerous early white country music artists—for example, Dave Macon, Jimmie Rodgers, and Roy Acuff—started careers playing *blackface* parts in minstrel-type shows, and many of these white musicians openly gave credit to black artists for teaching them how to sing or play in country style. Related musical efforts, such as fiddle playing and square dance calling, have drawn often from the tunes and styles of African American musicians.[51] Significantly, too, over the decades since the 1920s, whites in the country music industry have discriminated against the black musicians who pioneered in, or taught whites, important country music playing styles.

In addition, some prominent white musicians and producers have argued that "enlightened" and compassionate white record-company owners have been the only people who could expose black musicians to wider markets and thus help them "to gain exposure and success, thereby establishing new relationships between previously divided races."[52] During the decades before, during, and after the Harlem Renaissance (see below), white executives and their assistants spent much time with black musicians and in black clubs to exploit black musicians' talent and draw from the black musical traditions in creating black-influenced music sanitized for white ears.[53] As Franklin and Higginbotham note, during the 1920s and 1930s Harlem Renaissance, the popularity and profitability of black creativity did not escape the attention of the white-dominated entertainment industry, wealthy white art patrons, and publishers and literary agents. The renaissance of black musicians, writers, filmmakers, painters, and sculptors captivated . . . white audiences with its vibrant, colorful appeal.[54]

White executives commodified much black music and other artistry for white audiences. In this process, white musicians, record producers, and corporate executives regularly discriminated against black musicians in contracts. Gordon Hancock, a black dean at Virginia Union University, wrote in his influential newspaper column that such whites were the "world's greatest mongrelizers" as they were stealing black music and dance for their own profitability.[55]

Additionally, white executives in the recording industry have tried to counter arguments about their discriminatory dominance by noting the rare early black-owned record companies, such as Black Swan Records. Yet, Black Swan Records lasted for less than three years—substantially because of competition from white-run companies that did not face racial discrimination.[56] Black-founded record and publishing companies that had germinated and fostered much of the new black artistry stemming from the Harlem Renaissance frequently found themselves displaced by white firms seeking to cash in on the national popularity of creative black music, writing, and other cultural arts.

Enduring and Pervasive Cultural Effects: Black Music and Musicians

Over the decades since the 1940s, black musicians—and a few black record companies like Motown Record Corporation (1959)—have continued to generate and innovate in popular music, including in the areas of blues, jazz, gospel, rhythm and blues (soul), rock and roll, and hip hop (rap). Not surprisingly, more contemporary African American music and related cultural practices have been influenced by earlier music and musicians. Researcher Charles Keil has assessed the discernible impact of the blues background on numerous contemporary black musical, choreographic, and rhetorical practices, including in a "performance by B. B. King, a sermon by the Reverend C. L. Franklin, a Moms Mabley comedy routine, or a John Coltrane saxophone solo."[57] One can extend this insight to continuing blues, jazz, gospel, and rock impacts on a great array of contemporary artists whose music is often described with the hybrid labels of "soul music" or "rhythm and blues"—such as the great artists Michael Jackson, Stevie Wonder, Mariah Carey, and Aretha Franklin ("Queen of Soul").

This African American music, too, has continued to have major effects on the music of white America, especially as it is widely recorded and circulated by the large white-run recording companies. The latter have also encouraged and accented white musicians "borrowing" (again) from these innovative black musicians. For example, in the 1950s and 1960s, white rock-and-roll musicians, such as Elvis Presley, borrowed and stole heavily from black musical groups, including the innovative musical traditions covered by the term "rhythm and blues." They crafted music appealing greatly to younger whites, and genres such as rock and roll (later, rap) spread dramatically across the country and the globe.[58] In many white minds since then, especially those of white youth, much black and black-influenced musicality is greatly enjoyed, even while it is also frequently associated (especially by older Americans) with notions of black music being "immoral" and hedonistic. What Marian Mair notes about certain white British reactions to African American music has applied to younger white Americans: During the twentieth century "anti-puritanical associations of black musicality" led to identifying black musicians, often favorably, as "symbols of dissent."[59]

The post-1960s young black hip hop (rap) artists did not initially create their genre for white consumption. Rap music emerged, yet again, as creative community music reflecting inner-city perspectives on families, street life, urban conflicts, and discrimination such as police brutality. As with nineteenth century spirituals, hip hop signaled the ability of African Americans to create something significant and beautiful in spite of impoverished conditions. In areas with few music programs and instruments, they innovated by using what they had, including old turntables and records. As Tricia Rose underscores, hip hop began as

a locally inspired explosion of exuberance and political energy tethered to the idea of rehabilitating community. It wasn't ideal by any means: Carrying many of the seeds of destruction that were part of society itself, it had its gangsters, hustlers, misogynists, and opportunists.[60]

Jay-Z, a prominent rapper, has noted that those who complain of rap's "immorality" have not considered seriously enough structural realities

that spread poverty and racism and gun violence and hatred of women and drug use and unemployment. People can act like rappers spread these things, but that is not true. Our lives are not rotten or worthless just because that's what people say about the real estate that we were raised on. In fact, our lives may be even more worthy of study because we succeeded despite the promises of failure seeping out from behind the peeling paint on the walls of every apartment in every project.[61]

Thus, Tricia Rose also insists that much hip hop has had

> a love of community, a drive toward respect and mutuality that served as a steady heartbeat for hip-hop and the young people who brought it into existence. These inspirational energies kept hip-hop alive as a force for creativity and love, affirmation and resistance. [62]

Sociologist Michael Eric Dyson has underscored that the hip hop community is now a major African American institution, one that for many people has replaced the church and older leaders in articulating "their hopes, frustrations, and daily tribulations, it is fast becoming men like Jay-Z and Nas, and women like Missy Elliot and Lauryn Hill, who best vocalize the struggle of growing up black and poor in this country."[63] Indeed, there is a very important political dimension to much hip hop. The more socially conscious rappers, today and in the past, have rapped

> about racial injustice, police brutality, over-incarceration, political prisoners, rampant poverty, radical educational inequality and more. . . . At their best, hip hoppers have the potential to raise people's awareness. And I think hip hop, if it will challenge and renew itself in the cycles of history and social struggle, can continue to play a vital role in inspiring young folk to become politically astute human beings and citizens. [64]

Clearly, the black hip hop musicians have broken dramatically with the older established musical reality—yet again initially within, and for, their own black communities. Moreover, their musical and linguistic innovations have reinvigorated the national and international music scene. The enormous increase in the popularity of rap music since the 1960s signals not only the significant creativity of black songwriters and other musicians but yet again the borrowing of African American music by whites. As in the past, mostly white executives in large record companies and other media firms (e.g., Viacom, Time/Warner, General Electric, News Corporation, Bertelsmann) have decided to accent certain rap music, especially the rap (e.g., gangsta rap) that heralds street criminals, hyper-sexuality, or violence. Not surprisingly, much of this type of rap music today is bought by young whites.[65]

Critical questions need to be raised about this white cooptation, channeling, and debasing of black music. One Public Broadcasting System report asked, "Why do white kids in the suburbs listen to rap? . . . Does the distance of most whites from the black urban culture that spawned rap mean that whites cannot truly appreciate rap music and its content?"[66] By focusing mostly on a limited range of rap music, the mainstream recording industry has once more reinforced the white-racist framing of black Americans, especially the youth, as problematical, criminal, and poor. In reality, as suggested earlier, contemporary hip hop includes not only the highly commercialized gangsta rappers, but a diversity of socially conscious rappers. The latter include female rappers, religious rappers, political rappers, and academic rappers. Indeed, much early and some contemporary hip hop is quite critical of white racism and other oppressions, yet most of it is not well known to whites or widely commercialized.[67]

Not surprisingly, white musicians and companies have borrowed heavily from black rap musicians. White rappers such as Eminem, the Beastie Boys, Macklemore, and the Australian woman Iggy Azalea have drawn on black hip hop to become successful. Black rap artists have affected older music genres, including in regard to their language and production styles. Note, too, the impact of the historical civil rights movements on an array of white and other musicians. Not only have white musicians, such as Bruce Springsteen and U2, made use of speeches of Martin Luther King, Jr., but musicians overseas (such as African-French and African hip hop artists) have also used his speeches in lyrics as well as the speeches of other civil rights leaders.[68]

African American hip hop artists have had much international impact. Musical styles and lyrics, dance styles, dress, and hair styles of these and other young African Americans have influenced the cultural practices of youth in other countries. The world's youth cultures are substantially African American–ized. As Ian Condry notes, "In urban centers throughout Asia, Africa, Europe, South America, Australia, and beyond, hip hop is performed in clubs and on the streets, prompting some artists and fans to proclaim the emergence of a 'global hip-hop nation.'"[69] For instance, numerous Japanese hip hop artists and many youths in Japan have been greatly influenced by hip hop. Some Japanese rappers have been so influenced by U.S. rappers' critiques of U.S. racism that they, too, rap about the racialized atrocities of Japan's past and the need to teach an honest history of that past. One young rapper, Utamaru, who has been inspired by black rappers and the civil rights movement, has strongly accented the irresponsibility of government officials, which in his view requires younger generations "to do a pile of homework, or else we are all going to fail."[70] The now international rap music scene has opened new spaces for critical debate, especially among young people, of suppressed social issues in numerous other countries.

Note, too, the importance of African Americans to the development of distinctive U.S. and global dance traditions since the days of slavery. As Joseph Holloway has explained, the influential dance called "The Charleston" stemmed from an African dance:

> It is a form of the jitterbug dance, which is a general term applied to unconventional, often formless and violent, social dances performed

to syncopated music. Enslaved Africans brought it from the Kongo to Charleston, South Carolina, as the juba dance, which then slowly evolved into what is now the Charleston.[71]

Over the years since, African American dance music and dancing techniques have had a great impact on U.S. whites and people overseas. To take a contemporary example, the dance steps and techniques of black hip hop music have influenced much of the U.S. dance scene of white and other nonblack Americans. Indeed, there is a great impact on people of many backgrounds overseas as well as millions of comments and photos in social media show. Throughout these music, dance, and other artistic examples, we observe how aesthetic values, innovations, and experiments within African American communities have undergirded their joyful and celebratory life responses even in the face of recurring racial degradation.

A Note on European "Classical" Music

Over the last century or so, often working against substantial discrimination, African American musicians have also contributed to "classical" music traditions, especially in the area of opera and concert singing. Educated at a historically black college, by the 1920s Roland Hayes was the first black male opera singer to become well recognized as such by predominantly white U.S. "classical" concertgoers. For a time, however, he received greater respect in Europe. He emphasized the importance of African Americans taking pride in their heritage of song innovations and singing abilities, including before "white folks."[72] Collecting African American songs, he performed them along with European songs before white audiences. In this era, the great black singer, Marian Anderson, slowly became famous for European opera and other singing performances but also had a period when she was better regarded in Europe. Along with European songs, she too introduced African American songs to white audiences. In this era, Paul Robeson, prominent actor and civil rights activist, became well known as a singer in musical theater and opera, including performances inspired by black musical traditions. Slow in coming, early successes before mostly white concert audiences laid the groundwork for later black achievements and creativity in European-origin musical traditions. By the 1960s, major U.S. opera companies were accepting a few black singers into principal roles. More recently, great artists such as Leontyne Price, Grace Bumbry, Shirley Verrett, and William Warfield have attracted attention in Europe and the United States for extraordinary singing abilities and have done well in the opera concert world—thereby repeatedly demonstrating the greatness of the African American musical heritage.[73]

While there have been numerous black musicians working in other European-origin musical areas, only a few have become well known outside their communities. One is William Grant Still. Drawing on both European traditions and black folk music for his great creativity, William Grant Still has been one of the few black composers who performed regularly for traditional "classical" audiences.[74] These examples of African American creativity and success in traditionally white music worlds reveal again important legacies of the centuries-old African American musical heritage.

Major Achievements in Science and Technology

Unsurprisingly, a serious study of U.S. history beyond the conventional white perspectives reveals there are many other areas where Africans and African Americans have had major impacts on U.S. cultural practices. Historically, thus, African Americans have long played a significant role in the development of this country's scientific and technical knowledge. There is deep historical background to this role. We do not have space in this book to dig deeply into the African background and the many important scientific, technological, and engineering contributions made over millennia there, but we can note one summary of these by research scientist Hunter Adams:

> We examined man's earliest beginnings in the heart of Africa—how he discovered time and fire, domesticated animals, developed writing, agriculture and calendars. We learned how he developed religion and why he intensely studied the stars. We then focused our attention on some of the many achievements of the ancient Egyptians. We discussed their scientific paradigms and their impact in the Nile River Valley area, as well as on other Northeastern African people for centuries. We took note of their astronomy and the legacy they left: The 24-hour day, equal hours of the day and the 365-day year. We talked about their achievements in medicine, metallurgy and aeronautics.[75]

Clearly, many of those enslaved in the Americas brought much scientific and technical knowledge with them that had been gained over thousands of years, indeed long before there were such developments in Europe. Once forced into slavery they regularly drew on this cultural background.

Even during the extreme oppression of the slavery era, there were significant achievements. For example, the largely self-educated Benjamin Banneker (1731–1806) was the son and grandson of enslaved Africans, yet was allowed enough freedom during the eighteenth century to develop his substantial talents as an astronomer, surveyor's assistant (e.g., in laying out the District of Columbia), and author of a series of best-selling science-based almanacs. Banneker also engaged in a famous exchange with then U.S. Secretary of State Thomas Jefferson over freedom and slavery, to which I return in a later chapter. We should also note that among enslaved and free black workers in the eighteenth and nineteenth centuries, there were hundreds of thousands of skilled workers who worked in employment on plantations and in cities as skilled carpenters, painters, shipbuilders, iron workers, and goldsmiths. As they worked, they frequently innovated in the development of new tools and new skills (including some that were patented) that were adopted by white slaveholders, other white employers, and white workers as well.[76]

In the eighteenth and nineteenth centuries, African American knowledge and expertise on medical matters often rivaled or exceeded that of whites, although for both groups much was lacking in their knowledge. Working in their home communities, numerous African American medicinal practitioners dealt with the medical needs of fellow enslaved and free African Americans while often at the same time having significant impacts on the health and health practices of whites. These practitioners often had a more sophisticated conception of diseases and their causes than did European immigrants of that era.[77] For instance, African medical practitioners introduced the practice of vaccinating people against smallpox, thereby helping the European colonists to deal with smallpox epidemics—and assisting fundamentally in the development of this persisting type of important medical practice. During the eighteenth century, an important African American doctor, Thomas Derham, practiced medicine extensively in New Orleans. Born enslaved, he learned medicine initially by assisting two slave-owning physicians to whom he had been sold. Once freed, because of his talents, he set up a medical practice, mastered French and Spanish, and became a prominent New Orleans physician with expertise in southern diseases. His medical knowledge was praised by the country's most famous physician, Pennsylvanian Dr. Benjamin Rush, who reported thus: "I have conversed with him upon most of the acute and epidemic diseases of the country where he lives. I expected to have suggested some new medicines to him, but he suggested many more to me."[78]

Over the intervening years since the eighteenth century to the present day, there have been numerous African American doctors and scientists, including inventors, who have shaped this country's scientific and technological development.[79] These huge contributions of these men and women are almost unknown to most people today. Though we do not have the space here to track their substantial numbers, historian Jeffrey Stewart has provided a listing of just some of black Americans' major scientific and technical achievements during and after the slavery era. Over the nineteenth and early twentieth centuries, enslaved and free African

Americans invented a dry cleaning process, seed planter, sugar processing equipment, sailing and fishing devices, a grain reaper and an array of other agricultural inventions, a telegraph system, adding machine, gas mask, automatic stop sign, several medical devices, and devices to improve train lubrication, coupling, and ventilation.[80]

An enslaved African American worker probably helped with the early development of the cotton gin, which allowed the U.S. cotton economy to create much wealth and international influence. In spite of the extreme oppression of Jim Crow segregation, some black scientists gained national recognition in this era. Perhaps the most famous was George Washington Carver, who was an extraordinary scientist working on *many* new agricultural techniques and products, although conventional white accounts have mainly focused on his work with peanuts. Howard University professor Ernest Just completed pioneering research on cell ectoplasm. Scientist Ralph Gardner was a pioneer in plastic chemistry and joined several other African American scientists in working on the atomic bomb during World War II. Other black scientists have achieved much in mathematics, physics, and space sciences, and in the medical sciences. In this latter area, one of the more famous achievements was that of Charles Drew, a medical researcher who did pioneering research on blood plasma in the Jim Crow era that led to the development of widespread blood transfusions, blood banks in all countries, and the saving of many lives. [81]

Although rarely recognized in mainstream discussions, a number of African Americans have played a pioneering role or other important role in the more recent development of U.S. information and cyberspace technology. Yet, the mainstream media have almost entirely ignored these African Americans, usually instead accenting the "digital divide," the inequality in technological access and development across the racial line. Researcher John Barber has shown that this digital inequality is but one part of the history of information technologies. Indeed, the "Black digital elite are among the growing number of Black computer scientists, mathematicians, analysts, cybercommunity developers, activists, and businesspersons who are leaders in the Information Revolution."[82] Barber details the lives of more than two dozen little-known African Americans who have had cutting-edge achievements in all these important occupations. For example, since the 1970s, African Americans such as Roy Clay, Clarence Ellis, Mark Dean, and Philip Emeagwali have helped to make several Silicon Valley firms the pioneers in computer hardware and software development. More recently, other African Americans have played significant roles in the development of the U.S. telecommunications industry, both within major telecommunications firms and in passing key communications-related legislation in Congress. They have been very important in the development of various digital innovations and networks used for major business purposes, and some have been especially important in pressing for the education of young people for occupations in information technology areas.[83]

Let me reiterate the point that these African American achievements are more than tangential "add-ons" to a dominant white culture. Though I do not intend to overstate the cultural impact that African Americans have had on this society, I do want to accent that, as Du Bois long ago emphasized, African Americans have been more than just "contributors," for they have regularly been "co-creators" in many areas of this society's important cultural developments.

Creating and Reshaping Agricultural Technologies

Let us examine one area of technological contribution in more detail— the development of important U.S. food staples, cooking practices, and agricultural technologies. The Africans forced to come to the Americas by slavers frequently came from African areas with well-developed botanical knowledge and indigenous agricultural technologies. They brought seeds and roots from their homelands, and much more, for many were experts in tropical cultivation. Although unknown to most buyers, a large array of consumer products today—"Coca-Cola, Palmolive soap, Worcestershire sauce, Red Zinger tea, Snapple and most soft drinks—rely in part on plants domesticated in Africa."[84] As one scholarly analysis has explained, enslaved Africans developed at least a hundred species of foodstuffs that became part of "global food supplies." These included "millet, sorghum, coffee, watermelon, black-eyed pea, okra, palm oil, the kola nut, tamarind, hibiscus, and a species of rice."[85]

These plants, and innovative cultivating and cooking styles, led to many foods—for example, fried chicken, cornbread, okra, collard greens, yams, eggplants, black-eyed peas—that not only spread among the African-origin groups but became central to the food of most southerners. A racially stereotyped image of a black cook, named "Aunt Jemima" and still pictured on commercial food packages, became a well-known symbol of this "southern" cooking. During the slavery and Jim Crow eras, especially in the South, whites borrowed many African American foods and cooking styles (e.g., deep fat frying, gumbos), and later on this food and cooking (in effect, "soul food") spread to the rest of the United States. As one expert has put it, black-origin food has had much greater socioeconomic mobility than have African Americans themselves, as it has "gone up and down the social ladder, but a disproportionate number of African Americans remained mired in the lower socioeconomic strata of U.S. society."[86] Most ironically perhaps, our commonplace Fourth of July foods stem from African American sources.

Numerous analysts have reported on the slavery era products such as tobacco, rice, and cotton that enslaved workers on farms and plantations and were produced in huge quantities, thereby creating significant income and wealth for an array of whites. However, this story of Africans' and African Americans' agricultural knowledge and innovations is *much* bigger than popular analysts and even many historians of slavery have indicated. To take one extraordinarily important case, many of those enslaved worked under the auspices of a paddy-rice system, much of the agricultural technology of which had been brought by their ancestors and peers from Africa, a continent almost never portrayed as knowledgeable and advanced in white accounts. Europeans did *not* have this highly productive rice knowledge and technology but had to *import* it thus from Africa. Unsurprisingly, whites in control of agriculture claimed to have invented this critical technology, a mythology that has lasted to the present. Judith Carney has noted that African achievements in the southern rice economy are still seen, inaccurately, by whites as minor: "Little ground in fact has given way over the issue that slaves transferred crucial technologies to the Americas, such as milling devices or systems of water control for irrigation." The reason is that recognition of this important African technological knowhow destroys the racial framing of whites that "attributes the political-economic hegemony of Europe and the United States to a preeminent mastery of technology, which in turn distinguishes Europe and its culture from all other societies."[87]

The whites most in control of this country's dominant racial framing have retained that frame's heavy accent on European superiority in technology and civilization. This has been, all too easily, adopted by whites more generally. Note a significant pathological aspect of how this white framing operates—that is, how whites often erroneously and arrogantly claim to have invented or developed a cultural or social innovation that was actually developed by people of color.

Unsurprisingly, during the slavery and Jim Crow eras, black workers supplied much labor for this rice industry. North American rice, generally of high quality, was mostly cultivated on farms and plantations by enslaved (later, free) black men and women. Rice and its byproducts were exported to Europe as food for people and animals and for industrial purposes.[88] In this manner, enslaved Africans and African Americans developed and implemented a North American technology that generated the very *first* important food product traded extensively across the Atlantic basin by white capitalists "who would later take complete credit for the innovation."[89] Indeed, African men and women generated significant aspects of the agricultural technology enabling white colonists and their descendants to build up the wealth necessary to break with the British empire, and thereby to stay at the top of the U.S. racial hierarchy to the present day. Ironically, a contemporary white-run food corporation has long implied the importance of African Americans to rice cultivation in the stereotyped image of an older black man, "Uncle Ben," on commercial rice packages.

Additionally, enslaved workers from different ethnic groups in Africa worked together in this rice and other slavery economies, and constantly drawing on African agricultural knowledge helped them to maintain significant aspects of their home cultures and thus an integrated and persisting African American identity as well.

African Americans provided numerous important innovations for other agricultural developments across North America. Much early ranching in the Southwest involved Mexican ranch owners and ranch hands, before and after the Mexican American war of the 1840s. Yet, during the later years of slavery, and throughout the early decades of the Jim Crow era, African Americans played a significant role in the development of southern and southwestern cattle raising and its cowboy culture. Enslaved people from Senegambia (especially the Fulani) were very skilled in raising cattle and, by the 1730s, were introducing numerous important animal husbandry skills to North American colonizers, skills that are still being used. These included the first use of artificial insemination for breeding cattle and the development of some cattle to provide dairy products for consumption. Later on, in the nineteenth century, African Americans came to constitute an estimated one-fourth of Texas cowboys. Indeed, much cattle ranching in Texas, with its famous cattle drives, was similar to that of African (Fulani) herders from Senegambia to the Sudan.[90] (Interestingly, "doggies" in the cowboy song with the line "get along little doggies" stems from an African word.) Some historians have suggested that early longhorn cattle and African cattle egrets probably came in with enslaved workers. In addition, certain customs of cowboy life and work seem to have significant West African antecedents.[91] Not surprisingly, thus, one of the most famous rodeo figures in the late nineteenth century was Texan Bill Pickett, whose father had been enslaved and who developed modern techniques of bulldogging, such that he was often billed as the "world's colored (rodeo) champion."

Black Achievement and Impact: Centuries of Literature

African Americans have extensively influenced this country's literature, both directly and indirectly. In the 1920s, James Weldon Johnson, a major author and civil rights activist, argued that black Americans had long proven their artistic powers by creating the "only things artistic that have yet sprung from American soil and been universally acknowledged as distinctive American products." Black writers had the power "to suck up the national spirit from the soil and create something artistic and original," an ability with "universal appeal" and one signaling a "remarkable racial gift of adaptability" and "transfusive quality."[92] He noted, too, that Europe had great writers of African descent, such as Russia's celebrated poet Alexander Pushkin, France's major novelist Alexander Dumas, and England's classical composer Samuel Coleridge-Taylor.

Even facing the extreme degradation of slavery and Jim Crow for centuries, a remarkable number of African American poets, novelists, and essayists accomplished much in pressing U.S. literature in new directions. Many more have made such substantial achievements to the present day. By developing their own distinctive literatures, African Americans have not only asserted strongly their cultural values and self-chosen identity but developed a substantial counter-framing against how they are racially portrayed by whites and in pressing for major change in the system of racial oppression.

In 1761, the country's first recognized African American author, Jupiter Hammon, published a significant poem on a broadside poster. Hammon was enslaved in New York but allowed an education and freedom to write. In 1787, he published "An Address to the Negroes in the State of New-York," where he used numerous Christianity references and urged those enslaved to work hard, insisting they would be rewarded in a (racially egalitarian) heaven. Though some have seen his address as too deferential, Hammon was clear

That liberty is a great thing we may know from our own feelings, and we may likewise judge so from the conduct of the white-people, in the late war. . . . I must say that I have hoped that God would open their eyes, when they were so much engaged for liberty, to think of the state of the poor blacks, and to pity us.

Recently, an unpublished poem dated 1786 was found in the Yale archives, and there Hammon is strongly critical of slavery as a "manmade evil"— suggesting his slaveowners did not want it published.[93] From the earliest known writings of enslaved African Americans, we see the emphasis on slavery's immorality and the need for full liberty and justice in this society.

One of the country's very first published female poets was Phillis Wheatley, an enslaved black woman who wrote poems in the 1770s, a number of which were replete with Christian symbolism and directed to prominent whites. As Johnson notes, she has not been given her rightful place in the history of North American literature, for she is

kept out of most of the books, especially the text-books on literature used in the schools. . . . Her importance, if for no other reason, rests on the fact that, save one, she is the first in order of time of all the women poets of America. And she is among the first of all American poets to issue a volume.[94]

When literature collections have reprinted her poems, those published are usually the ones inoffensive to whites. Yet in her writings, Wheatley protested white oppression of black Americans. In one letter to a colonial newspaper during the American Revolution, she protested the use of the slavery metaphor by white revolutionaries for themselves as they accented their goal of "freedom," yet "whose Words and Actions are so diametrically opposite."[95] Wheatley was soon followed by many African American writers who continued the struggle against racialized enslavement in words and actions.

Essential Analysts of Racism: Centuries of Black Literature

Over centuries now, one of the great and far-reaching achievements of African American authors in regard to the North American intellectual tradition is their recurring critical analyses of this society's deep and systemic racism. Since the late 1700s, critical black authors and writer-activists have forced issues of racial oppression into mainstream discussions. We return in detail to numerous such freedom-fighters in later chapters, but let us note here a few who provide milestones in the development of the African American literary tradition. Writing soon after Wheatley were Absalom Jones and Richard Allen, who had bought their freedom from enslavement and were leaders in Philadelphia's black community. In 1794, they published an anti-slavery pamphlet, the first major one by African Americans, aimed at the city's white community. It ended with "An Address To those Who Keep Slaves and Uphold the Practice." In pointed and eloquent terms, they emphasized the oppressive character of slavery in the North and South: "We do not wish to make you angry, but excite attention to consider how hateful slavery is in the sight of that God . . . . Men must be willfully blind, and extremely partial, that cannot see the contrary effects of liberty and slavery upon the mind of man."[96]

The first head of the newly created African Methodist Church, Allen also published an important autobiography in 1793, one of the first in this country's literary history. Soon thereafter, numerous blacks who had fled slavery also wrote autobiographical accounts of their experiences—to "tell a free story" as some put it. One dilemma for early black authors was stated eloquently in the narrative of runaway Henry Bibb:

Reader, believe me when I say, that no tongue, nor pen has or can express the horrors of American slavery. Consequently I despair in finding language to express adequately the deep feeling of my soul, as I contemplate the past history of my life.[97]

Over the first decades of the nineteenth century, African American communities produced powerful, aggressive, and extensive critiques of the living hell that was slavery. These included author-activists David Walker, Martin Delany, and Frederick Douglass. By the end of the nineteenth century and early twentieth century, other important black male and female author-activists, especially W. E. B. Du Bois, Ida Wells-Barnett, and Anna Julia Cooper, were among the early social science and other social analysts who dealt powerfully with the complexity of Jim Crow segregation. With celebrated literary skills, they not only made significant advances in U.S. literature but wrote substantial articles and books providing the first detailed and accurate analyses of the country's white racism and making the first use of the analytical language of "subordination," "repression," and "despotism." Cooper and Wells-Barnett were also pioneers in early analyses of the conditions of black and white women, thereby helping to develop the early U.S. feminist (womanist) analytical tradition.[98] These African American author-activists brought much new insight into the U.S. literary tradition, including a new and dramatic honesty about the deep realities of continuing racial oppression.

Since the early twentieth century, African American movements against oppression have often given us yet more great African American writers, thinkers, and advocates, including James Baldwin, Richard Wright, Ralph Ellison, Malcolm X, Martin Luther King, Jr., Kwame Ture, Maya Angelou, Angela Davis, and Toni Morrison, among many others. Indeed, one of the greatest contributions of African American writers and author-activists to world literature is their extensive literature of resistance to oppression. Few other groups have produced such a deep and penetrating set of texts that guide and force reflection on resistance values, strategies, and tactics.

Literary Revolutions: The Harlem Renaissance

During the era from the 1910s to the 1940s, there was an explosion of African American literature, drama, visual art, dance, and music often called the Harlem Renaissance. This dramatic outpouring of U.S. artistic talent was distinctive and unprecedented, even more so because it came from a sector of Americans long framed by whites as incapable of such great creativity and genius. The literary mix of this Renaissance was complex. Many of these creative artists drew heavily on important elements of the dominant European American culture and thereby signaled the desire, especially among those of middle-class status, to be a well-assimilated part of the white-dominated cultural mainstream. In addition, because most U.S. book and magazine publishers and other mass media were mostly controlled by white men, these media outlets usually had to be used in circulating products of the Harlem Renaissance to wider audiences.

Nonetheless, much of this new black productivity sought to establish a distinctively black American artistic world and frequently involved a black counter-framing of this racist society. This counter-framing moved an old respect for *real* democratic virtues and freedom values assertively into a public sphere where whites were forced to confront them and where white-racist framing of black Americans was explicitly and implicitly challenged. Black-produced shows increased on Broadway, and white-produced shows also used more blacks in their casts.[99] One very important thrust of several important black writers, such as Alain Locke, during the Harlem Renaissance was an increased accent on the old folk sources and backgrounds of African Americans. As in other racial and ethnic renaissances, these writers and other artists sought to move away from reliance on the inspirations of white society and history to that of black society and history. Prominent poets such as James Weldon Johnson were greatly influenced in their free-verse and other poetry by cadences and expressions of African American preachers.[100] In this era, we also see an increase in important black women poets such as Alice Dunbar Nelson, Angelina Weld Grimké, and Gwendolyn Bennett, who also made much use of African American experiences and materials.

This intellectual and artistic movement "helped to establish the authority of black writers and artists over the representation of black culture and experience, and it created for those writers and artists a continually expanding space within Western high culture."[101] An impressive array of creative and innovative African American writers, artists, and musicians were central to the Harlem Renaissance and later on, including figures such as W. E. B. Du Bois, Paul Robeson, Mary McLeod Bethune, Josephine Baker, Richard Wright, Langston Hughes, and Zora Neale Hurston. For example, Hurston was a novelist and anthropologist. She, too, made much use of African American and Afro-Caribbean folklore and accented African American women's experiences. As with many other Harlem Renaissance figures, she has had a significant impact on later African American writers and researchers to the present day.[102]

These intellectuals were usually civil rights activists and worked alongside important civil rights organizers such as A. Philip Randolph (Brotherhood of Sleeping Car Porters) and Walter White (National Association for the Advancement of Colored People) and the rare black federal officials such as Ralph Bunche and Robert Weaver. Distinctive to the Harlem Renaissance, and unlike almost all other literary flourishing, is the fact that many major literary figures were active in the important civil rights organizations and efforts of this era. They circulated widely the goals of the growing black rights movements, setting in place a secure foundation for yet later movements—including their often outspoken emphases on black pride and an anti-racist counter-framing of society. The explosion of creativity in the Harlem Renaissance thus added to the forces reshaping the U.S. racial landscape that were already at play since the late nineteenth and early twentieth centuries, such as expanding education for African Americans and the migration of African Americans out of the Jim Crow South. These forces together were bringing changes in how African Americans saw themselves and viewed their ability to bring change through human rights movements—and in how many white Americans and Europeans regarded African American communities.

Significant elements of the work of Harlem Renaissance intellectuals and activists gained international visibility, especially among African-origin leaders in anti-colonial movements. The era from 1900 through the Harlem Renaissance decades to the 1940s laid some of the intellectual and resistance basis of the U.S. civil rights movements of the 1950s to 1970s and also of numerous anti-colonialism movements across the globe. One review of the scope of the Harlem Renaissance accurately views it as including "social movements, popular cultures, and public behavior [that] spanned the globe from New York to New Orleans, from Paris to the Philippines and beyond."[103] Yet again, we see clearly that a major aspect of African American history that has usually been viewed as a local or timed phenomenon turns out to be *global and timeless*.

Pervasive Effects on White Literature

Not surprisingly, given the systemic and foundational character of U.S. racism, black Americans and associated white-black racial matters have been central to white thinking and writing about this society since the seventeenth century. Du Bois long ago noted this centrality of the African American: "In the South he is everything. You cannot discuss religion, morals, politics, social life, science, earth or sky, God or devil without touching the Negro."[104] What the prominent African American novelist Toni Morrison has noted for our contemporary era has been true for centuries:

Race has become metaphorical—a way of referring to and disguising forces, events, classes, and expressions of social decay and economic division . . . . it has a utility far beyond economy . . . . the metaphorical and metaphysical uses of race occupy definitive places in American literature, in the 'national' character . . . .[105]

There would likely be less truly distinctive "American literature" without this white engagement, for good and ill, of the central presence of African Americans in this country's history. The impact of the black presence on white writers has taken several forms. Some early white writers, such as powerful Massachusetts judges, wrote for and against the enslavement of African Americans. Massachusetts Judge Samuel Sewall's 1700 anti-slavery pamphlet was entitled the "Selling of Joseph," while numerous other early white leaders and authors wrote essays and pamphlets defending the enslavement of African Americans.[106] Over ensuing decades, black folk tales had a major impact on U.S. literature, a point I return to below. Many famous white writers in the decades before and after the turn of the twentieth century—from Ralph Waldo Emerson, Walt Whitman, and Harriet Beecher Stowe to George Cable, Thomas Dixon, Thomas Wentworth Higginson, Joel Chandler Harris, and Mark Twain—wrote fiction and nonfiction dealing centrally with African American characters and issues.

However, as Du Bois long ago noted, white portrayals of black Americans were rarely accurate in this era:

> As a normal human being reacting humanly to human problems, the Negro has never appeared in the fiction or the science of white writers, with a bare half dozen exceptions; while to the white southerner who 'knows him best,' he is always an idiot or a monster, and he sees him as such, no matter what is before his very eyes.[107]

Many of these authors, including those such as Mark Twain, who are supposedly liberal and now iconic, used openly white-racist perspectives in their writings. Only a tiny few, such as the long-forgotten, but then best-selling, white novelist Albion Tourgée, wrote from a substantially anti-segregation and anti-racist perspective that presented a much more favorable and honest view of African Americans. Unlike Twain and most other white writers of his day, Tourgée had extensive collegial contacts with African Americans. To the present day, many white writers' images and accounts of African Americans are fabrications, stereotyped distortions, or substantial revelations of racial fears.[108]

A few decades later, during the Harlem Renaissance, resurgent black creativity and artistry, together with racially integrated urban nightclubs, attracted much attention from some white writers and artists. Still, most were operating to a substantial degree out of a racist framing of African Americans as having a deviant cultural uniqueness—which "conformed to racially charged notions of 'the primitive' and constituted a crucial part of [white] modernism's desire to extricate artistic creativity from what were condemned as stifling old Victorian conventions."[109] That is, whites frequently drew on black artistic creativity only selectively and for the purpose of moving beyond old Puritan cultural straightjackets. In this process, some of the popular cultural landscape of modern America changed significantly if gradually. Reflecting on major twentieth-century white authors significantly influenced by African American history, folklore, and language, some analysts have suggested that there would have been no William Faulkner or Ernest Hemingway without that influence.[110] Nonetheless, the important African American influences on numerous profound cultural developments such as these remain concealed and rarely recognized in most discussions of U.S. history.

Black Sources of Folklore and Language

From the beginning of slavery, and of necessity, African Americans developed a strong oral culture to pass along critical information in group settings and across the generations. Linguistic talents were well honed among enslaved (later, Jim-Crowed) African Americans substantially because they had to survive lifetimes of physical and verbal oppression. An important part of this oral culture involved folk stories, including those that used humor as resistance against oppression, humor often involving creative use of the English language. As Mel Watkins explains "Misdirection, pretense, cryptic speech, in fact, a land of homespun Socratic irony . . . loom prominently as characteristics of early authentic black humor."[111] This humor was often couched in a creative dialect that those enslaved developed in dealing with the English forced on them. Their satirical wit can still be observed in the numerous trickster and animal folk tales they regularly recounted. In these stories, a physically weaker creature often outfoxes a stronger creature, as in the famous Br'er Rabbit tales. These folk tales portray the "triumph of physical weakness, hypocrisy, mischievousness, trickery, and cunning over brute strength and guilelessness."[112]

The white journalist, Joel Chandler Harris, published many folk tales gathered from enslaved African Americans that he had encountered, including those published with a fictional Uncle Remus interacting with a white child. These folk stories of the slavery era are still published and have been beloved by generations of white and other Americans. However, the reality of slavery's brutal oppression is missing from Harris's books; his romanticized folk tales generally suggest fictitious "happy slaves" and idyllic plantation settings. Together with other African-origin folk tales, such as the "Chicken Little" tales, these became a very important source of the relatively distinctive U.S. nursery rhymes and stories that persist in use to the present day.[113]

In contrast, however, African American folk stories recorded elsewhere did reveal the oppressiveness of enslavement; they mix accounts of slavery's troubles with those of slave resistance. As African American historian Sterling Stuckey explains, the folk tales of enslaved African Americans (usually people of West African origin, such as the Hausa, Fulani, and Mandinka peoples) were not designed for white children's amusement but represented a universe of African American culture that unfolded

with dance and music at times brilliantly on display together with unsung heroes. At times, the storyteller is challenged to maintain the respect and admiration of the audience of slaves, young and old, recoiling from if not contemptuous of the master's point of view.[114]

Undoubtedly, too, most saved their commentary critical of the slavery system for private conversations and settings, and they were unlikely to make that manifest for white observers such as Joel Chandler Harris.

A central aspect of this oral culture—its wit, humor, and satire—survived slavery and has endured across the Jim Crow decades to the present day. In this centuries-old process, black wit and humor, with its often distinctive speech patterns and rhythms, has recurringly appeared in the work of black preachers, authors, musicians, and comedians and has long buttressed the long black struggles for equality.[115] Numerous African American novels and short stories have used the humorous trickster and other folk stories for inspiration since the nineteenth century, including novels by Charles W. Chesnutt (*Conjure Woman*, 1899); Ralph Ellison (*Invisible Man*, 1952); and Toni Morrison (*Love*, 2003); and a short story by Alice Walker ("The Revenge of Hannah Kemhuff," 1973).[116] Indeed, this satirical humor, including that of trickster tales, seems to have had a distinctive impact on the humor of Americans generally, especially in comparison with that of Europeans.

A number of African American literary analysts such as Ellison have long suggested that the sound of U.S. English has been significantly shaped by the "timbre of the African voice."[117] This view has been buttressed by scholarly research indicating that some of the tone and character of U.S. English, especially in the South, has been significantly shaped by traditional African American ways of speaking. One reason is that during the slavery and Jim Crow eras, black women (less often men) frequently played important roles in raising millions of white children, especially in southern middle and upper classes. In regular interactions they taught the children certain distinctive ways of speaking English and important values and social manners. As one white observer put it in 1864, white southerners' speech is "clipped, softened, and broadened by the Negro admixture. The child learns its language from its Negro nurse, servants, and playmates, and this not unpleasant patois is never quite eradicated."[118]

Citing various linguists, Shelley Fiskhin has listed some of the many U.S. English words and distinctive expressions that have their origins in the African languages brought by enslaved Africans or in derivations from them:

bad-mouth, banana, banjo, "be with it," bogus, booboo, bronco, coffee, cola, cool, "do one's thing," guff, gumbo, guy, honkie, hulla-ballo, jam (as in music), jazz, jiffy, jive, kooky, okay, okra, phony, rap, ruckus, tote, uh-huh, mhm, uhh-uh, and you-all.[119]

Notice that one of the most common words in English, and the first learned by many non-English speakers, is African in origin: "Okay." Numerous African-origin, African-influenced, or African American-coined words have gained wider use beyond black communities as black music such as jazz, blues, rock, and rap have spread across the United States.

Black Spirituality and Religion

W. E. B. Du Bois was likely the first social scientist to accent the important African cultural influences on the home culture developed by African Americans as they adapted to North America, which influences he saw especially in the area of religion and spirituality. Even the oppressiveness of slavery had not destroyed their spontaneous humanity and spirituality or left those enslaved "no means of expression for their common life, thought, and striving."[120] Undeniably, much spontaneous expression took the form of deeply religious spirituals and other sorrow songs. In his path-breaking, *The Souls of Black Folk*, Du Bois argues that African Americans blended elements of their African background with elements of their Eurocentric environment to create distinctive African American religious beliefs and practices. This soulful religion provided both daily solace from racial tyranny and avenues to express their desires of resistance to it.[121]

Since this long slavery era, African Americans have enhanced and sustained a broad home culture, one incorporating religious and other cultural elements from their African backgrounds and reworked aspects of European American culture, and always one shaped and reshaped in the crucible of white oppression. With significant African infusions, enslaved African Americans created their own religion, art, and music and a strong resistance counter-framing on issues of oppression, freedom, and justice. This distinctive framing has involved critical understandings and values supportive of everyday life in personal and family settings, from slavery days to the present.

Additionally, in research on the slavery era, Du Bois shows how the emergence of African American religion shaped the history of group leadership. Early on, the African priest became a leader on slave plantations and operated as the "interpreter of the supernatural, the comforter of the sorrowing, and as the one who expressed . . . the longing and disappointment and resentment of a stolen people."[122] Out of this background emerged an important African American tradition of religious leadership, not only in meetings among those enslaved but in northern churches that were emerging in free black communities. Influential African American leaders emerged out of these churches—for example, the previously noted Richard Allen, who had been enslaved in Philadelphia but eventually secured his freedom and became a major minister and civil rights leader.

From the slavery era to the present, black ministers and their churches have often been leaders in local and national movements against racial oppression. Major slave rebellions were led by black men, such as Nat Turner (Virginia, 1831) and Denmark Vesey (South Carolina, 1822), who had strong religious views that guided them in their anti-oppression actions. Black abolitionists drew on deep religious roots. They included, among many others, the Presbyterian minister Samuel Cornish (New York, cofounder of American Anti-Slavery Society); Frederick Douglass (Washington, DC, major national leader); Harriet Tubman (New York, underground railroad leader); and Sojourner Truth (Massachusetts, women's rights activist).[123] Later on, twentieth-century civil rights movements were strongly rooted in black religion and churches and were regularly led by influential ministers such as Dr. Martin Luther King, Jr.

In addition, countless white churches and their ministers, in the United States and overseas, have been influenced by the religion-linked liberation movements of African Americans, especially those that have stressed nonviolent resistance and goals of reconciliation and inclusion. As I show in a later chapter, African American religion has long been closely associated with an authentic liberty-and-justice framing of this society, and as a consequence black churches have played a pivotal role in much black community organizing against oppression in all sections of the country. We will also see that this black liberty-and justice-framing has had very important impacts on religiously-based resistance in other countries.

Originating and Shaping Evangelical Religion

Significantly, from the first decades of black residence in North America, black religious movements have had important effects not only on black communities but on religious movements in the larger society. Over the centuries, religious practices among whites have been greatly affected by African American religious practices. Du Bois described the spiritual quality that African Americans brought into North American religion generally as a "spiritual joyousness; a sensuous, tropical love of life, in vivid contrast to the cool and cautious New England reason . . . an intense sensitiveness to spiritual values." African Americans thus established an influential religious heritage "of fruitful labor, of joy and music, of the free spirit, and of the ministering hand of wide and poignant sympathy with men in their struggle to live and love, which is, after all, the end of being."[124]

In the eighteenth and early nineteenth centuries, successful attempts by white ministers and evangelists to recruit enslaved African Americans to Christianity generally involved adapting to the latter's demand for emotional preaching and joyful services unlike the boring styles of most European churches. Most conspicuous among the black impacts on white religion is the centuries-old impact on white Pentecostal, Methodist, and Baptist denominations of the black evangelical tradition—with its typically more informal and spiritual-emotional church services, strong emphasis on love and sympathy issues, anthropomorphic view of God, and less hierarchical form of church leadership. Social scientists have demonstrated the impact of African Americans on the demonstrative and expressive religion characteristic of white Pentecostal and other evangelical groups. Certain joyful, expressive, often musical religious practices such as ritual drumming and dancing, speaking in tongues, and spirit possession and trances are likely to have been drawn from or influenced by African and African American practices.[125] Practices resembling this expressive, much less formalistic religious style were uncommon in European areas from which white Protestant, Catholic, and Jewish immigrants to North America have come. In the U.S. case, this is very substantially the result of the African American presence. Ironically, too, African Americans, although coming into Christianity only since the early 1600s, have remained the major carriers of some of the most central values prized in Western Christianity—especially the values of charity, compassion, and communalism.[126]

There are other important, yet unrecognized, African and African American impacts on certain aspects of North American culture. For example, in spite of its oppressive racial history, the U.S. South has long been known for a distinctive accent on manners and hospitality, features often celebrated by southern whites. Africans and African Americans have significantly shaped these famous "southern values." For example, I noted previously the importance of black women in raising white children, including in teaching them about certain manners. Moreover, one little-known reality of North American slavery is that many who were enslaved in the southern colonies (later, states) were people of royal and noble lineages in Africa, in contrast to the European immigrants and their descendants who much less often then had such upper-class backgrounds. Not surprisingly, enslaved African Americans often brought "gentility, manners, and honor into the American South—not the other way around."[127] Indeed, it is African Americans today who are probably more likely to be the distant descendants of nobility and royalty than are white Americans.

African Americans and Sports

Major national sports are much more than just games that people play in their spare time with no larger societal significance. They are central to U.S. society in many ways, and their racial patterns and dimensions generally reflect those of the entire society. African Americans have been pioneers in breaking down racist barriers in numerous sports arenas and, more broadly, in moving this racist country in the direction of some real desegregation. In this process, they have changed the character of sports arenas that they entered. Although few know this history, in the last half of the nineteenth century, numerous black athletes participated in, and often did well in, an array of sports–rodeo events, boxing, horse racing, bicycling races, track and field events, and early baseball games. Thus, black jockeys won at least 110 important horse races between 1880 and 1905, including thirteen Kentucky Derby races. Nonetheless, they were forced out of these sports events by the late nineteenth or early twentieth century by extensive Jim Crow racial segregation backed up by the anti-black violence and the aggressively racist framing of whites.[128] Additionally, African American athletes were increasingly stereotyped as inferior in their athletic abilities.

Still, this Jim Crow segregation did not end black athleticism. In the late nineteenth century and several decades up to the mid-twentieth century, segregated black communities had their own high school and college teams in segregated institutions and their own Negro professional leagues in baseball, football, and basketball. In these settings, many demonstrated major athletic talent. Gradually, they began to participate in some white-controlled sports events in the early decades of the twentieth century. Especially important was their participation in the international arenas of boxing and track and field events and in sports programs at some historically white colleges in the North. Boxing was one of the most prestigious sports in the early twentieth century, and John "Jack" Johnson beat a white boxing champion to become the world heavyweight boxing champion in 1908. This enraged many white Americans, some of whom murdered at least thirteen African Americans in white race riots protesting Johnson's victories and self-assured opulent lifestyle.[129] Indeed, after Johnson's dramatic victories over white boxers and over the segregated boxing system, white opposition to black boxers was so great that it would be 1935 before another black boxer, the low-key Joe Louis, was allowed to fight for the heavyweight title. His most famous matches were against the German boxer Max Schmeling just before World War II. Louis's successes again opened up the boxing world to a series of prominent African American boxers, including Floyd Patterson, Sonny Liston, and Muhammad Ali.[130]

Early on, too, black athletes pioneered in track and field events. George Poage and John Taylor were the first black Americans to win medals in the Olympics, in 1904 and 1908. At the 1936 Olympics in Berlin, Germany, the famous Jessie Owens was the first person to win four gold medals in track and field events and one of only two ever to do so. His great achievement flatly contradicted the white myths of black inferiority in athletics in the United States and in Europe. The other person to win four gold medals was also African American—Carl Lewis in the 1984 Los Angeles Olympics.[131] Black women also pioneered in track and field. Alice Coachman was the only U.S. woman to win a gold medal in the 1948 Olympics, while Wilma Rudolph won three gold medals at the 1960 Olympics. (About the same time, Althea Gibson became a major tennis star, appearing as the first black player at Wimbledon and Forest Hills tournaments.) Black sprinters John Carlos and Tommie Smith won medals in the 1968 Olympics but became more famous, around the world, for raising their fists in protest during the playing of the U.S. national anthem (ironically, a nineteenth century song written by a slaveholder).[132] As with Muhammad Ali's fierce resistance (see Chapter 6), their assertive actions signaled the recurring significance of black athletes in the organized efforts of African Americans to make the United States more just and democratic.

By the 1930s, sportswriters at major black-run newspapers, such as the *Pittsburgh Courier*, were pressing hard for the desegregation of other historically white sports arenas. For example, journalist Wendell Smith of the *Courier* took his protests against segregation in baseball to white owners, including a suggestion that the talented player Jackie Robinson be considered by the Brooklyn Dodgers management. By the 1950s and 1960s, an increasing number of African American athletes were finally accepted into the NBA, NFL, and major league baseball leagues. These included legendary basketball players such as Elgin Baylor and Wilt Chamberlain, football players such as Paul Robeson and Jim Brown, and baseball players such as Larry Doby, Roy Campanella, and Jackie Robinson. The most famous of the pioneers was Jackie Robinson. When the Brooklyn Dodgers executive Branch Rickey called him up in 1947 as the first modern black ballplayer in (white) major league baseball, the country's most popular sport, Robinson became the target of extreme racist hostility. Yet, like many pioneering black athletes, he performed at a high level of excellence and, in his case, at a time when sports were being televised. Ever since, Robinson has been a national symbol of the better side of U.S. society—the emphasis, if often rhetorical for most whites, on implemented liberty-and-justice values. A Hollywood film, *The Jackie Robinson Story*, celebrated him, and the U.S. government used his story to help to fight the former Soviet Union in the globalized Cold War. [133] By the late 1950s, all major baseball teams had black players, and the desegregation of historically white major sports was finally well under way.

Note, too, that behind many of these male athletes' achievements lay much hard work by their families, most especially their mothers and wives. Such was the case for Jackie Robinson. His wife, Rachel Robinson, was a pillar of support during the years of threatened violence against her husband and herself. In 1973, she created the Jackie Robinson Foundation to honor her husband and to support black youth. On the fiftieth anniversary of his breaking through baseball's racial barrier, outspoken then as previously, she made it clear that she was critical of continuing white racism: "I think he'd be very disturbed about it. We're seeing a great deal of divisiveness, a lot of hatred, a lot of tension between ethnic groups, and I think he'd be disappointed." Operating out of a strong black framing, she added,

> We would expect to be further along by now, and we're seeing it worldwide, . . . I don't feel despair about it because I think despair and cynicism only undercut our ability to address these issues and do something about them. So I've maintained a certain level of optimism, but it's restrained by a realistic knowledge of what's going on in the world.[134]

In another savvy interview, she noted the decreasing number of black Americans in the baseball leagues today and in the professions as a serious societal problem.

The national myth about this sports desegregation accents its moral and civil rights dimensions, but there was much more to these changes than that. Powerful whites who did increase black involvement or re-involvement in what were all-white sporting arenas typically did so to profit substantially from it. As sports analyst Dave Zirin underscores, "How can we praise baseball for Jackie Robinson's breaking of the color line without pointing out that Branch Rickey was the lone vote for integration among his peers, with quotas existing on black players for years thereafter?" Zirin also points out the major monetary interest of white men such as Rickey. In the process of securing numerous black players, they destroyed the Negro League, the largest black-owned U.S. business, by buying off players without compensation to owners.[135]

Significantly, this racial desegregation of historically white sports was generally well in advance of racial desegregation in other institutional areas. Not surprisingly, the desegregating sports world generated much enthusiasm and pride in black communities and opened up new social linkages between blacks and whites, at a time when other major institutions were still highly segregated. To some degree, these courageous efforts of black athletes—who often faced myriad threats and much violence from whites—had begun to reshape the ways that blacks and whites interacted, more cooperatively at least in sports arenas. They had also begun to challenge and reshape some aspects of the white framing of black Americans. As we have seen, by at least the 1950s and 1960s, black professional and college athletes were speaking out for more desegregation of white organizations, including for more black coaches and administrators, with the latter also speaking out for more African American studies programs. David Wiggins has noted that these black athletic rebellions occurred at an array of different white institutions, including

Syracuse University, Oregon State University, Michigan State University, San Francisco State University, University of Washington, University of California, Berkeley, University of Kansas, University of Wyoming, University of Texas at El Paso, University of Arizona, and Oklahoma City University.[136]

As Earl Smith suggests, even before Jackie Robinson, numerous African American athletes had begun to create a new image of a "strong, confident, capable African American athlete" in many white minds.[137] The grudging white recognition of these important black achievements did bring possibilities for later racial change, even though many developed a rationalizing notion of innate black athletic ability as being substantial but linked to their "primitive" origins. More important, this partial desegregation of sports arenas generated much pride among black Americans and optimism about possible societal changes, thereby helping to unify the black community in regard to building up civil rights organizations and increasing demands for the full racial integration of U.S. society.[138] Moreover, numerous black athletes were becoming successful businesspeople, lawyers, and other professionals. Over several decades, many have been leaders in their communities and worked to provide programs and funding that have enabled black youths and others to become upwardly mobile in socioeconomic terms.[139]

Conclusion

Historically, whites have applied phrases to African Americans and Native Americans that involved words such as "savages," as in the notions of "black savages" and "red savages." In counterpoint, this same white-racist framing often portrays white Americans as "white saviors" civilizing these and other Americans of color. Recall that leading white intellectuals such as Thomas Jefferson spoke of African Americans as being much less intelligent, rational, and sophisticated than whites. These early white supremacists played up whites as highly virtuous and civilized and, thus, as the cultural saviors of black people. Even today, the openly white supremacist commentaries of conservative Republican luminaries such as Patrick Buchanan play up the notion that African Americans should be thankful that they were rescued from being "primitive" Africans and brought by violent enslavement into the allegedly superior Anglo-American culture.

There is much that is wrongheaded in such white-aggrandizing notions. These analysts ignore the reality of the real "savages" in U.S. history most often being violent whites. Whites were, and are, the ones responsible for centuries of genocide targeting Native Americans, centuries of violent slavery and Jim Crow segregation targeting African Americans, long decades of historical discrimination against other Americans of color (e.g., World War II concentration camps for Japanese Americans, discrimination against Middle Eastern Americans since 2001), and the creation or support of much racialized oppression across the globe. In this country's history, whites, especially the elite, have been responsible for much violent crime (e.g., lynchings), economic depressions, and most continuing capitalistic exploitation (e.g., low-wage sweatshops today). They are principally responsible for a corporate-capitalistic culture commonly focused on greed and self-indulgence. They are responsible for this country's war involvements—including the bloodiest war for Americans, the Civil War. White presidents have been supportive of much racialized oppression overseas, including extensive U.S. support for bloody autocratic political regimes in South Africa, Iran, and Chile. Whites are also responsible for the extensive system of individual and systemic racism still aggressively targeting Americans of color in the present. One example today is the still-extensive environmental racism seen in the highly disproportionate placement of toxic waste dumps in or near communities of color. Sadly, there are many more examples that could be listed here. Who indeed have been the true uncivilized "savages" in U.S. history?

As we have seen, the Africans who were enslaved in the North American colonies brought much that has been significant and positive to North American culture and society. They and their descendants have generated so much innovative and creative music and musicality that much of U.S. music is now, at base, a form of African American music. Enslaved Africans and African Americans also brought much important agricultural knowledge to the colonies and, later, United States, including the early development of rice and other important food production. Directly or indirectly, African Americans have had profound impacts on the distinctive character of much U.S. language and speech and on many key themes and developments in U.S. literary efforts. They have also profoundly affected the character of much U.S. religion and even the character of things considered "southern," such as southern food, cooking, hospitality, and manners. Additionally, African Americans have often changed the character of U.S. sports, both as pioneers forcing the integration of sports—thereby meaningfully implementing U.S. liberty-and-justice rhetoric—and as talented athletes advancing the level of sports achievements.

In this chapter, I have attempted to help to restart a more public and contemporary discussion of the many important and positive impacts of African Americans on the development of a distinctive and important African American community culture, and on broad areas of the general U.S. culture and society. Some cynics still might ask why nonblacks should care much about these many black cultural and community achievements or the larger societal contributions. Reviewing these impacts on U.S. society, one historian of Africa, John Philips, has argued that

> A fuller appreciation by whites of their own African backgrounds would probably make them more willing to accept blacks as equals.... Pride in their African heritage is something that white children should be taught along with blacks. It could help improve not only black self-images but also white images of blacks, black images of whites, and perhaps some whites' images of themselves.[140]

While this sentiment is overly optimistic, it does at least move the discussion, especially for whites, of U.S. culture's great and lasting *debt* to Africans and African Americans in a more accurate and progressive direction.

4
Black Counter-Framing
Real Freedom, Justice, and Democracy (1600s–1910s)

Over the centuries since the first American Revolution, many people have asserted that the United States has been through, or is facing, a "second American Revolution." Many events, from the War of 1812 to Tea Party efforts in the twenty-first century, have been characterized by that catchy phrase. Most often, perhaps, that phrase has been applied to the overthrow of slavery and the passage of key constitutional amendments in the Civil War era. Indeed, one of the first uses of this phrase was for the fight for freedom and ending slavery in the first black newspaper in the South, the *New Orleans Tribune*, during the Civil War era. In my view, the actual second American Revolution *for liberty and justice* has been that begun by the courageous "black founders," who by their liberatory actions over the centuries before and after the Civil War have forced whites to pay serious attention to realizing their liberty-and-justice rhetoric. This contrasts dramatically with the views of numerous white analysts, such as Gordon Wood, who wrote in a Pulitzer prize-winning book that the white founders are the source for "our current egalitarian thinking."[1] In 1970, Ralph Ellison emphasized that the experiences of black Americans provide the "most stringent testing" of U.S. democracy and its rhetoric about freedom. The test of real democracy is the "inclusion—*not* assimilation—of the black man."[2] Unmistakably, most whites advocating the ideals of liberty, justice, and democracy have regularly failed this testing.

Since before the first American Revolution, African Americans have usually been the collective conscience and prod for the most significant racial changes to this white-racist society. The largest group that whites utilized for centuries as highly exploited and enslaved labor, African Americans were the largest racially exploited group *within* the new United States that was created in 1787—and the one that early on regularly petitioned and pressured the government for authentic "liberty and justice for all" (See Chapter 5). As W. E. B. Du Bois put it, black Americans were the ones "that raised a vision of democracy in America such as neither [white] Americans nor Europeans conceived in the 18th century, and such as they have not even accepted in the 20th century."[3] Very rarely, outside their own communities, have African Americans gotten credit for these counter-framing efforts forcefully pressing this country well beyond its racially totalitarian institutions of the slavery and Jim Crow eras to a much freer and more democratic country. Over centuries, African Americans have been a major and constant catalyst for social justice changes—by means of millions of individuals' bravery in words and deeds and by fearless organized actions against oppression. They have repeatedly been among the country's foremost truth-tellers on the deep realities of that racial oppression, on the contradictions between that oppression and the liberty-and-justice rhetoric, and on resistance strategies and change policies necessary to make this country into a real multiracial democracy.

White Framing, Black Counter-Framing

Recall from Chapter 1 that there have long been several categories of important racial frames in everyday use. These include (1) the dominant white racial frame, (2) the anti-oppression counter-frames of Americans of color, and (3) the older home-culture frames that Americans of color draw on in everyday life and in developing anti-oppression counter-frames. In Chapter 1, I emphasized the central role of the dominant white racial frame in rationalizing white oppression of Americans of color over the centuries.

In addition to these frames dealing directly with racial matters, there is a prominent white-crafted liberty-and-justice frame that we have periodically observed. This old liberty-and-justice frame is significant in this country's history because most Americans have professed some version of it since the seventeenth century. It appears in founding documents, such as in the "life, liberty and the pursuit of happiness" rhetoric of the Declaration of Independence and the "establish justice" and "secure the blessings of liberty" rhetoric of the U.S. Constitution. Liberty, freedom, equality, and justice were terms used, occasionally or often, by the white framers of the U.S. Constitution. Remarkably, these and other whites' professed statements about liberty were strongly contradicted by their extensive oppression of indigenous peoples and enslaved Africans. From the revolutionary era to the present, most whites have accepted some version of this liberty-and-justice frame but usually one that is only rhetorical and hypocritical when it comes to seriously redressing systemic racial oppression.

As noted earlier, two other categories of perspectival frames are essential in making sense of systemic racism and everyday resistance to it by African Americans and other Americans of color: their anti-oppression counter-frames and the home-culture frames from which they regularly draw in crafting anti-oppression counter-frames. For nearly four centuries, African Americans as a group have developed a major anti-oppression counter-frame designed to call out, oppose, and survive racial oppression. With its shared consciousness of oppression and its distinctive morality of *real* liberty and justice, this collectively generated black counter-frame has provided an important framework and tool kit enabling black individuals and groups to counter racial oppression at its roots, including whites' immorality in asserting fraudulent liberty-and-justice ideals. Additionally, as we have seen previously, since the slavery era African Americans have created a home culture incorporating a shared justice morality and important cultural features from their African backgrounds and have reworked aspects of European American culture—all shaped together collectively as they deal with everyday oppression. Important African aspects of the home-culture frame *preceded* encounters with whites, and African Americans often operate out of it in home settings without paying much attention to white Americans. The home-culture frame and anti-racist counter-frame lie behind most collective and individual black consciousness of, and action against, discrimination.[4]

Note, too, that people of all racial and ethnic backgrounds vary in the elements of these broad perspectival frames that they adopt and use. These racial frames are large and complex, and they have important sub-frames. People adopt elements of a frame to assist in interpreting social realities, and they frequently operate out of more than one frame over the course of their daily lives.

In this and the next few chapters, I assess thoroughly what is one of the most beneficial impacts that the perspectives and actions of black Americans have had on this country's long-term development. Black Americans were arguably the first major group within the European colonies, and later the United States, to widely utilize an extensive counter-frame to combat the white racial frame and other aspects of systemic racism—for example, in the form of thousands of black-authored pamphlets, books, speeches, and conventions. As Francis Adams and Barry Sanders have emphasized, one major reason for this has been whites' exclusion of black Americans from access to *full citizenship rights* for most of this country's history.[5] The large-scale, recurring resistance and counter-framing of black pamphleteers, abolitionists, Civil War soldiers, and civil rights activists have been critical factors in the significant progress this country has made in implementing, if still only partially, its much-heralded ideals of freedom, justice, and democracy. Indeed, most black Americans have sought much more than "civil rights." They have worked and protested to secure full citizenship and full democratic participation in all major aspects of a truly democratic society.

Early Letters of Protest

Recall that in the eighteenth century and early nineteenth century, substantial liberty existed almost exclusively for northern European men.

Then, from the 1830s to the 1920s, new European immigrant groups entered the country, insisted on their freedom and rights, and gradually moved up in the economic and political institutions, often successfully challenging the dominance of northern European Americans. However, African Americans, who had usually been Americans longer than these white immigrants, largely remained "un-free" and locked into great inequality and injustice in historically white institutions. From the beginning, enforced racial subordination and inequality have been foundational and systemic. Over four centuries, thus, African Americans and other Americans of color have had to regularly and forcefully insist on their own freedom and civil rights, thereby challenging this systemic racism.

In his path-breaking collection, *The Mind of the Negro*, the pioneering historian Carter Woodson reproduced 254 letters of African American writers, including leaders and activists writing from about 1800 to 1860. These African American writers alluded to freedom and liberty more than 400 times in their letters and to justice and equality another 120 times.[6] Unmistakably, the large number of times that African American writers, in many different contexts, have insisted on this country's fully implementing liberty-and-justice ideals shows over and over again that they are regularly employing a powerful counter-frame to the dominant white racial framing of society.

Let us examine in detail several of the many letters, pamphlets, slave narratives, and speeches of African Americans on liberty and justice issues from the 1700s to the early 1900s. In each of these examples, we will observe very important efforts at constructing key elements of the powerful black counter-frame. To take one major example, just three years after the 1787 U.S. constitutional convention, there was a debate in a New York newspaper's letters column between a white man who signed as "Rusticus" and a black man who signed as "Africanus." Operating from a strong version of the white racial frame, Rusticus wrote about the "wool hairy negro in the order of nature" and described black Americans in racially stereotyped terms as very inferior to whites.[7] Rusticus got a sharp satirical reply from Africanus:

> I am a sheep-hairy negro, the son of an African man and woman; by a train of fortunate events I was left free, when very young, and by the interposition of the most generous of mankind, I have received a common English school education, and have been instructed in the Christian religion—I am master of a trade. . . . I shall oppose the arguments of such as have written against the idea of *our* inferior nature.

He then added that

Europeans, Asiatics, Americans and Africans are all the descendants of Noah. . . . the [white] American and the African are one species— The law of nature declares it—And I . . . being free and in some degree enlightened, feel myself equal to the duties of a spirited, noble, and generous American freeman.

In reply to another racist letter from Rusticus arguing yet more aggressively that "wool hairy" Africans were born to be enslaved, Africanus provided this pointed reply:

[H]ow absurd is the notion, that nature should form an animal, endue him with reasoning powers, and place him in a clime congenial to his frame; only that he should be torn away from that climate to serve another animal differing from him only in the colour of his skin and length of his hair. Our philosopher [Rusticus] tells us, that amongst animated beings, the weakest is ruled by the strongest . . . No, this is not the nature of man. . . . 'tis the civilized European that takes advantage of the . . . untutored African, and robs him of his liberty to indulge himself in luxury. . . . according to our philosopher's principle, the most powerful nation has a natural right to seize on the property and persons of the weaker. So not only the sheep hairy negro is born for slavery, but the horse hairy native of America, or in short, people of black, brown or red hair, if another people have force or cunning to subdue them. . . . When my daily work is done, and I put on my Sunday's clothes to myself for the converse of those unphilosophic men who patronize me; as I pass through the street . . . another curses the damn'd proud negro! . . . If [white] pride must be the consequence of human wisdom, may I still remain in simplicity of heart, a plain, unphilosophic, black, sheep hairy, free citizen of America.[8]

With barbed sarcasm and logical argument, Africanus proves to be the superior analyst of racial oppression: African Americans are not inferior, are talented like Africanus, and are of the same human species. "Civilized" Europeans have robbed them of their natural freedom and, if an immoral European American is the best result of "human wisdom," it is better not to be one. Like many African Americans before and after him, Africanus insists that he is a proud American *citizen*, a designation a great many whites denied to African Americans until well into the twentieth century. We already observe in the insightful analysis of Africanus important features of the black counter-frame to the white racial frame and other aspects of white oppression. On the one hand, this counter-framing attacks stereotyped notions about black Americans; on the other, it also insists on the virtuousness of, and *liberty* and justice for, hardworking black *citizens* of the new nation.

Shortly after this early and revealing newspaper debate, in summer 1791, Benjamin Banneker—the black astronomer and almanac creator discussed previously—penned a forthright letter on liberty issues to none other than Thomas Jefferson, the principal author of the Declaration of Independence and, in 1790, the first U.S. Secretary of State. In this well-crafted letter, Banneker argued out of the black counter-frame and assertively countered whites' racist framing of African Americans—which Jefferson had proclaimed loudly in a recent book—as lacking in virtue and humanity. He vigorously criticized the white "prejudice and prepossession, which is so prevalent in the world against those of my complexion," and added that

> we are a race of beings, who have long labored under the abuse and censure of the world; that we have long been looked upon with an eye of contempt; and that we have long been considered rather as brutish than human, and scarcely capable of mental endowments.

Next he forthrightly urged the powerful Jefferson to recognize the

> indispensible duty of those, who maintain for themselves the rights of human nature, and who possess the obligations of Christianity, to extend their power and influence to the relief of every part of the human race, from whatever *burden or oppression* they may unjustly labor under.[9]

Then, drawing on whites' common slavery metaphor, he cited British efforts to reduce white American revolutionaries to "a state of servitude" and suggested that was a period when Jefferson himself must have seen "into the injustice of a state of slavery, and in which you had just apprehensions of the horrors of its condition." Banneker boldly added that, even as Jefferson had articulated in a Declaration of Independence some condemnations of British violations of whites' liberty, Jefferson and his slaveholding colleagues had detained "by fraud and violence so numerous a part of my brethren, under groaning captivity and cruel oppression" and thus were "guilty of that most criminal act, which you professedly detested in others, with respect to yourselves."[10]

In this forceful counter-framing of U.S. society, Banneker, like Africanus, attacks the commonplace white image of "brutish" black Americans. He likewise insists on making *real* the human rights language of the white American revolutionaries, for black Americans are morally virtuous and deserving of freedom. In fact, both Banneker and Africanus are directly challenging the view of superior white virtuousness that is at the center of the white racial frame. Banneker makes clear that *true* Christian morality obligates whites to free black Americans from brutal enslavement, thereby asserting a lack of white virtuousness. Similarly, Africanus accents the lack of white virtue in sarcastic comments such as it is "better not to be white if this is the best they can do." For both men, if there were real white virtue—an authentic commitment to liberty and justice—they would not have enslaved black Americans. Cogently accenting the morality unmistakably present in the liberty-and-justice rhetoric of the white "founders," Banneker makes a point central to this book: Very few racial or ethnic groups in the last four centuries have contributed so much to humanity, and yet faced such enormous and persisting "abuse and censure of the [white] world" as have African Americans.[11] At this early period in the nation's history, it is Banneker and *not* Jefferson who is insisting on full recognition of the "rights of human nature," a phrase echoing Jefferson's hypocritical language in the Declaration of Independence a few years earlier.

Already, in these constitutional-era letters, two black Americans fearlessly assert a vigorous black counter-frame against the prevailing white-racist framing of white and black Americans. This counter-frame included these important elements: (1) a strong moral critique of white racial oppression and the assumption of white virtuousness; (2) an aggressive countering of anti-black stereotyping; (3) a positive assertion of the humanity of black Americans; (4) an assertion of the American-ness of African Americans; and (5) a powerful accent on liberty, justice, and equality for *all* Americans.

White Framers and Black Founders

In Chapter 5, I describe in more detail many black *actions* that were informed by this black counter-framing. These included petitions to northern legislatures and, beginning in the 1790s, to the new U.S. Congress. However, in spite of the new U.S. Constitution's First Amendment right of Americans to petition the government for redress of grievances, the all-white-male Congress ignored or rejected numerous anti-slavery and pro-freedom petitions it received in its first decades. Some of the most fervent petitions were from free African Americans. Rather conspicuously, the white leadership of the new U.S. republic did not believe in implementing such freedom ideals for all Americans. Most white legislators worked to suppress efforts by all African Americans to petition the country's legislatures for their freedom. Not one major white political leader envisioned a truly democratic country in which not only white men could vote and hold office but the majority of Americans—women, black Americans, Native Americans—would have political, social, and economic equality.

For instance, in the numerous *Federalist Papers* written in support of the new U.S. Constitution, key members of the white elite—James Madison, John Jay, and Alexander Hamilton—constantly refer to the "principles of liberty," with the word *liberty* appearing more than 100 times. Yet, this supposed liberty was generally connected to property-holding and societal stability, and at no point in the *Federalist Papers* is the extreme oppressiveness of slavery discussed.[12] There is likewise no discussion of black freedom and equality in the *Papers*. The U.S. Constitution, often called the first "democratic" constitution, actually created a highly undemocratic nation-state on the backs of enslaved African Americans and the stolen lands of decimated Native Americans. Not surprisingly, thus, the white framers of the Constitution and other white leaders were actually hostile to *real* democracy. Many constantly worried about an "excess of political democracy" and "social leveling" in the new nation. "Real political, social, and economic equality were not what the framers had in mind."[13]

However, there were also numerous "black founders" in the emerging U.S. nation. These usually free black leaders, activists, and intellectuals worked hard to create strong African American communities (see Chapter 5). Recall Richard Allen's 1827 insistence that the emerging United States was indeed *theirs*: "This land which we have watered with our tears and our blood is now our mother country."[14] Numerous African American leaders insisted that the white political elite's rhetorical liberty-and-justice ideals be fully actualized. As historian Richard Newman has underscored,

> In New England, Phillis Wheatley, Newport Gardner, and Lemuel Haynes gave voice to African-American freedom dreams in the 1770s; in the mid-Atlantic region during the early 1800s, James Forten, William Hamilton, and Peter Spencer struggled alongside Allen for black equality; and in the early national South, Benjamin Banneker and Morris Brown attempted to put the cause of interracial democracy before white statesmen and citizens alike.[15]

Arguably, these and other African American leaders, together with ordinary African Americans, were the nation's authentic founders when it came to real liberty, justice, and democracy. One of the key themes of this book is that, from the beginning, it was African Americans who did the most to save this country from being just the slaveholding republic created by the white elite. Even the few more democratic white activists, such as the "radical" Tom Paine, did not go so far as to argue for liberty, equality, and justice *for all*. It was the black founders, those who spent long years of resistance to slaveholding conditions, who forced this country onto a path accenting a commitment to *real* multiracial democracy and implementing concrete societal changes on the road to that goal. Indeed, since this era, many progressive whites have been greatly indebted to the efforts at real "liberty and justice for all" pursued by these and other generations of African American freedom-fighters.

Anti-Slavery Pamphlets

In the decades after the U.S. Constitution was ratified, many African Americans wrote newspaper essays, autobiographies, sermons, fictional works, and pamphlets pressing for freedom and social justice. Many engaged in pamphleteering in which they attacked slavery, especially the slave trade and the fugitive slave law, and the growing Jim Crow segregation already common in northern states. The pamphleteers made frequent reference to the concepts of freedom, social justice, and equality, again with recurring references to the Declaration of Independence and U.S. Constitution.

In one example in 1794, Absalom Jones and Richard Allen, who had bought their freedom from enslavement and were leaders in Philadelphia's black community, produced a boldly worded pamphlet (the first major pamphlet by African Americans) directed to the city's white community. It ended with "An Address To those Who Keep Slaves and Uphold the Practice":

> The judicious part of mankind will think it unreasonable, that a superior good conduct is looked for, from our race, by those who stigmatize us as men, whose baseness is incurable, and may therefore be held in a state of servitude, that a merciful man would not deem a beast to; yet you try what you can to prevent our rising from a state of barbarism you represent us to be in, but we can tell you, from a degree of experience, that a black man, although reduced to the most abject state human nature is capable of . . . can think, reflect, and feel injuries, although it may not be with the same degree of keen resentment and revenge, that you who have been and are our great oppressors, would manifest if reduced to the pitiable condition of a slave. . . . Men must be willfully blind, and extremely partial, that cannot see the contrary effects of liberty and slavery upon the mind of man. . . . If you love your children, if you love your country, if you love the God of love, clear your hands from slaves, burden not your children or your country with them. . . . Will you, because you have reduced us to the unhappy condition our colour is in, plead our incapacity for freedom, and our contented condition under oppression, as a sufficient cause for keeping us under the grievous yoke.[16]

Jones and Allen are using the penetrating language of the anti-oppression counter-frame. Here they vigorously counter stereotypes of black Americans as incapable of thought and reflection and fearlessly characterize whites as "great oppressors" and slavery as "oppression." Throughout their writings here and elsewhere, they accent the importance of liberating those enslaved and thus of whites living up to U.S. freedom ideals, yet they also make the case that the abolition of slavery is good for the country as a whole, including for the younger generation of whites.

Writing in the early 1800s, numerous other leaders were among those in this first generation of African Americans to so publicly assert a strong black counter-framed perspective. Writing in a slave state, the courageous Maryland pamphleteer, Daniel Coker, used a scholarly dialogue format to attack slavery in an 1810 abolitionist essay aimed at white slaveholders, while the Pennsylvania business leader and pamphleteer, James Forten, more directly attacked the racially discriminatory Jim Crow laws in the North. Like many operating out of the black counter-frame, James Forten accented the American Revolution and its liberty-and-justice ideals, arguing that these ideals must encompass "the white man and the African" and that white legislation and other actions taken against this ideal violated the "letter and spirit of our Constitution."[17] In 1804, Pennsylvania's white politicians tried to pass laws blocking blacks from even migrating to the state. Forten published five strongly worded letters, including one with these words: "It has been left for Pennsylvania to raise her ponderous arm against the liberties of the black, whose greatest boast has been that he resided in a state where civil liberty and sacred justice were administered alike to all."[18]

Forten and Coker were just two of numerous brave African Americans who took a forceful public position on behalf of their liberty in the North and the South, in this way going well beyond white anti-slavery activists in articulating a black counter-framing of systemic racism. Their determined counter-framing was personally situated and vigorously expressed and, not surprisingly, even many white abolitionists found it difficult to accept this black-framed view of systemic racial oppression. That is, these black advocates of full freedom for black Americans had to battle not only against the majority of whites who were supportive of slavery but even against those whose opposition to slavery did not include a frontal attack on racial oppression, especially in northern states. Indeed, these bold black advocates and activists openly pressed white abolitionists and other whites to live by their professed ideals and speak out on behalf of freedom for black Americans, thereby sometimes becoming a crucial impetus for belated, often reluctant, white actions against the entrenched slavery system.[19]

In addition to the publication of pamphlets, black activists and entrepreneurs established newspapers in which they provided news for black communities and published articles, editorials, and letters dealing with liberation from enslavement and Jim Crow oppression. Between the 1820s and the 1860s, at least 100 of these newspapers were in operation.

Their owners and editors provided space for black Americans to speak for themselves on racial and other issues. Among these were strong abolitionist newspapers and journals, including *Freedom's Journal, The Rights of All, Mirror of Liberty, Impartial Citizen, Herald of Freedom*, and, perhaps the most famous, Frederick Douglass's *The North Star*. For example, in 1827 John Russwurm, a college graduate, and Samuel Cornish, a Presbyterian minister, set up the abolitionist newspaper, *Freedom's Journal*. Interestingly, black editors such as Russwurm and Cornish spoke out with accuracy and insightfulness on numerous social issues—not only on human rights and against slavery and organizations pressing for returning African Americans to Africa but on trade unionism, European conflicts, and self-improvement.[20] These editors had reasoned and critical views of the dominance of the white racial frame and its highly problematical accents on alleged white virtuousness and alleged black failings. These newspapers did have some larger impact, for their "vision destabilized whiteness itself in the new republic. Had history run differently, their path might have delivered the nation from the bloody struggles that the [racist] ideology produced."[21]

David Walker's Path-Breaking Pamphlet

In 1829, the well-traveled young Boston abolitionist, David Walker, circulated widely the first substantial analysis of U.S. racism, again viewed from an anti-oppression counter-frame. He published the revolutionary pamphlet *Appeal to the Coloured Citizens of the World*, and it soon became one of the most influential anti-slavery pamphlets of the antebellum era. It set forth an assertive manifesto shared by many blacks, free and enslaved, for racial unity among black Americans—including mass organizing—and for authentic justice and equality. Writing fiercely to black (and white) Americans and drawing frequently on Christian religious language, Walker lays out aspects of an old black counter-framing of real liberty and justice in the new United States. Most whites are "cruel oppressors and murderers" whose oppression will eventually be overthrown. They are "an unjust, jealous, unmerciful, avaricious and blood-thirsty set of beings." He examines the well-institutionalized character of white oppression and aggressively calls for its replacement. He accents how unjust enrichment and unjust impoverishment are reproduced over generations: Whites seek for African Americans to be slaves to them "and their children forever to dig their mines and work their farms; and thus go *on enriching them*, from one generation to another with our blood and our tears!" In addition, he critically assesses how whites emotionally stereotype black Americans, such as by framing them as "ungrateful." However, "what should we be grateful to them for—for murdering our fathers and mothers? Or do they wish us to return thanks to them for chaining and handcuffing us, branding us ... or for keeping us in slavery ... to support them and their families." Walker, like Banneker before him, recognizes who the leading white intellectual is and assertively critiques Thomas Jefferson's highly racist views. With penetrating reasoning, he refutes Jefferson's extensive racist framing of black Americans in *Notes on the State of Virginia*— for instance, by reasoning that his argument that enslaved blacks have naturally limited abilities and are by nature inferior to whites makes as much sense as saying that a deer in an iron cage can "run as fast as the one at liberty."[22]

Repeatedly, with devastating logic, Walker underscores the contradictions between the extensive oppression of African Americans and whites' rhetorical liberty-and-justice framing of U.S. society. Quoting the famous phrase "all men are created equal" from the Declaration of Independence, he boldly challenges white readers:

> Compare your own language above, extracted from your Declaration of Independence, with your cruelties and murders inflicted by your cruel and unmerciful fathers and yourselves on our fathers and on us— men who have never given your fathers or you the least provocation! . . . I ask you candidly, was your sufferings under Great Britain one hundredth part as cruel and tyrannical as you have rendered ours under you?[23]

Once again, Walker's accurate and penetrating analysis does not stop with a critique of white framing of African Americans but emphasizes a *positive view* of African American humanity: "Are we *men*!!—I ask you, O, my brethren! Are we *men*?" This assertion of black humanity, and thus moral virtue, is one of the oldest elements of black resistance framing. Furthermore, Walker scolds his fellow African Americans for not taking more assertive action against white oppression. Throughout the *Appeal*, he accents a framing of U.S. history and society that is non-mythological and insists on genuine liberty and justice for all.

Unsurprisingly, white political and economic leaders in the South and North were very disturbed by Walker's strong appraisal of black freedom and white immorality and oppression. Slaveholders put a huge monetary bounty on his head, and he died in mysterious circumstances in Boston. Fearful of slave networks and communications, slaveholders and their allies also blamed Walker's widely circulated pamphlet for stimulating slave revolts, including the major revolt of Nat Turner and his fellow freedom-fighters in Virginia 1831 (see below). Also in response to Walker's pamphlet and other abolitionists' actions, white officials in various southern areas put yet harsher restrictions on the movements of their black residents and on circulation of anti-slavery publications.[24]

In Walker's revolutionary analysis, we once more observe that in the early decades of the nineteenth century, African Americans were vigorously asserting and enhancing a counter-frame to the dominant white frame, one that encompassed elements like those of earlier African American freedom-fighters: (1) a forceful and critical analysis of racial oppression as unjust and immoral; (2) significant countering of whites' anti-black stereotyping and other racial framing, including the racist sanitizing of the country's history; (3) accents on the humanity and moral virtue of African Americans; (4) forceful assertions of black American-ness; and (5) frequent emphases on real liberty, justice, and equality. He mixed what later would be termed "black nationalist" views with a clear view that black Americans had to somehow come to terms with oppressive whites and force a truly integrated society. Note, too, that Walker's logical, fearless, and non-deferential insistence on the realities of oppression and on the necessity of efforts toward genuine liberty and justice noticeably influenced many other activists and authors, from Henry Garnet and Maria Stewart in this antebellum era to W. E. B. Du Bois, Malcolm X, and many others in more recent decades.[25]

Other Early Abolitionists

By the 1830s, numerous black activists and writers were insisting that aggressive and organized efforts at gaining political power were more important than verbal entreaties to whites, even if that involved revolutionary violence against slavery. Among these were fearless women such as Maria Stewart, a Bostonian inspired by Walker's *Appeal*. She wrote pamphlets and gave speeches, including lectures to Boston's African-American Female Intelligence Society. She framed her revolutionary analysis by accenting her religious motivation in speaking out, much like Old Testament prophets, against extreme oppression. She cited the French and Haitian revolutionary traditions and called on black Americans, especially men, to be more ambitious, and to organize and engage in organized efforts to overthrow racial oppression. Like Walker and other black writers, she heavily accented that she was a "true born American" and that the American "spirit fires my breast." Accenting African Americans' proud background of great African societies, she heavily criticized whites' forcing them into menial work and excluding them from public education. In an 1833 speech, she made what probably is the first public insistence on the critical role of black women in the struggle for justice. Women should have a public role, and she cites historical examples of women church leaders and scholars. Thus, she insisted that people should not be stereotyped on gender or racial grounds.[26] As Horton and Horton summarize, Stewart argued that black women should promote their own welfare, the strength of their families, and the elevation of their race not only in the private world of the home but also in the public world. . . . [and] that black women would not be constrained by the dictates of all the gender ideals of politics.[27]

Again, we observe a striking stress on implementing genuine liberty and freedom, even as there was a constant denial of those ideals by whites.

Black leaders were often influenced by one another's writings. In 1843, another prominent black abolitionist, Henry Garnet, spoke to those enslaved in a fiery speech to a northern National Negro Convention. Influenced by David Walker's *Appeal* (which he republished), Garnet's anti-slavery counter-framing was aggressive, calling on them to actively rebel against their structural "oppression." In his view, the white "oppressor's power is fading," and like Walker and others before him, Garnet emphasizes that African Americans like "all men cherish the love of liberty. . . . In every man's mind the good seeds of liberty are planted." Additionally, he advocated violence against white oppression: "There is not much hope of redemption without the shedding of blood. If you must bleed, let it all come at once—rather die freemen, than live to be slaves."[28] Garnet's address was published and widely disseminated, creating much debate within black and white communities. Just before the Civil War ended, he gave another address in the U.S. House chamber itself, one in which he addressed the question whites often ask: "When will the Negroes end their demands?" His reply was that this will happen "When all unjust and heavy burdens shall be removed from every man in the land. When all . . . holding allegiance to the government shall enjoy every right of American citizenship."[29]

During the next decade, another major abolitionist, Martin Delany, wrote books developing an anti-racist counter-framing of U.S. society. Writing to all Americans in an 1852 book, he underscored the dramatic contradictions between whites' words and practices: The U.S.,

untrue to her trust and unfaithful to her professed principles of republican equality, has also pursued a policy of political degradation to a large portion of her native born countrymen, and that class is the Colored People. . . . There is no species of degradation to which we are not subject.

Delany makes clear that his anti-racist framing accents meaningful freedom and justice goals: "We believe in the universal equality of man, and believe in that declaration of God's word, in which it is positively said, that 'God has made of one blood all the nations that dwell on the face of the earth.'"[30]

Like David Walker, Delany takes on anti-black notions in the common white frame, countering the "absurd idea of a natural inferiority of the African" that was dreamed up by "slave-holders and their abettors in justification" of extreme oppression. Attacking anti-black stereotypes, he provides a detailed list of important achievements of African Americans, including successful entrepreneurs and professionals. He further describes some of the major accomplishments of enslaved African workers that I discussed in Chapter 3, such as in farming and animal husbandry. Black workers are the "bone and sinews of the country," the very "existence of the white man, South, depends entirely on the labor of the black man—the idleness of the one is sustained by the industry of the other." Slaveholding whites lazily profit off others' labor. Furthermore, Delany emphasizes whites' unjust enrichment and that black Americans, as old Americans, should not be forced to emigrate to Africa (a common white idea) but seek out their freedom within the society they helped so much to build. "Our common country is the United States . . . and from here will we not be driven by any policy that may be schemed against us. We are Americans, having a birthright citizenship."[31] Delany's strong accent on black self-determination and building up black communities has led to his being termed the "father of black nationalism." Indeed, in this era, there were a number of such black nationalists, most of whom advocated black self-determination and substantial black community-building—but not a fully separate black nation. Another example of such an advocate was Alexander Crummell, first black graduate of Queens' College, Cambridge (England). In the 1850s, he gave important anti-slavery speeches there, seeking European support for the abolitionist cause. Insisting on black self-determination and Pan-African unity across continents, in the 1890s he also established the American Negro Academy in Washington, DC, the first such organization designed to foster black scholarship and literature.[32]

In this book, I use "black nationalism" to refer to black counter-framing and action that heavily and openly stresses black unity and self-determination, black pride, and substantial economic or political independence from white Americans. Black nationalist perspectives vary considerably in emphasis on the character and extent of separation from whites deemed necessary and in preferred protest strategies, and they often have overlapped with elements of aggressive civil rights perspectives.

The 1850s: More Courageous Protests

In the 1850s decade, during which the slaveholder-dominated U.S. Supreme Court issued its infamous Dred Scott decision that blacks had "no rights," the black opposition to oppression intensified. In one 1858 Boston speech,

Dr. John Rock, a brilliant young physician and lawyer, described how millions of "weak" white men had long kept blacks enslaved, backed up by "a rich oligarchy" of whites in that horrific process. He declared, too, the right of black Americans to revolt as black Haitians had done in the successful 1790s Haitian revolution against major European armies. In this era, African Americans also issued several important group declarations for freedom and abolition of slavery. For example, the 1853 Colored National Convention issued a Declaration of Sentiment insisting that whites live up to their liberty-and-justice ideals in regard to the treatment of black Americans.[33]

This was a decade when some black women bravely raised their voices publically against slavery and for group freedom. Charlotte Forten Grimké was a free black woman who grew up in Philadelphia and later went to the South to teach children during the Civil War. She taught recently freed black children about the heroes of African Americans' history, including the successful Haitian revolutionary, Toussaint L'Ouverture. In her diaries she, too, was adamant about the injustices of slavery and the goals of real liberty and justice for enslaved African Americans. In one diary entry in 1855, she spoke this way:

> I wonder that every colored person is not a misanthrope. Surely we have everything to make us hate mankind. ... Let us take courage; never ceasing to work,—hoping and believing that if not for us, for another generation there is a better, brighter day in store,—when slavery and prejudice shall vanish before the glorious light of Liberty and Truth; when the rights of every colored man shall everywhere be acknowledged and respected, and he shall be treated as a man and a brother![34]

The contemporary writer, Elizabeth Chittenden, has quoted Grimké with regard to Christian support of slavery: "How can I be a Christian when so many in common with myself, for no crime, suffer cruelty, so unjustly?" She decided she could no longer be a Christian. Grimké was also quite critical of the white racism she saw around her, at one point saying, "Oh, it is hard to go through life . . . fearing with too good reason to love and trust hardly anyone whose skin is white—however lovable, attractive, congenial in seeming."[35]

Another courageous black woman, Mary Ann Shadd, grew up in the North and was likewise a teacher of black children in southern areas. She was a civil rights activist, feminist, abolitionist orator, and the first black female editor of a newspaper, the anti-slavery paper *Provincial Freeman*. After the Civil War, she went to law school, becoming the second black female lawyer ever and continued to write for progressive newspapers.

During the 1850s, when she was residing in Canada, she became famous for advocating black self-reliance and emigration to Canada.[36] Her 1852 pamphlet, *A Plea for Emigration*, laid out the economic and civil rights advantages of Canada for fleeing African Americans:

> The conclusion arrived at in respect to Canada, by an impartial person, is, that no settled country in America offers stronger inducements to colored people. . . . the laws of the country give to them, at first, the same protection and privileges as to other persons not born subjects. . . . there is an increasing anti-slavery sentiment, and a progressive system of religion.

She added that the objection that this emigration would slow the move to abolition in the United States is unsupported. In the United States,

> more territory has [already] been given up to slavery, the Fugitive Law has passed, and a concert of measures, seriously affecting their personal liberty, has been entered into by several of the Free states . . . and the end may not be yet.[37]

Just a few years later, she demonstrated her strong revolutionary orientation when she assisted the black and white freedom-fighters who, under the leadership of John Brown, attacked the federal arsenal at Harper's Ferry (then Virginia) to secure weapons for slave rebellions (see Chapter 5).

Frederick Douglass: Brilliant Analyst of Oppression and Justice

One of the very greatest Americans, of any background, prior to the twentieth century was Frederick Douglass—an enslaved youth who emancipated himself, a major abolitionist, a major anti-racist orator for decades, a leading anti-racist editor and widely read intellectual, the key advocate and organizer of critical black volunteers for the Union military, and an outspoken feminist in a time when few men took such a public position. Even in early writings and speeches after his enslavement, the abolitionist Douglass made clear that liberty could come only with major national struggle and conflict, which he early on had termed the "second American Revolution." In his 1845 autobiography, *Narrative of the Life of Frederick Douglass*, he spoke specifically of freedom and liberty about forty-one times and of justice and injustice another five times. In a later autobiography, *My Bondage and My Freedom* (which includes speeches), he explicitly used the terms *freedom* and *liberty* about 155 times, and the terms *justice* and *equality* about 60 times.[38] In this antebellum era, there was a surge of pamphleteering and other protest writings, including dozens of influential slave narratives like these—all connected to growing black protests of the pre-Civil War era. One of this era's autobiographies was written by an enslaved black woman, Harriet Jacobs; she too frequently uses the concepts of freedom and liberty (about fifty-eight times) and justice and injustice (about seven times) in her important 1861 autobiography, *Incidents in the Life of a Slave Girl*. In her account of years in slavery, she provides details of the everyday brutality and moral corruptness of most whites associated in any way with the slavery system.[39] The large number of times these and other African Americans used forceful concepts of authentic freedom and justice shows just how developed and powerful is their black counter-framing against the morally corrupt white-racist framing of the last several centuries.

By the 1850s, many black and white abolitionists were regularly arguing that this second revolution for genuine black freedom had to be implemented soon. In a famous address entitled "The Meaning of July Fourth for the Negro" and given at an 1852 event commemorating the Declaration of Independence, Douglass raised these barbed questions directed at white America:

> What have I, or those I represent, to do with your national independence? Are the great principles of political freedom and of natural justice, embodied in that Declaration of Independence, extended to us? . . . Would you have me argue that man is entitled to liberty? That he is the rightful owner of his own body? You have already declared it. Must I argue the wrongfulness of slavery? . . . How should I look to-day, in the presence of Americans, dividing, and subdividing a discourse, to show that men have a natural right to freedom? . . . What, to the American slave, is your 4th of July? I answer; a day that reveals to him, more than all other days in the year, the gross injustice and cruelty to which he is the constant victim. To him, your celebration is a sham; your boasted liberty, an unholy license; your national greatness, swelling vanity; your sounds of rejoicing are empty and heartless; your denunciation of tyrants, brass fronted impudence; your shouts of liberty and equality, hollow mockery; your prayers and hymns, your sermons and thanksgivings, with all your religious parade and solemnity, are, to Him, mere bombast, fraud, deception, impiety, and hypocrisy. . . .[40]

This powerful black-framed argument extends David Walker's analysis in asserting the injustice and cruelty to blacks from whites fraudulently and hypocritically celebrating a Declaration of Independence that enshrines hypocritical ideals of liberty. Like most of his speeches and writings, Douglass's powerful Fourth of July address centers around solid arguments for truly meaningful and implemented freedom and justice for enslaved African Americans, in this case framed as a matter already settled, in theory and white rhetoric, by the Declaration of Independence.

Douglass regularly attacked the brutality and degrading character of slavery for all involved. Just a few years after achieving his freedom, he was a well-regarded lecturer on slavery in northern states and regularly published damning indictments of slavery and slaveholders in abolitionist newspapers, including his own *The North Star*. Over the 1840s and 1850s in his newspaper and in speeches, he argued that enslaved black Americans were treated with cruelty and classified by whites "with four footed beasts and creeping things." In this dehumanization process, the slaveholders degraded themselves, for indeed the "genuine American Negro hater surpasses the pig in piggishness."[41]

Like many other African American analysts of his day and since, Douglass was an excellent social analyst whose analyses of U.S. trends were usually on target. In one significant speech, presented in summer 1857 in Canandaigua, New York on "West India Emancipation," he asserted that, "If there is no struggle, there is no progress." Urging aggressive resistance to enslavement, he made these penetrating assessments:

The whole history of the progress of human liberty shows that all concessions yet made to her august claims have been born of earnest struggle. . . . If there is no struggle there is no progress. Those who profess to favor freedom and yet deprecate agitation are men who want crops without plowing up the ground; they want rain without thunder and lightning. . . . Find out just what any people will quietly submit to and you have found out the exact measure of injustice and wrong which will be imposed upon them, and these will continue till they are resisted with either words or blows, or with both. . . . In the light of these ideas, Negroes will be hunted at the North and held and flogged at the South so long as they submit to those devilish outrages and make no resistance, either moral or physical. . . . If we ever get free from the oppressions and wrongs heaped upon us, we must pay for their removal. We must do this by labor, by suffering, by sacrifice, and if needs be, by our lives and the lives of others.[42]

After listing a number of black men and women who made huge sacrifices, individually and collectively, in the name of resistance and liberation, he noted that he is fully aware

that the insurrectionary movements of the slaves were held by many to be prejudicial to their cause. . . . The answer is that abolition followed close on the heels of insurrection in the West Indies, and Virginia was never nearer emancipation than when General [Nat] Turner kindled the fires of insurrection at Southampton.[43]

Indeed, in an 1860 letter praising John Brown and his black and white associates for trying to get arms from a federal arsenal, Douglass made clear his view of insurrectionary action:

A long course of peaceful slaveholding has placed the slaveholders beyond the reach of moral and humane consideration. . . . The only penetrable point of a tyrant is the Fear of Death. The outcry that they make as to the danger of having their Throats Cut, is because they know they de-serve to have them Cut. The efforts of John Brown and his brave associates, though apparently unavailing, have done more to upset the logic and shake the security of slavery, than all other efforts in that direction for twenty years.[44]

Violent black action against white enslavement actually fueled some northern and southern white support for slavery's abolition.

In an 1863 speech at New York's Cooper Institute, Douglass responded to President Lincoln's recently issued Emancipation Proclamation. First he pointed out that for more than sixty years, the federal government had itself been a "stupendous engine of Slavery and oppression, through which Slavery has ruled us, as with a rod of iron." He added that, if that federal government and the white majority do indeed support that Proclamation, then he viewed such support as a

complete revolution in the position of a nation. ... We are all liberated by this proclamation. . . . It is a mighty event for the bondman, but it is a still mightier event for the nation at large, and mighty as it is for the both, the slave and the nation, it is still mightier when viewed in its relation to the cause of truth and justice throughout the world. ... What a glorious day when Slavery shall be no more in this country, when we have blotted out this system of wrong, and made this United States in fact and in truth what it is in theory—The Land of the Free and the Home of the Brave.[45]

Douglass states here, as I have argued throughout this book, that the central problem of this country is the unwillingness of whites to make the sacrifices necessary to produce a United States that is in *fact* what it often is in the white liberty-and-justice rhetoric. In his view, if whites carry out the goals of that Proclamation, this will be revolutionary not only for those enslaved but for the nation as a whole, including whites. Similarly, in a previous 1862 New York speech, Douglass had argued that the destiny of the black

American was the "destiny of America," and he "likened the nation to an open book, its black ink giving meaning to the white pages and offering lessons about 'wisdom, power, and goodness' and the sacredness of 'human brotherhood.'"[46]

Ever the activist, for decades after the Civil War, Douglass worked against white violence (including lynchings and Klan groups), the debt peonage entrapping newly freed black people, and growing legal segregation. Late in his career, when asked by a young black man what advice he would give for living a good life, Douglass replied strongly, "Agitate! Agitate! Agitate!"[47] He wrote articles and gave speeches that counter-framed increasing legal segregation as yet another type of black enslavement. In one 1880s speech, he emphasized how Jim Crow segregation meets black Americans "at the workshop and factory, when they apply for work. It meets them at the church, at the hotel, at the ballot-box, and worst of all, it meets them in the jury-box." He put the reality quite accurately and succinctly: The African American has moved from being the "slave of an individual" to being the "slave of society."[48] Additionally, in an 1888 speech on the twenty-sixth anniversary of slaves' emancipation in the District of Columbia, he emphasized that this "so-called emancipation [was] a stupendous fraud" because the white-run nation had not honored its pledge to free blacks, who now faced extensive Jim Crow:

> My mission now, as all along during nearly fifty years, is to plead the cause of . . . millions of our countrymen against injustice, oppression, meanness and cruelty, and to hasten the day when the principles of liberty and humanity expressed in the Declaration of Independence and the Constitution of the United States shall be the law and the practice of every section, and of all the people of this great country without regard to race, sex, color or religion.[49]

Douglass remained a freedom-fighter to his death, with a vision of the country that was remarkably farsighted and inclusive. Note, too, that while his recurring focus is on freeing African Americans from oppression, he also accents liberty for all in terms of "race, sex, color or religion," one of very few U.S. leaders who articulated such an inclusive view of justice before our contemporary era. African Americans such as Douglass have been on the cutting edge of U.S. intellectual thought for many generations and often well ahead of white analysts and intellectuals in assessing the deep foundations and everyday contours of U.S. oppressions.

Douglass is an excellent example of how African American writers and activists have regularly had a great influence on other African Americans, the cooperative and communal ethic discussed previously. From the time of his first speeches and writings, he was widely read by peers, and he has been greatly influential on later African American intellectuals and activists (for example, W. E. B. Du Bois). In his time, he also influenced white abolitionists and the leaders of the Republican Party, newly organized in 1854 with Douglass as a rare but respected black member. He met with Abraham Lincoln three times during the Civil War era. No African American had previously been treated this respectfully by a president. At one meeting, Lincoln asked Douglass to help create an organization of black scouts to take word of the Emancipation Proclamation to enslaved people throughout the Confederacy. [50] Later on in his life, Douglass became a minor Republican official and has been criticized by some recent analysts for not speaking out often enough against Jim Crow segregation and U.S. imperialism in the Caribbean.[51]

Significantly, at Douglass's funeral in February 1895, which thousands attended, Albion Tourgée, the prominent white novelist, Reconstruction leader, and lead lawyer in the major 1896 *Plessy v. Ferguson* case, gave a eulogy indicating the impact that Douglass had on progressive whites. Tourgée made clear inspiring lessons learned from Douglass about courage, resistance to oppression, and justice. Critical of the rise of Jim Crow in the South, Tourgée noted that

> Three classes of the American people are under special obligations to him: the colored bondman whom he helped to free from the chains which he himself had worn, the free persons of color whom he helped to make citizens, the white people of the United States whom he sought to free from the bondage of caste and relieve from the odium of slavery.[52]

One can also see the impact on Tourgée of Douglass and other courageous African Americans of the nineteenth century in Tourgée's writings. As Carolyn Karcher has noted,

> No other white writer of Tourgée's time—and few since then—portrayed African Americans with such realism, treated them as independent political agents instead of as menials attached to whites, and . . . It was Tourgée's contact with fugitive slaves and black soldiers in union army camps during his Civil War service that converted him into an impassioned advocate of racial equality.[53]

In their turn, Tourgée's honest portrayals of African Americans in novels and his civil rights activism significantly influenced some black activists and scholars of his day and later on, including Ida B. Wells-Barnett, Anna Julia Cooper, Charles W. Chesnutt, and W. E. B. Du Bois.

Ida B. Wells-Barnett: Anti-Lynching Activist and Social Scientist

In the late nineteenth century and early twentieth century, two of these important activists were pioneering social scientists: Ida B. Wells-Barnett and Anna Julia Cooper. They worked to expand the black counter-frame to accent issues of gendered racism. They analyzed societal data on the oppressive segregation faced by all black Americans and the sexism and gendered discrimination especially faced by black women. They were among the first social scientists to make explicit use of counter-framed ideas and language of racial "oppression," "subordination," and "repression." Wells-Barnett and Cooper were among the first to emphasize the overlapping realities of institutional racism and institutional sexism in the everyday lives of black women and men.[54]

At the turn of the twentieth century, Wells-Barnett, who was born enslaved, was an important journalist, a social science researcher working on lynching issues, a major civil rights activist, founder of a women's suffrage organization, and a cofounder of the National Association for the Advancement of Colored People (NAACP) in 1909. She traveled to Britain and helped establish an anti-lynching society and from there sent back the first reports by a black journalist to a white-run newspaper. She helped organize nonviolent resistance to Jim Crow segregation in Tennessee, fought Jim Crow discrimination on railroad trains in federal court, and bought a gun to protect herself from recurring white violence. Suffering the loss of a friend to a lynch mob, she worked tirelessly in researching and fighting against white violence targeting African Americans. She was among the first social scientists to explicate how white violence and other oppression were grounded in the material reality of economic exploitation and in protecting the unjust enrichment of whites in a system of racial oppression. In the face of violent white threats, she courageously dissected white rationalizations of lynchings in the mythological gendering of black men as dangerous ("rapists") to white women. She published a book-length pamphlet on lynching in the 1890s, one in which she and her African American sources often speak of the need for authentic liberty, justice, and equality before the law for African Americans, especially in the essentially totalitarian Jim Crow South.[55]

As she noted in her 1895 sociologically-oriented pamphlet on lynchings, *The Red Record*, black Americans have faced the "unbridled power" of white men for centuries, power that during the Jim Crow era revealed itself in many "acts of conscience-less outlawry." In this pamphlet, Wells-Barnett argued that the anti-lynching crusade, in which she was a major leader,

> will determine whether [U.S.] civilization can maintain itself by itself, or whether anarchy shall prevail; Whether this Nation shall write itself

down a success at self government, or in deepest humiliation admit its failure complete; whether the precepts and theories of Christianity are professed and practiced by American white people as Golden Rules of thought and action, or adopted as a system of morals to be preached to heathen until they attain to the intelligence which needs the system of Lynch Law.[56]

She further insisted that in this critical anti-lynching crusade, "it is the white man's civilization and the white man's government which are on trial."

Moreover, as the philosopher Tommy Curry has pointed out, Wells-Barnett, like other black leaders before, during, and after her era, was strongly supportive of African Americans' actively defending themselves against white violence.[57] In 1891, she expressed this revolutionary perspective on white lynchers and their white defenders in an editorial in T. Thomas Fortune's anti-racist paper, the *New York Age*:

The *Jackson (Miss) Tribune and Sun*, and the *Memphis (Tenn) Daily Commercial Appeal* are squirming in great shape over the outspoken sentiment of the "Memphis Free Speech" comme[n] ding the retaliatory measures adopted by the Afro-Americans of Georgetown, Ky., in revenge for the lynching of one of its members. The *Sun* insists that the people of Memphis should proceed to muzzle the "Free Speech," and the *Commercial Appeal* drops into philosophy and declares that two wrongs do not make a right; and that while white people should stick to the law, if they do not do so, the blacks can hope for nothing but extermination if they attempt to defend themselves. . . . Fundamentally men have an *inherent right to defend themselves* when lawful authority refuses to do it for them; and when a whole community makes itself responsible for a crime it should be held responsible.[58]

She called on African American families to have *a Winchester rifle* at the ready in their homes to protect them against white violence. Additionally, her sociologically honed assessments and visions of the future were well ahead of those of most people, such as in her argument that the abolition of southern lynching was necessary for all southerners, white and black, because U.S. capitalists would not

invest where lawlessness and mob violence hold sway. Many labor organizations have declared by resolution that they would avoid lynch infested localities as they would the pestilence when seeking new homes. If the South wishes to build up its waste places quickly, there is no better way than to uphold the majesty of the law by enforcing obedience to the same, and meting out the same punishment to all classes of criminals, white as well as black. "Equality before the law," must become a fact as well as a theory before America is truly the "land of the free and the home of the brave."[59]

For more than 180 years now, African American activist-scholars have developed an accurate critique of fundamental flaws in Western "civilization" that highlights this need for real "equality before the law."

I do not have the space to discuss in detail the numerous other leaders of this era, but let us briefly note two with close ties to Wells-Barnett. One was T. Thomas Fortune, editor of the largest-circulation black newspaper, *New York Age*. He constantly called for black "agitation" and militant protests against oppression. Together with Wells-Barnett and other activist leaders, Fortune organized the militant Afro-American League (AAL). That organization dwindled but was resuscitated in 1898 as the National Afro-American Council (NAAC). Well before the founding of the NAACP in 1909, the AAL and NAAC lobbied for anti-lynching legislation, brought lawsuits against southern discrimination, and organized civil rights protests. Fortune and his associates insisted on respecting their African roots, as in their term *Afro-American*. Fortune was an important mentor for Wells-Barnett, taking her on as a journalist at *New York Age* when she was driven out of Memphis by white violence against her lynching writings. Later on, Fortune started other black newspapers and worked on Marcus Garvey's black nationalist newspaper (see Chapter 6), at the time becoming an important figure in the Harlem Renaissance.[60]

Another outspoken leader was William Monroe Trotter, cofounder in 1901 of Boston's black newspaper, *The Guardian*. He too wrote and spoke vigorously for racial equality and against white violence and other discrimination, including racist policies of Presidents Woodrow Wilson and Theodore Roosevelt and the Klan-inspired movie *Birth of a Nation*. He worked with Wells-Barnett, Du Bois, and others to develop the Niagara Movement that led to the founding of the NAACP and attended an international peace conference in spite of opposition from U.S. officials.[61] In all these cases, we observe repeatedly that, while there were on occasion major tensions between these leaders, there was generally much teamwork and cooperation in their collective efforts against crushing white oppression.

Conclusion

Whites have oppressed African Americans and other Americans of color to keep them in their societal "place" of extreme inequality. Thus, over the course of U.S. history, these Americans have had to engage in individual and group struggles against oppression and its mythologizing white frame.

First under colonial conditions and then in a supposed U.S. "democracy," African Americans have had a central place in the centuries-old struggle against racism and in forcing this country's white leaders to periodically take action to expand freedom, justice, and equality.

Since the eighteenth century, African American thinker-activists have provided many of the most sustained, critical, and deep analyses of the racial oppression foundational to and systemic in this society. Without their courageous scholarship and research and associated activism of thousands of African Americans, there would likely be no extensive anti-racist tradition for making sense of the country's foundational racial structure, past and present.

This vital structural analysis is imbedded in a centuries-old African American counter-frame that not only questions major aspects of the dominant white racial frame but establishes a truly just and authentically moral framing of the changes needed for what is still a racially immoral society. The writings and speeches of the black counter-framers critically evaluate the realities of racial oppression and constantly raise an array of empirical and theoretical issues that otherwise would not likely have been dealt with, especially by white analysts. These include the hypocrisy of the supposedly virtuous liberty-and-justice language of founding documents such as the Declaration of Independence and the U.S. Constitution. By contrasting the actual realities of white oppression with the white rhetorical hyperbole about liberty and justice, African American analysts have raised questions about the diversionary character and extraordinary hypocrisy of this old rhetoric. In this manner, they vigorously contest the claim of white virtuousness that is so *central* to the dominant white racial frame. Undeniably, whites are *not* actually the moral exemplars they so assertively claim to be, and whites' assertions about U.S. "democratic exceptionalism" turn out to be fraudulent beneath their surface of superficial democratic structures.

In addition, a second feature of that white racial frame is directly challenged and destabilized. White claims regularly inferiorizing and denigrating people of color in that dominant white frame are likewise shown by these African American thinker-activists to be irrational and mythological defenses set up mainly to defend and legitimate whites' unjust enrichment over the centuries. These thinker-activists have been among those few in society who have intensively focused on white racial mythmaking that has become accepted knowledge in much of the society, and they have challenged how that knowledge is produced and reproduced over generations. Only in these critical African American analyses does one find the essential concepts of institutional and systemic racism well developed and underscored early on in U.S. history. Indeed, the African American thinker-activists were generating significant social science analyses of institutional and systemic racism long before there was much social science in U.S. colleges and universities.

One can also see in these commentaries from African American analysts over the first century of this country's existence that there is a distinctively *collective* and *communal* sense of freedom and justice. That is, the openly critical and developed counter-frame guiding radical and revolutionary black analyses and movements is deeply rooted in a home-culture framing that has in part been brought from Africa and in part been created in African Americans' creative constructions of freedom and justice as they have collectively battled centuries of oppression. Scholars C. Eric Lincoln and Lawrence Mamiya have pointed out that the concept of freedom has varied somewhat for African Americans depending on the historical era: "During slavery it meant release from bondage; after emancipation it meant the right to be educated, to be employed, and to move about freely from place to place. In the twentieth century freedom means social, political, and economic justice." Yet, as they also note well, there has always been a *common core* that is distinctive and communally oriented:

For whites freedom has bolstered the value of American individualism: to be free to pursue one's destiny without political or bureaucratic interference or restraint. But for African Americans freedom has always been communal in nature. In Africa the destiny of the individual was linked to that of the tribe or the community in an intensely interconnected security system. In America, black people have seldom been perceived or treated as individuals; they have usually been dealt with as "representatives" of their "race," an external projection.[62]

5

Black Action
Accelerating Freedom, Justice, and Democracy (1700s–1800s)

Let us turn now to an analysis of numerous large-scale African American efforts to secure freedom and social justice over the eighteenth and nineteenth centuries, with a particular focus on organized resistance to oppression. Much of this black action for freedom and justice has been forgotten, but it has slowly been recovered of late in the research of several historians and civil rights organizations.

In earlier centuries, whites often oppressed Native Americans in external wars of aggression and expulsion, while they always oppressed African Americans by internally enslaving them *within* white communities—and often on stolen Native American lands. Not surprisingly, whites constantly faced major resistance from both groups. From Native Americans, the resistance frequently took the form of organized armed resistance to white incursions into traditional Native American lands or, if forced to do so by white violence, withdrawal to areas farther west if that resistance was insufficient. In contrast, confined within the boundaries of white society, the overt physical resistance by enslaved African Americans took the form of destruction of crops, livestock, tools, and houses and violent individual and collective resistance against overseers and slavemasters. For African Americans, there was also much nonviolent resistance in the form of a slow working pace, feigned illness, and work strikes. The white oppressors faced millions of individual and collective acts of resistance from both groups over the first centuries of white colonization and control.[1]

The white-framed fantasy of "contented slaves" has long been circulated in U.S. movies and other mainstream media, and it is still accepted by many. Thus, in the 1880s, the prominent Harvard historian, James Schouler, accented the commonplace white framing of those enslaved with these stereotyped phrases: "the innate patience, docility, and child-like simplicity of the negro," an "imitator and non-moralist," "easily intimidated, incapable of deep plots," and "a black servile race, sensuous, stupid, brutish, obedient to the whip, children in imagination."[2] This racist framing was centuries old. Actually, most of those enslaved were not contented but *did* seek their freedom as they could. Many openly rebelled. One observes the scale and importance of this resistance in the great extent to which slaveholders tried to prevent it, including by frequent whippings, hangings, and other extreme brutality, and by an assortment of slave-control laws and patrols.

Unmistakably, Native American and African American resistance involved much cognitive and emotional intelligence and labor, including much counter-framing, to resist and survive brutal white oppression. This extensive resistance also forced whites into much cognitive and emotional labor of their own to defend their violent oppression, which labor has long taken the form of an emotionally loaded white-racist framing accenting the racial superiority of whites and racial inferiority of Native Americans and African Americans.

As I have shown previously and demonstrate further in this chapter and in Chapter 6 and Chapter 7, the many black struggles for liberation and justice have included slave uprisings, antebellum black abolitionists, soldiers in the Revolutionary War and Civil War, activists and officials' Reconstruction efforts, activists' creation of civil rights organizations in the nineteenth and early twentieth centuries, 1960s civil rights protesters and black power activists, and more recent black anti-racism protests and protest organizations. The courageous agency and actions of these African American groups constitute a major reason for much of the progress that the United States has made on issues of democracy and social justice since its centuries-long slaveholding era.

Wartime Action against Slavery

In the decades before the official emergence of the United States in the 1780s, many African Americans sought their freedom by fleeing enslavement, which was often facilitated by U.S. war settings. They were anything but the contented and docile stereotypes of white imaginations. Some escaped to northern areas or Canada. Remarkably little known is the fact that a great many fled their enslavement by going to the British lines during the revolutionary era of the 1770s and 1780s and again during the War of 1812. For several decades now, historians have recorded that during the American Revolution, far more enslaved African Americans sought out their liberty by fleeing and fighting for the British side than by fighting for the American side. Offered *real* liberty by smart British authorities after 1775 if they would fight for the British army and navy, tens of thousands (perhaps 100,000) of enslaved black Americans fled to, and frequently to fight and work for, the British side. This large number was a significant percentage of those enslaved, and it included many enslaved by Thomas Jefferson and then General George Washington. The reason for this little-known rebellion is easy to understand: The British promised them *freedom*, the goal of most enslaved black Americans. This determination to be free indicates as well how committed to extreme black oppression were many "liberty loving" whites.[3]

Later on, during the War of 1812, many enslaved African Americans again took advantage of the British military's presence and offer of freedom. A British admiral offered freedom to black men who joined British military forces and to black families, who would be sent as free people to British territories. While some fought or were forced to fight for the U.S. cause, more than 4,000 chose freedom with the British. A unit called the Colonial Marines was formed of refugees from slavery and fought well in engagements against slaveholders and others defending the United States. One British commander noted that the black troops were "infinitely more dreaded" by U.S. forces than his white troops. In addition, thousands of black Canadians formerly enslaved in the U.S. fought for the British.[4]

Recall, too, that Francis Scott Key, a slaveowner who during this war wrote the *Star Spangled Banner*, with its numerous lines about a fictitious "land of the free," considered the new nation a legitimate white slaveholding "republic." Moreover, in that anthem's seldom-sung third verse, Key verbally attacked those enslaved Americans who courageously fought with the British for their liberty.[5] With some reflection, one can understand why this important part of U.S. history has been ignored by virtually all white Americans until very recently. Such rarely acknowledged historical events signal that this country's whites are still unwilling to face its enslavement foundations and that African Americans have long resisted that racial oppression and actively sought opportunities to create freedom for themselves.

Early Petitions against Enslavement

Another major type of protest action by African Americans involved the filing of important petitions for freedom and against slavery. The first of these petitions was filed in 1773, well before the white elite's Declaration of Independence, by enslaved blacks in an organized effort in the Massachusetts colony. They described enslaved lives as quite "embittered with this most intolerable reflection" of never being able to "possess or enjoy anything, no not even life itself."[6] A related type of protest in Massachusetts and other colonies (later, states) involved filing numerous lawsuits insisting that the enslaved black plaintiffs should be freed.

After the creation of the new United States, these petitions continued at state and federal levels, and white political leaders routinely rejected them. In one 1799 petition to the President, Senate, and House of Representatives, seventy free black Philadelphians protested aspects of the implementation of the inhumane Fugitive Slave Law. They emphasized their "natural right to Liberty," as described in the Declaration of Independence and in the

Constitution's preamble. They called on white officials to act as "Guardians of our Civil Rights, and Patrons of Equal and National Liberty" and concluded that government action "extending of Justice and equity to all Classes, would be a means of drawing down the blessings of Heaven upon this Land."[7] Again, this forceful black counter-framing drew attention to the great oppression faced by black Americans and also to the moral obligation of white leaders to implement their stated liberty and civil rights ideals.

In this founding era, we note the importance of the small percentage of African Americans who were officially free. Early free black leaders such as Richard Allen, Daniel Coker, and Prince Hall publicly insisted on black liberation from slavery and other oppression. They used the weapon of petitions and published writings and organized street protests to condemn white tyranny and to press adamantly for the liberties articulated in the country's revolutionary ideals. Using newspapers and pamphlets, the public media of the day, they vigorously argued that slavery "violated both secular and sacred creeds," and they forced some in the white public to pay attention to black counter-framing of slavery's oppression.[8] These free blacks firmly proclaimed that all African Americans should be treated as U.S. citizens with full civil rights.

In this era, a few of these leaders articulated the idea of black colonization overseas, especially in Africa, as a solution for the oppressed conditions of blacks who were free or might be freed in the future. However, at one important meeting of black Philadelphians in 1817, when several made the case for black colonization in Africa, *not one black person* in the large audience supported this idea. Although a modest number of black Americans did migrate to Africa (mainly to what became Liberia), the colonization idea was eventually abandoned by most black supporters even as numerous whites were supportive. By the 1830s, free black leaders were playing a key role in attacking colonization and lessening its support among white abolitionists.[9] Note, too, that the white supporters had a different set of reasons for support of overseas colonization, as many such as Thomas Jefferson were fearful of slave rebellions or of enslaved blacks being freed and socially merging with the white population.

Note, too, that free blacks in the North, led by these leaders emphasizing the goals of genuine liberty and justice for all, created numerous substantial communities of African Americans. As the United States developed in the 1790s and 1800s, these black northerners created numerous successful businesses and civic organizations. Beginning with few resources, they were "laboriously creating autonomous churches, benevolent societies, Masonic lodges, insurance groups, and literary organizations. Havens from racial oppression, these self-propelled groups allowed people of color collectively to demonstrate racial pride while simultaneously emphasizing principles of self-reliance and uplift."[10] In these efforts, they were collectively creating and maintaining not only a reinforced black home culture and national black identity but safe spaces largely beyond white control, spaces in which they often developed an aggressive black counter-framing of U.S. racism. Repeatedly over long decades, they thereby created an "African America" by their own vigorous efforts and in the face of great and persisting white oppression.

Individual and Collective Battles for Liberty

Historically, enslaved African Americans have been among the foremost freedom-fighters this country has produced. As we have already seen, these Americans often revolted against their enslavement, both individually and collectively. The slavery system was demonstrably one undergirded by millions of acts of torture by white slaveholders, their relatives, and their employees. The autobiographical accounts of those enslaved reveal U.S. slavery as an institutionalized system of racial oppression undergirded by routine violence and the socially sanctioned coercive or sadistic inclinations of many whites. There are many examples of enslaved individuals seeking liberation from enslavement's many types of everyday torture.

One dramatic example is given in his autobiography by the great abolitionist and civil rights leader Frederick Douglass. At one point in 1833, during his teenage years of enslavement, Douglass decided to resist openly and with all necessary violence the recurring white attempts to violently subordinate him. Threatened with whipping again by a hired white slave breaker named Covey, Douglass successfully defended himself. After an intense fight in which he got the better of Covey, the latter did not try to whip Douglass thereafter. For Douglass, this was not just a fight but an effort at increasing his freedom:

> This battle ... rekindled the few expiring embers of freedom, and revived within me a sense of my own manhood. It recalled the departed self-confidence, and inspired me again with a determination to be free ... and I now resolved that, however long I might remain a slave in form, the day had passed forever when I could be a slave in fact.[11]

Torturous enslavement required African Americans to use their skills, intelligence, and resilience daily in dealings with whites who threatened or used violence against them. Notice the focus on *freedom*, a concept throughout black writings that means what it says—freedom *from* coercion and torture and freedom *for* choosing one's life patterns. His confrontation gave him more control over his life, buoying his "long-crushed spirit."[12]

Enslaved African Americans also fought this country's oppressive slavery system collectively, frequently with physical force. Over centuries, they engaged in more than 300 recorded slave rebellions and conspiracies to revolt. From the seventeenth century onward, colonial whites, contradicting their conventional framing of docile slaves, were very fearful of these violent revolts against subordination. White fears can be seen in many letters and numerous commentaries in early newspapers. One accusation made against the British king by the white revolutionaries in the 1776 Declaration of Independence was that King George had "excited domestic insurrections amongst us," which in their minds included slave uprisings. In his original draft of the Declaration of Independence, Thomas Jefferson had gone even farther, accusing King George of encouraging those enslaved "to rise *in arms* among us, and to purchase that liberty of which he has deprived them, and murdering the people upon whom he also obtruded them."[13] These revealing comments signaled that Jefferson and his colleagues were well aware that African American enslavement was anti-liberty and that those enslaved were really human beings who would seek liberty if possible.

Not surprisingly, white slaveholders and their allies passed numerous laws trying to prevent such black uprisings. In June 1680, thus, a fearful Virginia General Assembly passed "An Act for Preventing Negroes Insurrections." Apparently, the first major all-black conspiracy to revolt was discovered and put down in Westmoreland County, Virginia in 1687. Enslaved African Americans were reported to be planning to destroy property and to kill slaveholders. While the plot was discovered, it created a very negative reaction from whites. After several more conspiracies such as the 1687 plot were discovered, more harsh legislation was passed, including allowing white colonists to kill any enslaved person who resisted or fled enslavement.[14]

Some black revolts occurred in northern areas that traded in enslaved workers. In spring 1712, a substantial group of enslaved workers, assisted by a few whites and Native Americans, violently revolted in New York City. They set fire to buildings and killed or injured fifteen whites who responded to the fires.[15] Put down violently by a white militia, those captured and convicted at trials were tortured and killed in brutal fashion, including twenty being burned to death. As in Virginia, white leaders in New York and adjacent states responded to this major uprising with more repressive laws targeting African Americans.

We do not have space to list more than a few of the hundreds of other slave revolts and conspiracies to revolt. One major revolt was the 1739 Stono Rebellion in the South Carolina colony. About twenty enslaved men raided a store, killed the owners, and burned houses nearby. By the time it was over, about 100 enslaved men had joined in, with many yelling "liberty" (often in African languages) as they tried to make their way to then Spanish-controlled Florida to the south, where the Spanish had promised enslaved workers their freedom. After several days of the uprising, white colonists organized and managed to kill in battles, or later execute, most of the insurrectionists. Just two years later, there was apparently another conspiracy to revolt in New York City. Numerous city fires were attributed to enslaved blacks who whites claimed were talking about setting fires. Eventually some thirty black men and a few poor whites were put to death for their involvement in the supposed insurrection.[16]

Though it did not take place in North America, the major slave rebellion (1791–1804) on the island of Saint-Domingue (Haiti) was the first successful one by an enslaved population in the Americas. This revolt against slavery was led by free and enslaved people of African origin and succeeded against the French leader Napoleon's mighty army and other European military interventions. Even the first U.S. President, George Washington, tried to help white leaders there to put down this large-scale slave rebellion. As word gradually spread of its success, it inspired some African Americans to rebel and led to increased fears of such revolts among U.S. whites (see below). Whites had the importation of enslaved workers from the island banned out of fear they would bring in revolutionary ideas. Ironically, the successful rebellion brought French leaders to the point of seeking to get rid of their lands in North America. In 1803, the Louisiana territory was sold to the U.S. government, thereby increasing the country's size and creating opportunities for slaveholders to expand westward.[17]

In 1800, a major conspiracy to revolt against U.S. slaveholders was begun by an enslaved blacksmith, Gabriel, in central Virginia. Excited by the successful slave rebellion in Saint-Domingue and using the motto of "Death or Liberty," Gabriel and his associates developed a plan to seize the arms at a Richmond armory and kidnap the governor, demanding their freedom for his return. However, after hundreds of armed black freedom-fighters gathered, heavy rains cut them off from Richmond, and they had to postpone their revolt. In the meantime, their plan was betrayed, and at least twenty-six black men were caught and hanged for the conspiracy.[18] At his trial, the courageous and eloquent Gabriel insisted on the human rights of African Americans:

> I have nothing more to offer than what George Washington would have had to offer, had he been taken by the British and put on trial by them, I have adventured my life in endeavoring to obtain the liberty of my countrymen, and I am a willing sacrifice in their cause.[19]

Also inspired by the successful Haitian revolution, the largest organized slave uprising prior to the Civil War took place in 1811 in the Louisiana territory. For decades, influential whites have managed to keep its history unknown or thoroughly whitewashed. This too was a large-scale revolutionary uprising for *real* liberty and justice organized by Americans within the United States. The large sugar plantations of the New Orleans area imported many enslaved African workers and, unlike those elsewhere, these harsh plantation regimes often worked their laborers to death. Hundreds of enslaved workers passionate for freedom and inspired by the Haitian rebellion were led by the courageous Charles Deslondes and two associates. These enslaved freedom-fighters sought to destroy slavery and bring liberty to many enslaved workers. On January 8, 1811, about twenty-six men attacked one major plantation, taking guns, horses, and other equipment. As they traversed a main road, beating drums and shouting for freedom, many of those enslaved at nearby plantations (eventually at least 200 people) joined their group.[20]

However, assisted by U.S. army troops, white planters organized a military force and confronted the black fighters in a pitched battle. More experienced in modern weaponry, the planters' force killed at least forty. Those captured were "tried" by a committee and savagely put to death, with bodies often being mutilated.[21] Yet again, we observe how extensive violence was essential to maintaining one of the world's most oppressive slavery systems. This was indeed a "land of death; a land of spectacular violence," as historian Daniel Rasmussen has put it. This brutal destruction of black insurrectionists, here and in other areas, was considered essential to preserving white domination and reducing the likelihood of more insurrections. In the slaveholders' framing, those enslaved were "little better than cattle" who violated their "racial order."[22] As a result of this rebellion, local white officials increasingly militarized their region. They worked hard to create the myth that this rebellion was "criminal" action by uncivilized individuals—a white-racist framing of such struggles for freedom espoused by most whites until recent decades. Contrary to this mythology, the New Orleans area rebellion was well organized and well led; at its peak, it involved many men from plantations over a large area.[23]

Like other southern areas, this Louisiana region was developed by whites who were expansionist and fearful of the Spanish, their European enemies occupying North American land in Florida and land in the Caribbean. This was an era of expansion of U.S. slavery, and it got much local, state, and national government support. Thus, the federal government supported "rogue adventurers and profit-hungry slavemasters, allying with those who sought first to conquer and then to farm the American frontier."[24]

Two decades later, in 1831, another major rebellion took place, this time in Southampton County, Virginia. This uprising was led by Nat Turner. Religious visions of deliverance from slavery inspired him to lead a liberation movement of about seventy enslaved men. These freedom-fighters killed at least fifty-five whites before a white militia managed to kill or capture them. Turner and his fighters had a strong framing of human liberty in their minds. Evidence for this can be seen in the fact that they had originally planned to begin the attacks, as Turner put it, against their white "enemies" on the independence day of July 4. As with other such rebellions, slaveholders and their allies reacted brutally. After a pretend trial, Turner was hanged, and whites decapitated him and skinned him for souvenirs. Many other men were executed for actually or allegedly participating in this major rebellion for human freedom.[25]

Given the opportunity, enslaved black men and women exercised their agency and openly fought for their liberty, sometimes meeting slavery's violence with liberatory violence. They held strongly to a black counter-framing insisting on the right of "those oppressed to use any means at their disposal."[26] Unmistakably, the leaders of these revolts took seriously the principle of real liberty and justice. Equally as clearly, they should be included at the front rank of the great U.S. revolutionary heroes. Again and again, these slave revolts contradicted white apologists' notion of "happy slaves." Contradictory of this notion, too, were some of the white reactions. Increasingly, the white framing of African Americans portrayed them as dangerous, and this resulted in increases in highly repressive state enslavement laws.

"The Underground Railroad": Dramatic Black Agency

Enslaved blacks kept pressure on the slavery system in many ways. From the late 1700s to the 1860s, an estimated 100,000 to 150,000 African Americans fled southern slavery and thereby helped to destroy the economic viability of the slavery system even before the Civil War. Until recently, most people thought of this metaphorically named "underground railroad" as something operated mostly by well-meaning whites. However, in recent years, much research has demonstrated that black Americans themselves were central to operation of this successful effort at substantial black liberation. Taking into account all those who assisted runaways, it seems likely that a majority of those in the underground insurrection against slavery were African Americans. Many who stayed on the slave plantations and many others along the way risked much to help those fleeing. Most "conductors" assisting people to escape slavery were black, as were many of those running hideout stations along the way north.[27] One famous conductor was Harriet Tubman, who had been enslaved, fled to the North, and went back many times, risking her life to deliver several hundred people to freedom. She certainly deserves recognition as a hero, but there were scores of other courageous African Americans (for example, Mary Ann Shadd and Josiah Henson) who made this freedom system work.

Historian Fergus Bordewich has emphasized the complexity and interracial character of the movement: "By the 1850s the underground had developed into a diverse, flexible, and interlocking system with thousands of activists reaching from the upper South to Canada. In practice, the underground was a model of democracy in action."[28] It also demonstrated the significant organizational skills of many black Americans. One result of this was that new black leaders emerged from this movement in northern and border states. Yet again, African Americans were actively shaping not only their own history but that of the entire country. Considering the scale of involvement by enslaved and free blacks in the southern, border, and northern states and Canada, this underground railroad was one of the great organized insurrections against slavery in U.S. history. As Bordewich has put it, the underground railroad

> physically resisted the repressive laws that held slaves in bondage . . . it engaged thousands . . . in the active subversion of federal law and the prevailing mores of their communities, and for the first time asserted the principle of personal, active responsibility for *others'* human rights.[29]

This great insurrectionary effort signaled southern and northern blacks' meaningful implementation of their counter-framed ideas of authentic black freedom and justice. Without the slave insurrections and this massive escape of those enslaved, including the extensive role of many other people along the escape routes, there probably would not have been a Civil War, and slavery might have lasted several more decades. These many thousands of resistance actions generated great fear among whites, and many in the South, especially powerful slaveholders and allied officials, were becoming political secessionists in part because of the runaway migration. Indeed, the first major secessionist "Declaration of the Immediate Causes" came from South Carolina; in it, the slaveholding leaders there insisted that northern states had "encouraged and assisted thousands of our slaves to leave."[30] Slaveholders at all levels were determined to keep enslaved "property" from leaving their farms and plantations, and they blamed northern abolitionists and the underground railroad for enticing and helping those enslaved to flee, thereby creating huge individual and collective economic losses for southern slaveholders.

Free blacks in the North were essential to the underground railroad, and they also protested or interfered with the slavery system in other ways. Free blacks in several northern cities engaged in armed and other group resistance to the enforcement of northern laws protecting the interests of southern slaveholders. For example, these black activists physically resisted the federal Fugitive Slave Law by rescuing runaways against official attempts to seize them. Again, they were clearly operating out of a strong counter-framing that vigorously insisted enslavement was contrary to the country's stated liberty-and-justice ideals. Additionally, in the critical 1860 election that brought Abraham Lincoln to the presidency, black northerners became active in the new Republican Party and northern politics. They were also increasingly active in the era's abolitionist activities, including in the short-lived Radical Abolitionist Party that advocated immediate emancipation.[31] This assertive political activity helped to bring a stronger criticism of the slavery system to the conscious attention of northern whites, many of whom would eventually support a war against slavery. Indeed, many black activists also worked in national and regional conventions to pressure influential whites to eliminate northern Jim Crow segregation laws.

The Harper's Ferry Rebellion: Centrality of Blacks

The radical white abolitionist, John Brown, had the active support of numerous black abolitionists, including Frederick Douglass and Martin Delany. Recall the prominent black leader, Martin Delany, from Chapter 4. He not only advocated powerfully for black liberation but acted aggressively out of his black counter-framing. In May 1858, he and John Brown gathered together a group of black and white abolitionists for a revolutionary anti-slavery meeting outside the United States, in the safer area of Chatham, Canada. Nearly four dozen Americans, the majority black, formulated a new anti-slavery Declaration of Independence and anti-slavery constitution to govern what they hoped would be a substantial band of armed revolutionaries drawn from the enslaved population. Black men were not the only ones who played a critical role in supporting these freedom-fighters in planning a raid on a federal arsenal. One black woman, Mary Ellen Pleasants, was once enslaved but later married a man from whom she subsequently gained an inheritance. Migrating to California, she became a successful businessperson. Boldly, she later supported John Brown with personal contacts and much monetary support.[32]

There is only one eyewitness account to the 1859 raid on the federal arsenal at Harper's Ferry (then Virginia) conducted by Brown and his black and white anti-slavery fighters. Osborne Anderson was one of five black men among Brown's original fighters. He was the only black man to escape and published a counter-framed narrative of the revolutionary events in 1861. Unsurprisingly, authentic black freedom is at the heart of his framing of events:

> The shaping and expressing of a thought for freedom takes the same conscience with the colored American whether he be an independent citizen of the Haytian nation, proscribed but humble nominally free colored man, a patient, toiling, but hopeful slave as with the proudest or noblest representative of European or American civilization and Christianity.[33]

In his narrative, he makes strong references to liberty, freedom, and equality and develops in his last section an assertive defense of the raid and of the hundreds of enslaved blacks who were in fact waiting for the arms that would be secured by it. He directly refutes the common slaveholders' depiction of the raid's failure as indicating a lack of support from enslaved African Americans for rebellion and of their supposed devotion to white slavemasters:

> On the Sunday evening of the outbreak, when we visited the plantations and acquainted the slaves with our purpose to effect their liberation, the greatest enthusiasm was manifested by them joy and hilarity beamed from every countenance. . . . they stepped forward manfully, without impressing or coaxing. . . . Of the slaves who followed us to the Ferry, some were sent to help remove stores, and the others were drawn up in a circle around the engine-house, at one time, where they were. . . . furnished by me with pikes, mostly, and acted as a guard to the prisoners to prevent their escape.[34]

He further insists that enslaved and free black fighters took a very active part in the raid and were well represented in the casualties. Reports varied in the number of insurrectionists killed (from seventeen to twenty-seven), and just ten of these were Brown's original plotters. Among the others killed were at least seven (and as many as seventeen) of the enslaved fighters from among the two dozen or more enslaved African Americans who joined the original Brown group as they went by local plantations.[35] According to Anderson's detailed report, just more than half of those killed were African Americans. He notes, too, that if the attempt to secure guns from the arsenal had succeeded, hundreds of slaves "ready and waiting would have been armed before twenty-four hours had elapsed."[36] This detailed account refutes the assertions of many whites who downplayed the larger-scale slave participation in uprisings that would have likely resulted if these brave revolutionaries had been successful in getting arms and spreading the word to slave plantations more effectively. Ironically, and unfortunately for their revolutionary cause, Brown had delayed such extensive slave recruiting so he could take better care of prominent whites whom they had already captured.

Few contemporary analyses provide much information on the local aftermath of the raid on the arsenal, but one analysis by Hannah Geffert notes that there was a major military presence in the area long after the raid, in part because of continuing black guerilla activity that included setting fire to plantation crops, agricultural implements, and barns. Indeed, the Virginia governor sent in 500 more troops to prevent guerilla activity. Geffert notes that standard histories of the Harper's Ferry raid have long neglected a careful examination of the available data. These data indicate that local blacks were significant participants in this raid, much more so than these histories record. She concludes with this very important point about the societal context:

> The significance of John Brown's raid should be analyzed not as an isolated event but in the context of the struggle for freedom that black America engaged in throughout the 19th century. Brown had found black allies in the region of Jefferson County who were willing both to stand with him at Harper's Ferry and to continue the struggle through the war and beyond. He and his black allies insisted that it was vital for African Americans to fight for their freedom and that they had the right to do so; Harper's Ferry showed, again, that they would.[37]

In northern areas, the black reaction to the defeat and execution of John Brown and the other black and white freedom-fighters was significant and extensive. In numerous cities, on December 2, 1859, the day of Brown's hanging, many free blacks joined with some white sympathizers in large gatherings to mourn Brown's execution. In great contrast, the conservative white reaction, in the North and South, was supportive of government suppression of the uprisings and the hanging of the white and black freedom-fighters. In the U.S. Senate, Virginia's slaveholding Senator James Mason, creator of the Fugitive Slave Law, led a Senate investigation that concluded that Brown's raid was a northern white conspiracy, intentionally playing down the major role of black Americans in this insurrectionary event. Not surprisingly, he and his all-white colleagues were unwilling to admit publicly the significant agency of African Americans in trying to bring down the slavery system.[38]

Black Rebellions in the Civil War Era

"General Strike": Black Agency Undermining Slavery

Seeking their freedom from slavery, many more African Americans fled southern areas during the Civil War. A very substantial proportion, about half a million, of the 3.8 million enslaved blacks and 258,000 free blacks in the South in 1860, had left by the end of the Civil War. By 1863, President Lincoln's Emancipation Proclamation in January and some Union military victories in the South had emboldened many enslaved black families to increase their protest activity—that is, to empower themselves by means of "escape, employment, enlistment, and education."[39] Many abandoned slave plantations and moved to Union-held areas, thereby gaining greater control over their own lives and futures. Many became spies and guides for Union armies. Much essential military intelligence came from those enslaved. In contrast, southern slaveholders, including top Confederate military officials, spoke of enslaved blacks as being "dumb" and unable to demonstrate personal autonomy without encouragement from Union officials. However, by the thousands, once in Union-controlled territories, formerly enslaved blacks demonstrated just how intelligent and courageous they were; they rebuilt their families, sought educations and employment, and enthusiastically enlisted in the Union military.[40]

This massive flight from slavery meant a major loss of labor for southern slaveholders and employers. Du Bois describes the reaction of these workers as a *general strike*. Those who could escape to Union-conquered territory often did so, and those who had to remain frequently slowed down the agricultural production that the white South needed to feed and clothe civilians and the military. Thousands of enslaved women rejected not only labor in slaveholders' fields but the slave breeding forced on them. In this manner, they doubly disrupted slavery in a gendered general strike and set the model for the development of African American feminist (womanist) rebellions later on.[41]

This general strike of laborers and their families had dramatic impacts on this country and its future. It helped mightily in ending the war with the United States still intact. It played a central role in destruction of one of the world's biggest slave societies. It was one of the greatest efforts at expanding democracy in this country's history, indeed in world history. It brought a new generation of African American leaders to the forefront, many with significant experience—in the underground railroad and Union military units—as managers and organizers.[42] All these assertive efforts proclaimed the black counter-frame of real liberty against the white racial frame of oppression, including the latter's infantile insistence that blacks were unintelligent and servile by nature.

The Largest Slave Rebellion: African American Soldiers

Clearly, the largest-scale African American rebellion and resistance to the slavery system took place during the Civil War years of the 1860s. Hundreds of thousands of formerly enslaved and free African Americans joined the Union army and navy or provided the support troops during Union military operations. Substantially more than half of those blacks who served in Union forces had formerly been enslaved, and a great many had fled to Union lines during the war. Including free blacks, about 210,000 blacks served as Union soldiers and sailors, winning twenty-five Medals of Honor for bravery. An additional 300,000 served in military support occupations. Black Americans made up one-tenth of the soldiers, about a fifth of black men of military age. As of fall 1864, there were 140 African

American regiments; by the end of the conflict, there were *more* blacks in Union military units than there were white Confederate soldiers. [43]

Substantial service in Union forces did not come easily because of white opposition, including in the military. Securing recruitment of black soldiers required pressure from abolitionists. An influential abolitionist, Frederick Douglass pressed President Lincoln on this matter. He had already pressed Lincoln and other officials to issue an enforced emancipation declaration. His reasoning suggested why this was so important: Southern slaveholders

> boast that the slave population is a grand element of strength, and that it enables them to send and sustain a stronger body of rebels to overthrow the Government than they could otherwise do if the whites were required to perform the labors of cultivation. [44]

Douglass visited Lincoln and pushed hard for recruitment of African Americans into the military. Activist-intellectual Martin Delany, later the only black major in the Union army, was among abolitionists who strongly urged Lincoln to take such action. When Lincoln's Emancipation Proclamation was finally issued, it freed those enslaved in southern areas still in secession and officially authorized the military employment of those thus freed. General Ulysses S. Grant, later in command of all Union forces, sent a note to Lincoln: "This [Proclamation], with the emancipation of the negro, is the heaviest blow yet given the Confederacy." [45] As of the date of the Proclamation's release to the public, black southerners who made it to Union lines would be set free and were to be treated as free by white officials.

The Lincoln administration's belated acceptance of black soldiers did not end the issue of northern discrimination, nor did it end assertive protests for equal treatment. For instance, one Union recruiter who met in 1863 with formerly enslaved men in an area of North Carolina taken by Union forces reported that they demanded equal pay if they were soldiers, Union support for their families, and Union efforts to protect black soldiers captured by Confederate armies. [46] In spite of such demands, in the first year or so of service (1863–1864), black soldiers did often get poorer equipment and were paid less. This brought significant protests. One courageous sergeant in the Third South Carolina regiment, one of the first black regiments, had his men stack rifles in mutinous protest against discrimination, for which he was shot. Such punishment did not end the soldiers' protests, and finally in June 1864, Congress acted to provide equal pay for black troops, who in spite of poor treatment were mostly performing well. [47]

Tens of thousands of African American soldiers volunteered at a critical time for the Union cause. White soldiers had been killed or wounded in very large numbers, and many others had served out their terms. There was major white resistance to Lincoln's new draft law and declining support for the war in some northern areas, and northern officials were very concerned about where additional soldiers would come from. In addition, many white officials, including army generals, thought blacks could not make good soldiers. Yet they proved, dramatically, that these doubts were quite wrong and racially framed. For example, black regiments were important in capturing Confederate positions in the fierce Petersburg fighting in the summer of 1864. Secretary of War Edwin Stanton commented that the "hardest fighting was done by the black troops. The forts they stormed were the worst of all."[48] Black soldiers' and sailors' service was important and extensive, as they took part in 449 battles and earned twenty-five Medals of Honor. Eventually, this military service was better recognized, and there were numerous celebrations by whites and blacks in the North when the black regiments returned home.[49]

These black military efforts dramatically shaped the all-but-inevitable result of the Civil War. In mid-1864, Lincoln himself wrote that without the black volunteers, he would have had to "abandon the war in three weeks." In a letter to a friend, he noted that these black men

> can remember that, with silent tongue, and clenched teeth, and steady eye, and well-poised bayonet, they have helped mankind on to this great consummation; while, I fear, there will be some white ones, unable to forget that, with malignant heart, and deceitful speech, they have strove to hinder it.[50]

Even some newspapers in the South accepted the reality that black soldiers could fight well. One editor commented that it is "useless to talk anymore about negro courage—the men fought like tigers . . . and the main difficulty was to hold them well in hand."[51]

The black troops often made clear why they had volunteered. Their view was generally different from that of white soldiers. John Washington, who volunteered for the Union's support troops, spoke of the joy of liberty:

> Before morning I had began to feel like I had truly escaped from the hands of the slaves master and with the help of God, I never would be a slave no more. I felt for the first time in my life that I could now claim every cent that I should work for as my own. I began now to feel that life had a new joy awaiting me. I might now go and come when I please. This was the *first night of freedom*.[52]

Another formerly enslaved volunteer similarly commented,

> The next morning I was up early and took a look at the rebels country with a thankful heart to think I had made my escape with safety after

such a long struggle; and had obtained that freedom which I desired so long. I now dreaded the gun, and handcuffs and pistols no more.[53]

Repeatedly in the volunteers' letters, we see clearly that for these formerly enslaved African Americans, liberty and justice were not abstract rhetorical slogans but concrete human objectives that were met, if often partially, only with great sacrificial efforts on their part.

Other Protest Organizations

During and immediately after the Civil War, African Americans organized significant civil rights organizations, conferences, and other meetings at which they again assertively pressed for much greater freedom, justice, and equality. Most were in the North. In October 1864 in Syracuse, New York, more than 140 delegates met at the National Convention of Colored Men of the United States, the first major national assembly including black northerners and southerners. The delegates issued a "Declaration of Wrongs and Rights" that demanded full civil and political rights. They aggressively articulated the wrongs blacks endured under enslavement. They asserted strongly that "all men are born free and equal" and "that no man or government" had a right to "annul, repeal, abrogate . . . this fundamental principle." Looking toward the future after the war, they further insisted that the main thing needed from whites was

> *Justice:* let that magic word . . . become all-controlling in all your courts of law. . . . let the halls of legislation, state and national, spurn all statesmanship as mischievous and ruinous that has not justice for its foundation; let justice without compromise, without curtailment, and without partiality, be observed with respect to all men, . . . then strife and discord will cease.[54]

This 1864 gathering created the National Equal Rights League, the first major U.S. civil rights organization, to press for these full citizenship rights for African Americans—a viewpoint increasingly asserted by the older and newly emerging African American leaders throughout the country after the war.

There was much more to these protests than statements about freedom and justice. The aforementioned Union recruiter who came to North Carolina in search of military volunteers also found, as one historian puts it, "Instead of freedpeople who were fragmented and disorganized, he saw recently liberated slaves who were carefully organized, with a command structure and strong leadership."[55] These included numerous black women such as the courageous Mary Ann Starkey, who headed a relief society supporting black soldiers and black families in need in North Carolina during the Civil War. Over the course of the Civil War, many black Americans, North and South, had organized and collectively played a critical role not only in ending the Civil War but in efforts to liberate black Americans from Jim Crow oppression in the North and the South after the war.

The "Second American Revolution": Reconstruction Restructuring

As the Civil War was coming to a close in February 1865, the radical black minister, Henry Highland Garnet, gave a sermon in the chamber of the U.S. House of Representatives. He answered the common white question about when the demands of reformers would end thus:

> When all unjust and heavy burdens shall be removed from every man in the land. When all invidious and proscriptive distinctions shall be blotted out from our laws, whether they be constitutional, statute, or municipal laws. When emancipation shall be followed by enfranchisement, and all men holding allegiance to the government shall enjoy every right of American citizenship.[56]

Philadelphia's *Christian Recorder*, published by the African Methodist Episcopal Church, urged black citizens to press aggressively for full civil rights and fair economic opportunities:

> Fellow Citizens of America! *Awake to Action* .... Lay claim to every available opportunity of amassing property, increasing wealth, becoming stockholders, merchants and mechanics, that our foothold may be strengthened upon the soil of our native land.... We demand, therefore, like all other citizens.... The right to go and to come; The right to vote; The right to public instruction; The right to hold public office; The right to be judged, treated and governed according to the common law.[57]

After the war, free blacks set up numerous newspapers to advocate for full citizenship rights. Indeed, they probably generated more extensive writing about freedom and justice issues in their many newspapers, speeches, sermons, books, and pamphlets than did the white revolutionaries in the era of the 1776 Declaration of Independence.

By the Civil War's end, many whites in Union states were convinced of black soldiers' importance in ending this country's bloodiest war. Because of this war service and, even more important, the renewed black activism, progressive changes came to many northern and southern areas in the Reconstruction era (ca. 1865–1877). Some northern and border officials acted to reduce anti-black discrimination. Manning Marable notes numerous examples: "In 1865, Illinois finally permitted blacks to testify in courtrooms.... Philadelphia blacks fought successfully to bar segregation in the city's streetcars. Rhode Island blacks forced state officials to desegregate public schools in 1866."[58] In Massachusetts, black activists succeeded in getting civil rights legislation enacted and a few legislative seats. In addition, black activists succeeded in pressuring northern representatives in Congress to vote for the federal Civil Rights Act in March 1875, the most powerful such act passed there before the 1960s. In many areas, free blacks were becoming much more active in local and state political life.[59]

Many accounts of racial change before, during, and after the Civil War ignore or downplay the role of African American women in political struggles. However, Sojourner Truth was a leader in a major 1865 boycott of segregated streetcar facilities in Washington, DC. Other African American women were very important in struggles for freedom and equality across the South, including many efforts to improve the education and health of newly freed black Americans. For example, traveling in the South, the courageous Frances Ellen Watkins Harper raised much money to build schools and hospitals for these black southerners, often in the face of violent white opposition.[60]

In the 1870s, numerous areas of the Reconstruction South saw the emergence of a substantial degree of multiracial democracy at state and local levels. Because of the Fifteenth amendment to the U.S. Constitution, black men were officially granted voting rights protection, and many were now able to be active in local and state politics. New state constitutional conventions and legislatures included black representatives. During Reconstruction, about 2,000 black men served as local, state, and federal officeholders. Some twenty-two black men served for a time in the U.S. House and Senate. Mississippi's now racially diverse voters elected a legislature that put talented black men into the U.S. Senate—Hiram Revels and Blanch Bruce—the first ever to serve and the only ones to serve before the 1960s.[61] In the U.S. Congress and in state legislatures, black legislators attempted to implement greater political democracy. Thanks in substantial part to their active presence, the new biracial governments brought desperately needed political reform to much of the South, including prison reform, public schools, and modern constitutions accenting (male) political equality and the rights of free speech, assembly, and due process. Together with non-elite white southerners, black southerners sought to achieve significant democratic reforms in southern states, yet they have often not gotten the credit they deserve for this heroic effort to the present day.

The great black activism against racial oppression before and during the Civil War—the black abolitionists, underground railroad activists, participants in slave uprisings, soldiers and support troops in the Civil War, and those who fled or rebelled on slave plantations—did in effect create a "second American Revolution." To a substantial degree, their courageous, often life-sacrificing, actions made possible the destruction of the slavery system and putting into place the anti-slavery and democracy-enhancing (Thirteenth, Fourteenth, and Fifteenth) Amendments to the U.S. Constitution during the Reconstruction era. Indeed, only in July 1868, with the bold Fourteenth Amendment's passage, did African Americans finally become full U.S. citizens. These extraordinarily important amendments not only signaled the greater freedom that had been won by African Americans but the significant expansion of democratic laws and institutions that affected all Americans. This was truly a second American Revolution.

Conclusion

Unfortunately for the expansion of democratic norms and institutions, the Reconstruction experiment in reform was brief and soon destroyed by violent actions of thousands of whites. The latter were frequently led by the old slaveholding gentry and operated through white supremacist organizations such as the new Ku Klux Klan. Northern supervision of southern Reconstruction efforts, including the few Union troops still there, was terminated; the near-slavery of Jim Crow segregation was soon in place.

Today, the mainstream media or most school textbooks fail to recognize the real plot of nineteenth-century racism. As Du Bois reminded us, this plot involved the "sheer moral courage and sacrifice" of black abolitionists and the spirited struggle of the oppressed "black millions in their fight for freedom and their attempt to enter democracy."[62] The Reconstruction experiment in expanding democratic institutions in the South was destroyed by the barbarousness of state-supported Klan-type terrorism. Even an accurate history of black efforts and advances in this era was suppressed; until the 1940s, most popular and scholarly analyses by whites accepted the southern gentry's racist rationalizations for losing the Civil War and the white-racist framing of the impoverishment of African Americans and enrichment of white Americans there and elsewhere.

Over the decades after the end of Reconstruction in 1877, white paternalism toward African Americans dominated almost all white discussion of racial matters in the North and the South. Elites reiterated a positive framing of white virtues, including of white-led capitalism and overseas imperialism. They reinforced and expanded the old framing of black Americans as an inferior race in need of white discrimination and guidance. Even white leaders more sympathetic to the oppressive conditions faced by black Americans could not see past this white-racist framing. For example, in 1890, some eighty white leaders from various religious, philanthropic, educational, and journalistic organizations gathered in upper New York state to assess what they termed the "Negro Question." No African American leaders were invited, and only one or two of the white leaders seemed concerned about widespread racial discrimination. The most concerned delegate was apparently the white lawyer, Albion Tourgée. He was very rare among whites in that he was an anti-racist northerner who fought with black soldiers in the Civil War and moved to North Carolina after the war to fight for black equality. His experience learning from African Americans clearly influenced his framing, for example about education: "I am inclined to think that the only education required is that of the white race. The hate, the oppression, the injustice are all on our side."[63]

A few years later, Tourgée's friend, Frederick Douglass, commented to him on the worsening conditions for African Americans as Jim Crow crystallized in the 1890s:

The strange claim that a white, intelligent, Christian people makes of right dependent on race or color—of a right to oppress, to degrade, to subjugate, or destroy another people, merely because they are not as white or as wise or as strong as themselves. Will it never end?[64]

While the transformation of the United States into a real democracy is still far from complete, it was greatly reinvigorated in the Civil War and Reconstruction eras by courageous actions of hundreds of thousands of African Americans such as Frederick Douglass. All Americans should be eternally grateful.

6
Black Counter-Framing and Liberatory
Action (1900s–1970s)

With Jim Crow segregation firmly in place by the 1890s, a strong collective black pushback gradually emerged. By the early twentieth century, numerous organized efforts were pressuring increasing numbers of whites to reflect on the country's liberty-and-justice ideals and to move toward significant racial desegregation. Recall from the preface that Ralph Ellison once reflected insightfully on the 1960s civil rights movement, noting that it has been the "black American who puts pressure upon the nation to live up to its ideals" and to fully implement social justice.[1]

From the beginning of the centuries-long march of African Americans against racial oppression, black freedom movements have been about much more than gaining civil rights, for they have centrally been about gaining full citizenship and egalitarian participation in major institutions. Especially after the massive, mostly white "welfare handouts" and "affirmative action" programs after World War II (e.g., Federal Housing Administration home loans, GI Bill financing college educations[2]) that effectively created the white middle class, African Americans in civil rights movements have sought similarly supportive social and economic programs. Clearly, too, there has long been a strong emphasis on the collective interests and needs of African Americans.

Whites have regularly blocked significant change in their racial power and privilege. I have earlier emphasized the massive, violence-backed, and well-institutionalized structures that have for centuries maintained racial oppression. Much conventional analysis of the long civil rights era, from the 1910s through the 1960s, underestimates the constant level of this white violence. While numerous analysts have noted that dozens of black Americans involved in freedom movements lost their lives to lynchings, bombings, and other insurrectionary violence, this usually publicized violence was the tip of the iceberg. Indeed, white racial violence was foundational and central to southern segregation and to much informal northern segregation. In this long era, hundreds of thousands of African Americans were violently threatened, assaulted, or killed by ordinary whites and white officials such as police officers. This state-backed racial totalitarianism made much use of violence and the threat of violence to keep black people, as whites regularly proclaimed, "in their place." Thus, one recent interview study of nearly 100 elderly black southerners who lived under Jim Crow segregation found that about eight in ten reported one or more physically violent attacks by whites on someone in their family or acquaintance networks in that era.[3] Beyond this physical violence, many millions also suffered recurring threats of violence from the well-institutionalized racial etiquette that was the everyday reality of legal segregation.

We should keep this violently oppressive reality in mind as we assess the bravery, intelligence, and ingenuity exhibited in recurring African American resistance to such oppression. One revealing dimension of the freedom movements discussed in this chapter is the insistent *agency* of black individuals and their social networks. Their efforts routinely revealed the "creativity of a people who have had to engage in a chain of struggles to survive relentless oppression and to maintain their dignity."[4]

Organizing against Jim Crow Oppression

African Americans continued to organize and protest oppression over decades of brutally harsh Jim Crow segregation. By the early twentieth century, organized resistance efforts took two overlapping and interacting tracks—one mostly accenting civil rights, racial integration, and nonviolent strategies (often termed the *civil rights movement*) and the other heavily emphasizing black self-determination, black political-economic power, and aggressive self-defense (often termed the *black power movement* or *black nationalism*). Organized efforts in both tracks, however, demonstrated a recurring emphasis on black consciousness and a determination to bring major change in racist patterns. Both reflect a distinctive oppositional consciousness and strong black counter-framing of society.

Black civil rights activists working against Jim Crow segregation were already numerous at the turn of the twentieth century. They had been born in the Civil War and Reconstruction era and bridged that era's black activism to that of the early twentieth century. Recall from previous chapters courageous activist-researchers such as Ida B. Wells-Barnett, who started a crusade against lynching and spoke extensively against white violence. Another influential leader, Mary Church Terrell, organized and battled for decades against Jim Crow. A graduate of Oberlin College and early motivated to active resistance by a white mob's lynching of a friend, Terrell was a tireless civil rights activist for seven decades until the 1950s. Called a "living link between the era of the Emancipation Proclamation and the modern civil rights movement," she, like Wells-Barnett, was a founding member of the National Association for the Advancement of Colored

People (NAACP, founded in 1909), which soon became the leading civil rights organization.[5]

About the same time, Terrell was a key organizer of the influential National Association of Colored Women (NACW). Like black anti-slavery advocates before her, Terrell was outspoken in her framing of black Americans as collectively self-determining and gutsy in the face of white oppression. In an 1897 presidential speech to the NACW, she challenged "any other race to present a record more creditable and show a progress more wonderful than that made by the ex-slaves of the United States and that too in the face of prejudice, proscription, and persecution against which no other people has ever had to contend in the history of the world."[6] Moreover, in a speech to the National American Women's Suffrage Association, she highlighted black women's determination:

[I]n spite of the opposition encountered, the obstacles opposed to their acquisition of knowledge and their accumulation of property, the progress made by colored women along these lines has never been surpassed by that of any people in the history of the world.[7]

A tireless organizer, she attacked legal segregation in a 1906 talk to the Washington, DC United Women's Club:

Surely nowhere in the world do oppression and persecution based solely on the color of the skin appear more hateful and hideous than in the capital of the United States, because the chasm between the principles upon which this Government was founded, in which it still professes to believe, and those which are daily practiced under the protection of the flag, yawns so wide and deep.[8]

Moreover, using picketing, boycotts, and sit-ins, Terrell was an early and energetic leader in persistent fights for desegregation in Washington, DC from the difficult 1890s to victories in the 1950s. This accent on black courage, pride, and self-determination was commonplace among early black activists, who thereby anticipated the better known "black nationalist" themes of later decades. These remarkable women demonstrated how commitments to civil rights, black self-pride, and community self-determination were already present in early civil rights movements.

As Jim Crow segregation expanded even more in the early decades of the twentieth century, African Americans countered with increasingly powerful civil rights organizations such as the NAACP. From the 1910s to the 1940s, enlarged civil rights organizing, together with new electoral participation by southern black migrants now in northern cities, was substantially responsible for the white elite's increasing concern with taking some action against southern segregation. NAACP activist-lawyers worked aggressively to end any aspects of Jim Crow that they could and, by the 1940s, the NAACP had 1,000 local organizations and a half million members. Meanwhile, NAACP lawsuits resulted in major federal court decisions knocking down peonage in agriculture, some southern voting barriers, and some educational segregation—first in higher education in the 1930s and 1940s and then in public schools.[9]

Influential Black Nationalism: Marcus Garvey

Recall that the early twentieth century saw a great expansion of influential African American literature and art. Much of this productivity established a distinctive artistic world with a strong black framing respecting age-old African and African American heritages and values. Not surprisingly, new black nationalist organizations emerged in this era. They stressed black self-determination, black pride, economic independence, and the perspective called pan-Africanism.

Numerous African American intellectuals and other leaders supported a strong version of black nationalism, including for some the old idea of African emigration to create a separate nation as a solution to oppression. The most important was Marcus Garvey, a Jamaican American who was influenced by the self-reliance views of earlier black leaders, including Booker T. Washington. From the 1910s to the 1920s, Garvey's Universal Negro Improvement Association (UNIA) was influential, and millions joined in its self-determination efforts. The UNIA has been described as the "greatest mass movement of people of African descent in the twentieth century."[10] Garvey's accent on self-determination, critical stance on white-racist institutions, and respect for African origins had significant influences not only on the black population in the 1920s but on later nationalistic groups such as the militant Black Panthers and Nation of Islam. Additionally, in the 1960s, Malcolm X, among other leaders, gave Garvey's movement credit for helping to spur the civil rights movement and anti-colonial movements in Africa.[11]

Additionally, during the 1930s and 1940s, many African Americans were involved with other militant organizations. One was the U.S. Communist Party, the only major historically white organization that recruited black members and supported civil rights efforts. Black Communists were leaders in rights demonstrations, and black and white organizers were active in union struggles seeking better conditions for all workers. The Party's white activists risked their lives to end racial and class oppression. Some black activist-intellectuals, such as W. E. B. Du Bois and Paul Robeson, were connected to the Party and inspired by Marxist class analysis for a long period, while others such as Ralph Bunche, Richard Wright, and Bayard

Rustin were associated for shorter periods. In particular protest efforts, the mostly white Party's commitment to an anti-discrimination perspective brought it together in rare interracial coalitions with mainstream civil rights organizations.[12]

Critiquing and Protesting White Racism: W. E. B. Du Bois

Let us now consider one of the greatest of all U.S. activist-intellectuals, W. E. B. Du Bois, who early on expressed many key ideas associated with the black power and nationalist traditions developing over his lifetime. He and his allies were among the first to have a global impact in aggressively asserting black counter-framed views before international organizations such as the United Nations. Over the twentieth century and since, no analyst of systemic racism has made more significant contributions to understanding its critical dimensions. Living from the Reconstruction era through the late nineteenth- and twentieth-century Jim Crow eras, Du Bois had many roles in fighting racism. He was a path-breaking sociological researcher and historian of Reconstruction and a longtime editor of the NAACP's influential journal *Crisis*; a leading civil rights activist; and co-founder of a pan-African movement linking people of African descent across continents. Working as a young scholar in the era of Ida B. Wells-Barnett and Mary Church Terrell, Du Bois made major contributions to social science research and theory and to a critical black-framed societal perspective.

In 1899, he published the first field study of an urban U.S. community. His path-breaking book, *The Philadelphia Negro*, involved 2,500 field interviews and signaled he was an early founder of U.S. sociology.[13] In the 1890s, he was hired by Atlanta University to teach and develop a sociological research center, where he and other black scholars he mentored (for example, sociologists R. R. Wright, Jr., and George Haynes) did pioneering field studies of black workers, communities, families, religion, and class relations—much of it in policy-oriented reports for major journals and conferences. These social scientists were the *first* to do such empirical social science. They made it legitimate to research African Americans and to link empirical social science to policy matters. In 1910, Du Bois left to become the director of research at the new NAACP.[14]

Du Bois was a path-breaking historian who changed the study of U.S. racial history with an honest account of African Americans in the Reconstruction era. He was astute in understanding how mainstream analyses had missed a central plot of U.S. history—its deep and recurring oppression of black Americans and the courage of these Americans in fighting back. Mainstream analyses often miss the "triumph of sheer moral courage and sacrifice in the abolition crusade" and the "hurt and struggle of degraded black millions in their fight for freedom."[15] He generated many brilliant ideas and analyses that laid the foundation for what is now called "critical race theory" and "systemic racism theory." He once described how being black is, metaphorically, like being freedomless in a cave behind a glass wall. A black person views the

> world passing and speaks to it; speaks courteously and persuasively, showing them how these entombed souls are hindered in their natural movement, expression, and development; and how their loosening from prison would be a matter not simply of courtesy, sympathy, and help to them, but aid to all the world.[16]

Moreover, this well-institutionalized racism has long ensured that, in many circumstances, African Americans cannot openly express their true selves without risking white retaliation. Du Bois described the resulting double consciousness:

> It is a peculiar sensation, this double consciousness, this sense of always looking at one's self through the eyes of others. . . . One ever feels his twoness—an American, a Negro; two souls, two thoughts . . . in one dark body, whose dogged strength alone keeps it from being torn asunder.[17]

Unjust impoverishment for blacks has typically meant unjust enrichment for whites. Du Bois contributed significantly to a critical understanding of the strong "white" identity and of the acceptance of privilege by whites—the "public and psychological wage of whiteness." Since before the American Revolution, most ordinary whites have accepted unquestioningly a higher position in the racial hierarchy—and privileges historically provided by the white elite—in return for giving up much struggle against their own class exploitation by that capitalistic elite. Moreover, Du Bois was one of the first to emphasize that, as the dominant group oppresses others, it suppresses *vast* stores of human wisdom that can benefit all.[18]

Du Bois's actions matched his critical words. On October 23, 1947, the NAACP sent the new United Nations a dramatic document entitled "An Appeal to the World." Substantially written by Du Bois, this appeal laid out dimensions of the caste-like oppression in the United States and asked the United Nations for aid:

> A nation [the U.S.] which boldly declared "All men equal," proceeded to build its economy on chattel slavery; . . . Sectional strife over the vast profits of slave labor and conscientious revolt against making human beings real estate led to bloody civil war, and to a partial

emancipation of slaves which nevertheless even to this day is not complete. Poverty, ignorance, disease, and crime have been forced on these unfortunate victims of greed. . . . and a great nation, which today ought to be in the forefront of the march toward peace and democracy, finds itself continuously making common cause with race hate, prejudiced exploitation and oppression of the common man. . . . Peoples of the World, we American Negroes appeal to you; our treatment in America is not merely an internal question of the United States. It is a basic problem of humanity; of democracy; of discrimination because of race and color; and as such it demands your attention and action.[19]

In this call for international assistance in attaining justice for African Americans, Du Bois again manifested both his insightful global perspective and his strong adherence to a black counter-framing of a racist U.S. society. However, the prominent white liberal, Eleanor Roosevelt, served on the NAACP board and on the U.S. delegation to the United Nations. She refused to present this reasonable NAACP petition to the UN General Assembly, apparently because it might hurt the U.S. image globally.[20]

Again, in 1951, Du Bois and other African American leaders (especially William Patterson and Paul Robeson) delivered an even stronger indictment of U.S. racism to the UN General Assembly. This long petition, titled "We Charge Genocide: The Crime of Government Against the Negro People," detailed how the white-run government generated and assisted in Jim Crow's discriminatory actions against African Americans, judged as genocidal according to provisions of the UN Genocide Convention. Notice their black counter-framing here:

The responsibility of being the first in history to charge the government of the United States of America with the crime of genocide is not one your petitioners take lightly. . . . Your petitioners . . . submit evidence, tragically voluminous, of "acts committed with intent to destroy, in whole or in part, a national, ethnical, racial or religious group as such"—in this case the 15,000,000 Negro people of the United States.[21]

The many genocide-like aspects of legal segregation over the decades are fully documented herein, yet the petition and its data were almost entirely ignored by the mainstream U.S. media. In contrast, the petition's well-crafted arguments were widely covered in the overseas media. Again, the U.S. delegation to the UN attacked or downplayed the document, and it too was rejected.

Notice how many African American leaders, past and present, have been true *internationalists*. Working with other black internationalists, Du Bois was one of the first social scientists to analyze the global white supremacist order. In 1946, he wrote about how, from the sixteenth century to the twentieth century, the expansion of the resources and wealth of Europeans and European Americans was made possible by the bloody imperialism of European countries and the United States. His actions matched his words, for he became a leading U.S. advocate of a pan-Africanism—that is, united action by colonized peoples of African descent against Euro-American colonialism. In 1919, over objections from the State Department, he and others put together the first international Pan-African Congress. He pursued these internationalist efforts until his death in 1963.[22]

Weak White Analysis, Insightful Black Response

Interestingly, by the 1940s, a moderately liberal segment of the white elite had come to the view that the repression of civil rights in the Jim Crow South was a political liability for the United States. A major example of this response was the very important 1940s study of southern segregation, *An American Dilemma,* that I have touched upon in previous chapters. The author, liberal social scientist Gunnar Myrdal, was a member of the white elite and was funded by a major corporate foundation (Carnegie). The book critically dissected Jim Crow oppression, yet the individualistic view highlighted in the book presented racial segregation as primarily a matter of (southern) white prejudice. In Myrdal's view, white Americans were also under the spell of the "American creed," which accented "ideals of the essential dignity of the individual human being, of the fundamental equality of all men." However, this American creed was, the book argued, in great tension with Jim Crow discrimination—the American dilemma of the title.[23] Myrdal's prominence and official authorship of the book made him the central scholarly figure. This was deeply problematic, as numerous African American social scientists had provided research analyses necessary for his project, yet their major contributions were largely ignored in official discussions of the book. Myrdal's dependence on years of black scholars' well-crafted research contradicted his stated conclusions that black Americans had a "pathological" culture and that black thought was derivative, provincial, and inferior to that of whites.[24]

African American analysts, such as Du Bois and Ellison, were vigorously critical of Myrdal's analysis for leaving out whites' well-institutionalized material interests and the importance of black agency in bringing significant racial change.[25] Similarly, pioneering black sociologist Oliver Cox faulted the study for failing to recognize that the problem of U.S. racism is far more than prejudice. Central political-economic interests of whites lie in maintaining a well-institutionalized system of oppression that works to their advantage, and this greatly outweighs white commitments to egalitarian ideals.[26] Cox also underscored the links between capitalism and racism almost never made by white analysts, arguing that Western capitalism had expanded by exploiting people across the world and imbedded them "in a growing global capitalistic system."[27] About the same time, a leading historian, Rayford Logan, edited *What the Negro Wants* (1944), a book with numerous black-authored essays. His was a black-framed view of racism with global perspective: "We want the Four Freedoms to apply to black Americans as well as to the brutalized peoples of Europe and to other underprivileged peoples of the world."[28]

Black Migration Brings Progressive Change

At the turn of the twentieth century, the demographic center of the U.S. black population was still in the deep South, thanks largely to the geographical location of the earlier slave economy. Between the early 1900s and the 1970s, about 6 million to 7 million black southerners escaped the Jim Crow South, a great many during and after this World War II era. Usually operating out of a freedom-and-justice framing and much like the enslaved southerners who escaped North before and during the Civil War, they "voted" against Jim Crow tyranny with their feet. These African American workers and their families were attracted by economic opportunities opening up in the industrializing North. This courageous large-scale migration greatly changed the lives of millions of African Americans and their descendants and of this country's racial, geographical, and political landscapes.

The timing of this migration was such that it had significant impacts on both the receiving and the sending areas. Most people moved to the North and California, where they had much more freedom. They mostly went to larger cities—especially Chicago, Detroit, New York, Philadelphia, and Los Angeles—which were booming economically during this era (except for the 1930s depression). The nativistic 1920s immigration acts had ended much European immigration, and the return of large-scale overseas immigration did not come until the late 1960s. Thus, African American immigrants to northern and western cities mostly did not have to compete for jobs with new external immigrants, although they did face some competition from working-class whites who also left the South in these decades.

Accessing better jobs, in turn, enabled many African American families to build up some economic and educational resources unavailable to them in the South. Consequently, some of the migrants and their children were able to fund and participate actively in northern civil rights struggles. Fueled in part by growing black populations in northern cities, several northern-based civil rights organizations increased protest demonstrations against job and other racial discrimination. In 1941, for example, several black freedom activists led by A. Philip Randolph, the head of the black

Brotherhood of Sleeping Car Porters union, threatened a large-scale march in Washington, DC over wartime job discrimination. Operating out of a strong counter-framing of a racist U.S. society, Randolph assertively insisted that African Americans must bring their "power and pressure to bear upon the agencies and representatives of the Federal Government to exact their rights in National Defense employment and the armed forces of the United States."[29] In a reluctant response to the threatened civil rights march, President Franklin Roosevelt signed an executive order establishing a Fair Employment Practices Committee to oversee desegregation of defense-industry jobs. We should note, too, that the Brotherhood of Sleeping Car Porters union itself represented a courageous organizing effort by black men, a union that was the first to "successfully confront a major U.S. corporation and win the right of collective bargaining—and as a result to gain major improvements in wages and working conditions for porters."[30] It was also the first black union in the American Federation of Labor.

Black Voters: A New Political Force

Moreover, after World War II, under pressure from northern black voters and from northern and southern civil rights groups, President Harry Truman desegregated the armed forces and established a Committee on Civil Rights. Repeatedly, organized protests in the North pushed white leaders toward desegregation. Well before the 1960s civil rights movement, these spirited protests brought noteworthy changes in some segregation patterns in the North and South. Significantly, participating in these important 1940s–1950s protests were many African American veterans of World War II, a war fought "for democracy."[31] Once again, African American leaders were not the only theorists of their oppression. Centuries of oppression have long encouraged the majority of African Americans to develop an institutional-racism framing of society and to seek white racism's eradication.

Clearly, too, this great black migration out of the oppressive South had major national political significance, for it greatly expanded black freedom to actively support local, state, and federal political candidates. In the North, African Americans found political allies among whites and others, and they helped to increase local, state, and national Democratic Party strength. In this manner, they brought needed educational and other socioeconomic benefits to their communities.[32] Their greatly increased numbers often gave Democratic candidates a winning edge in states such as Illinois, Ohio, Michigan, California, and New York, especially in larger cities. Between 1940 and 1970, black voters increased their share of the voting age population from modest percentages to 14 percent to 38 percent in key cities such as Chicago, Detroit, Los Angeles, New York, and Philadelphia. They held the balance of political power in most mayoral elections in 1946–1962 in these cities and in a majority of senatorial elections in the states of these cities.[33]

From the beginning of significant black voting after the Civil War, a stereotype in a common white framing has been that of the black vote as "singularly ignorant, venal, and corrupt."[34] Yet, it was black voters who helped to bring much progressive social change to these areas. Significantly, there was a major shift of black voters to the Democratic candidate Franklin Roosevelt in 1936, and they voted heavily for him in subsequent elections, substantially for economic reasons. Unfortunately, no senior member of Franklin Roosevelt's administrative team showed interest in meeting with African American leaders about their problems with racism.[35] Nonetheless, during the 1930s, some white Democratic congressional candidates were getting substantial black votes because they did openly support civil rights reforms. Under pressure from these and other northern liberals, including black civil rights officials, the Roosevelt administration did employ small groups of black professionals as advisers in several federal agencies. The latter pressed, sometimes successfully, for greater racial fairness in the implementation of important New Deal programs.[36]

Concentrated in big electoral states of the North and in California, the relatively new black voters were increasingly sought after by white Democratic Party leaders, who provided strong Party civil rights platforms and worked to increase black voter registration. As political scientist Keneshia Grant has detailed, these voters were numerous enough to hold the balance of political power in several presidential elections from Harry Truman to Lyndon Johnson. Without them, Truman would not have won his close election, and his late-1940s desegregation of the military reflected the power of the black vote. In the 1950s, as the Democratic Party waffled on racial matters, some voters returned to the Republican Party, probably enough to insure the presidency to Republican Dwight Eisenhower. When the Democratic Party and its 1960 presidential candidate, John Kennedy, openly backed some civil rights groups' concerns, numerous black voters again shifted to the Democratic Party and gave him a margin of victory in key states. The efforts of Kennedy and Lyndon Johnson to support the 1960s civil rights movement and to pass civil rights laws helped to move the majority of black voters yet more solidly into the Democratic column.[37] Indeed, by the end of the great migration, northern black voters were helping to elect growing numbers of liberal Democrats to Congress, which significantly reduced the formerly great power of southern white representatives there.

The southern migrants and their descendants forever changed not only local and national politics but the social terrain, cultures, and institutions of northern cities and states and thus of the United States. As researcher Isabel Wilkerson notes, the geography of northern cities was substantially altered:

[The] social geography of black and white neighborhoods, the spread of the housing projects as well as the rise of a well-scrubbed black middle class, along with the alternating waves of white flight and suburbanization—all of these grew, directly or indirectly, from the response of everyone touched by the Great Migration.[38]

Indeed, this reconfiguring of U.S. urban geography revealed that white racism was not just a southern matter. The blatantly racist views and actions of many white northerners came to the forefront in their resistance to migrants' efforts to desegregate the de facto segregated job and housing patterns of northern and western cities.

Nonetheless, even with this white resistance, the millions of black migrants had much greater freedom to build up community institutions, both new ones and existing ones. The building of strong black communities by these southern migrants and their children was assisted by the substantial economic growth of northern and western cities and by freer cultural settings of these cities. They developed many new businesses, churches, sports facilities, and music clubs. The migrants and their children likewise helped to spur and foster the Harlem Renaissance (see Chapter 3) with its array of openly anti-racist African American artists, writers, musicians, activists, and professionals. Most of the latter overtly exhibited black pride and a sense of much greater personal and collective agency. Most had personal or parental roots in the northern migration. Over time, as noted in Chapter 3, urban black cultural creativity and artistic development in the North dramatically affected the country as a whole—as seen, to take just one major example, in the impact of black jazz geniuses Louis Armstrong, John Coltrane, Miles Davis, Anna Mae Winburn, Thelonious Monk, and Bessie Smith (jazz and blues). Black music and musicians originating in the South would not likely have become so remarkably central to the U.S. musical culture without this northward migration.[39]

These millions of courageous and determined southerners escaping Jim Crow for freer northern and western cities had profound and lasting impacts on this country. Over the decades, a great many blacks' lives and "life chances were altered because a parent or grandparent had made the hard decision to leave."[40] These have included a large array of prominent African Americans in many fields—including, to name just a few, James Baldwin, Toni Morrison, Spike Lee, Denzel Washington, and Michelle Obama.

In addition, this large-scale northern migration, which significantly improved the socioeconomic and political resources of migrants and their children, gradually helped to bring down the southern Jim Crow system. That racially totalitarian system of the South eventually buckled under the pressure of freedom movements populated by black southerners but substantially financed by northern black churches and supported by northern civic organizations, the latter benefitting substantially from the great migration in terms of many thousands of new black members in the North. Southern civil rights movements and northern black power movements, mostly financed by northern blacks, did much to press the United States in the direction of more commitment to and action on longstanding liberty, justice, and democracy ideals.

Interestingly, too, over the last few decades, a new migration back to the South, often including black children and grandchildren of those in the great migration, has helped to turn some southern states such as Virginia, North Carolina, and Georgia—for a long time controlled by conservative white Republican officials in part because of white voters' racial fears—into occasional Democratic-column states, at least for presidential elections. If this new migration to the South—likely motivated by deep family roots, lower living costs, and an improved racial atmosphere in some areas—accelerates, southern demographic and political diversity may yet expand more in these and other southern states.

Suppressing Freedom Activists: Anti-Communism

From the 1930s to World War II, many black African Americans openly operated from a critical black counter-frame. Many also had global connections and impacts, as their anti-racist efforts in the United States influenced colonized peoples' rebellions overseas in their efforts to break down Western colonialism. Yet, once President Harry Truman and the overwhelmingly white U.S. Congress committed to a Cold War with the Soviet Union in the late 1940s, most African American leaders moved to a position much less anti-colonial and internationalist. One reason was the large-scale anti-Communist repression of left-leaning Americans conducted by the white-run policing agencies. From the 1940s to the 1960s, white officials labored to suppress civil rights, black nationalist, and other anti-racist movements, especially their leaders who spoke out critically about U.S. racism. Courageous black intellectuals and other leaders—such as Du Bois, Richard Wright, Paul Robeson, and Claudia Jones—were aggressively investigated and attacked in numerous ways by openly racist government officials, including in witch-hunt trials that violated First Amendment rights.

Thus, the brilliant black activist, Claudia Jones, served time in prison and was deported just for being a Communist Party activist working against racism and capitalistic exploitation. She was outspoken and emphasized what are now intersectionality (racial-gender) issues, in this case the importance of women to black communities and movements against oppression:

> An outstanding feature of the present stage of the Negro liberation movement is the growth in the militant participation of Negro women in all aspects of the struggle for peace, civil rights, and economic security. . . . As mother, as Negro, and as worker, the Negro woman fights against the wiping out of the Negro family, against the Jim-Crow ghetto existence which destroys the health, morale, and very life of millions of her sisters, brothers, and children.[41]

Jones further underscored the reality of 2.5 million black women being very active in a large array of activist organizations working against racism and for black communities.

Similarly, gifted black male leaders Du Bois and Robeson were involved in Communist organizations working against racial and class oppression and for overseas anti-colonialism movements. Because of their principled political activism, white officials periodically harassed them, tapping their phones and revoking their passports. In the 1950s, they arrested the elderly Du Bois in handcuffs for work with the liberal Peace Information Center. Operating out of a white-racist framing of black anti-racism activists, they charged the courageous Du Bois with the absurd charge of "treason."[42] As a result of this political repression, leaders in mainstream groups mostly moved into the anti-Communist faction in the society, apparently in the mistaken hope that this would increase their ability to work successfully against legal segregation. Significantly, too, U.S. government repression of these black activists increased important linkages between the U.S. civil rights movement and anti-colonial movements overseas. Before this political repression, "colonial peoples owed more" to African Americans than African Americans owed them, yet after this repression started the successful ending of overseas colonialism by Africans and other people of color "reversed the debt."[43]

The Civil Rights Movement

The civil rights movement did not arise suddenly in the 1950s. Organized pushback against forced segregation had a long history. From the 1920s through the 1960s, southern civil rights leaders worked together in numerous organizing efforts, periodically with supportive whites. During World War II, the prominent black educator, Gordon Hancock, worked with the white liberal, Jessie Daniel Ames, in setting up a Durham, North Carolina conference. There, sixty southern black leaders drew up a "New Charter of Race Relations" calling for reforms to reduce Jim Crow discrimination in education, agriculture, and military service. Subsequently, a group of moderate white southern journalists, university presidents, and religious leaders held an Atlanta conference and responded to this Charter with a supportive statement. Out of this rare biracial collaboration arose the Southern Regional Council, established in 1943 with black and white co-chairs and a motto of "We seek to find and to tell the truth."[44] The Durham meeting was one of the first southern civil rights meetings, marking a major achievement for black community leaders.

Because these southern efforts did not call for a complete eradication of Jim Crow, they were criticized by northern black leaders, including editors of the *Chicago Defender* and the *Pittsburgh Courier*. During the World War II era, these editors directed spirited protest against Jim Crow violence, periodically suggesting that white southern editors covered up racist attacks on black people because they feared "race war."[45] The long-term significance of this northern advocacy of ending all segregation should not be underestimated, for it kept pressure on moderate white leaders and reinforced the determination of many black Americans, North and South, to press hard for their civil rights.

Repression Backfires: Male and Female Activists Respond

The 1940s and 1950s successes of the NAACP in bringing some desegregation to the South by means of lawsuits and efforts such as the mid-1950s Montgomery bus boycott resulted in much white backlash. Some came from southern politicians who sought to suppress the freedom-seeking NAACP organization and, for a time, they were successful. However, this suppression stimulated the activity in the South of other rights organizations, including the Southern Christian Leadership Conference (SCLC), the Congress of Racial Equality (CORE), and the Student Nonviolent Coordinating Committee (SNCC). These organizations, coupled with more local groups, engaged in hundreds of sit-ins, freedom rides, and other nonviolent protests across the southern states. In addition, CORE accelerated protests against white housing and employment discrimination in the North. There, black freedom-fighters engaged in school boycotts, picketed construction sites, and engaged in rent strikes. These southern and northern protest efforts garnered much local support. By 1963, one national poll found that about half of African Americans were willing to participate in a civil rights demonstration.[46]

Unmistakably, one great contribution that black men and women have made to the long *global* struggle for real liberty and justice has been the development and honing of nonviolent protest strategies. These courageous efforts have often been treated superficially in mainstream textbooks, and numerous civil rights heroes, especially black *women*, have been neglected or forgotten. The contemporary civil rights movement is often dated as beginning in the 1955–1956 Montgomery bus boycott. Rosa Parks, a seamstress and NAACP activist, refused to be mistreated and is deservedly celebrated for resisting racial segregation. However, there is a larger story, one that makes obvious the central role of numerous black women in the civil rights movement. The Montgomery bus boycott idea began with Jo Ann Robinson, a faculty member at a local college, and Montgomery's Women's Political Council (WPC). In a May 1954 letter—well before the conventional dating of boycott events—to the white mayor of Montgomery, Robinson demanded bus desegregation, threatening a boycott. There was no action by the mayor, and months later, when Parks was arrested for not adhering to bus segregation, Robinson and other black women (some from the WPC) began implementing the boycott.[47] This protest made a local young minister, Martin Luther King, Jr., a leader in the black freedom movement.

As we have often seen, African American women have been extraordinarily important to the growth and successes of black freedom movements. Consider two more examples. Mississippi's courageous Fannie Lou Hamer, a major civil rights activist in the 1960s, registered black Mississippians to vote, was violently attacked by whites, and was a key organizer of the Mississippi Freedom Democratic Party. At the 1964 Democratic convention, this latter group challenged the official all-white Mississippi delegation, pressing hard for its own inclusion. Hamer later ran for Congress and is famous for her comment about the long black rights struggle: "I am sick and tired of being sick and tired."[48] Another often forgotten woman hero of the rights movement was Ella Baker, a Virginian who served as NAACP branches' director and was one of the most effective civil rights organizers. For decades she dedicated her life to grass-roots democracy, working tirelessly to expand NAACP branches. In southern travels from the 1930s to the 1960s, she built extensive activist networks, what she termed the necessary "spade work" among ordinary people. In the 1950s and 1960s, she played pivotal roles in organizing voting rights and other anti-discrimination efforts for the Southern Christian Leadership Conference (SCLC) and in helping found the SNCC, with its successful organizing, voting, and protest efforts.[49] She, too, had a global vision of the human rights struggle: "Over the course of her life, she was involved in more than thirty major political campaigns and organizations, addressing such issues as the war in Vietnam, Puerto Rican independence, South African apartheid, political repression, prison conditions, poverty, unequal education, and sexism."[50] Together with the efforts of numerous other forgotten female and male civil rights organizers, Hamer's and Baker's work was also extraordinarily important in increasing black consciousness and pride in the critical decades before and during the powerful 1960s civil rights movement.

Black rights activists added much to contemporary strategies of nonviolent resistance. Already during the 1950s, activists such as James

Lawson, John Lewis, and Diane Nash had developed concrete strategies of nonviolent resistance, preparing the groundwork for expansion of nonviolent civil rights demonstrations then and later in the 1960s.[51] Because nonviolent protests often precipitated extreme white violence, resisting segregation involved incredible courage and sacrifice. Manning Marable has underscored this reality in his discussion of Mississippi NAACP leader, Medgar Evers, who was assassinated in 1963 by a white supremacist: "What we, as Americans, owe Medgar and Myrlie Evers can scarcely be put into words. To sacrifice everything—personal safety, income, and life itself—for the cause of democracy and equal justice is monumental."[52] Evers and his wife Myrlie endured years of death threats and attacks before one succeeded.

Thousands Marching for Racial Change

One major victory for the civil rights movement involved greatly expanded voting rights. In the strong counter-framing of those in the civil rights movement, African Americans should have full citizenship rights. Because white officials aggressively blocked these rights, well-organized registration efforts, marches, and other forceful protests were necessary. In the 1940s and 1950s, significant registration efforts by the NAACP and other groups increased black voters in several southern areas, frequently triggering official and unofficial white violence. Fearing bad international publicity, in 1961 the John Kennedy administration agreed to provide some support for black voting efforts. Nonetheless, the voting rights organizations still faced extensive white violence, especially in Georgia, Louisiana, Alabama, and Mississippi. Significantly, too, registration workers did not get the federal protection they expected from the Kennedy administration.[53]

Thus, in March 1965, several voting rights marches were attempted between Selma, Alabama, where few blacks had been allowed to register, and the Alabama capital of Montgomery. The first march was met with violence from state troopers, and many protesters were injured. Much publicity was given to the police brutality, a day soon called "bloody Sunday." Another march, with thousands more protesters, was protected by federal troops and successful in generating national support for the civil rights movement. President Lyndon Johnson submitted a voting rights bill to Congress, which passed in the summer of 1965 as the Voting Rights Act. In a speech to a congressional session, Johnson showed the influence of the civil rights movement's counter-framing:

And we shall overcome. . . . The real hero of this struggle is the American Negro. His actions and protests, his courage to risk safety, and even to risk his life, have awakened the conscience of this nation.

His demonstrations have been designed to call attention to injustice, designed to provoke change; designed to stir reform. . . . And who among us can say that we would have made the same progress were it not for his persistent bravery and his faith in American democracy?[54]

As Thomas Sugrue has noted, these African American movements did not directly change public policies, but government policymakers were frequently affected: "Most protestors did not draft civil rights laws, propose legislation, or enact regulations. But they raised the issues of racial exclusion in public forums, through demonstrations, pamphlets, and newspaper articles."[55] The Voting Rights Act was effective in sharply increasing black voters and black elected and appointed officials at the local and state levels in the South. In addition, the civil rights and black power movements (see below) spurred a significant increase in northern black officials who were, to varying degrees, able to improve the socioeconomic and de facto segregated conditions faced by black urbanites in the North.

Again, we observe that little change in systemic racism takes place without substantial organization and major protest. Black freedom movements have regularly elevated the entire society's discussion and periodically forced change in overtly racist practices. This was true in the decades immediately after World War II. In this era, the anti-Communist (McCarthyist) ideology became dominant in white political circles and among elites who had convinced themselves that the Soviet Union was a major threat to U.S. imperialism overseas. From the late 1940s to the 1980s, black activists and intellectuals who connected the civil rights cause to necessary changes in U.S. racist patterns or to anti-colonial uprisings overseas often found themselves accused of being "Communists," "anti-American," or "subversive." Regularly, white politicians and other white leaders hammered black leaders, including Dr. King, in these political-attack terms, which operated to take the focus from eradicating racial oppression in the United States.[56] As Mary Dudziak has put it, "Civil rights groups had to walk a fine line, making it clear that their reform efforts were meant to fill out the contours of American democracy, and not to challenge or undermine it."[57] However, black leaders and their millions of followers knew that international Communism was not their main enemy. As one leader noted at the time,

The black folk of America know the enemy, the real enemy. They have looked into his hard white face. It is the fiendish face of reaction. The face of death—death to the spirit as well as to the body. . . . They have met him face to face in the villages of South Carolina, in the swamps of Florida, on the banks of the Potomac, on the plains of Texas and Kansas, and in the dark ghettos of Detroit, Chicago, and New York.[58]

Not surprisingly, the black freedom movements repeatedly created *legitimation crises* for the white elite, who in the 1950s and 1960s were aggressively competing in a "Cold War" with the Soviet Union for worldwide influence. Thus, one U.S. attorney general commented on the 1954 *Brown* Supreme Court desegregation case, arguing that Jim Crow segregation had to be eradicated because it "furnishes grist for Communist propaganda mills."[59] White elites could successfully meet these increasing international critiques only with racial reforms such as civil rights laws. As Derrick Bell perceptively observed, the white elite has acted to substantially reduce racial discrimination only when whites benefit, in a process called "interest convergence." International publicity on U.S. racial violence and insistent civil rights pressures coming from black freedom movements gradually moved the moderate wing of the white elite to support significant racial desegregation and civil rights laws, at least for a time. Eventually, protests by civil rights groups succeeded in getting a majority of the elite to support major legislation officially prohibiting racial discrimination in voting, schools, employment, and housing.[60]

The 1960s Democratic presidents, John F. Kennedy and Lyndon Baines Johnson, felt much social and political pressure from the accelerating black freedom movements. As a result, Kennedy supported the first modest remedial (named "affirmative action") efforts for Americans of color and some significant actions to aid southern civil rights demonstrators. A few months after "bloody Sunday," Johnson gave a remarkable address at historically black Howard University titled "To Fulfill These Rights." There he dramatically emphasized the "devastating heritage of . . . a century of oppression, hatred, and injustice" as explanations for inequality, then insisted:

> You do not wipe away the scars of centuries by saying: Now you are free to go where you want, and do as you desire, and choose the leaders you please. . . . We seek not just legal equity but human ability, not just equality as a right and a theory but *equality as a fact and equality as a result*.[61]

Such reparative phrasing was clearly drawn from the counter-framed language of the black freedom movement. Briefly in U.S. history, a few white political leaders took important anti-discrimination action. Moreover, in speeches such as Johnson's, we observe why a U.S. perspective sharply accenting racial justice and equality for all is identified by many here and overseas as something distinctively "black." Within this society, black Americans have frequently been the most visible group carrier of the liberty-and-justice ideals, which they have regularly implemented in anti-oppression organization efforts now over several centuries.

Dr. Martin Luther King, Jr.: Dramatic Freedom Counter-Framing

In both the southern civil rights movement and the northern black power movements (see below), the leaders and rank-and-file protesters were operating out of a strong black counter-frame to the dominant white racial frame. Many regularly and effectively asserted an anti-racist framing of society that made effective use of elements of the old liberty-and-justice frame once strongly articulated by the country's white founding elite. Most significantly, these black freedom movements brought a serious emphasis on a *comprehensive* implementation of these ideals of liberty and justice for *all* Americans.

Speaking for a majority of black Americans, the brilliant and heroic activist leader, Dr. Martin Luther King, Jr., frequently emphasized a distinctive black counter-framing with its conception of oppression being countered by assertive black agency and action. For example, in his discussions of the critical Montgomery bus boycott he accented the role of tens of thousands of local black people, termed the "forces of justice," who walked to work instead of riding the buses in order to bring down Jim Crow segregation.[62] Justice, freedom, and equality were recurring themes in the civil rights movement: Both leaders such as King and their followers meant what they said. As King eloquently put it, justice means major change: "Justice for black people will not flow into society merely from court decisions. . . . White America must recognize that justice for black people cannot be achieved without radical changes in the structure of our society."[63] Just a few weeks before his assassination, King spoke at a New York gathering honoring W. E. B. Du Bois. He praised Du Bois's radicalism and strong commitment to "all the oppressed" and "all forms of injustice," thereby signaling how black activists and intellectuals have regularly read and drawn inspiration from justice-seeking predecessors.[64]

Over the 1960s, Dr. King and many other African American activists emphasized that achieving legal rights was insufficient. While their efforts brought an end to Jim Crow, they insisted on further structural changes providing first-rate educations, better-paying jobs, and considerably improved living conditions. King was assassinated in Memphis while helping the fight of unionized sanitation workers striking for better working conditions. As King put the matter to his staff right before he was assassinated, a large-scale *revolution* would be necessary to bring the required systemic changes:

> The black revolution . . . is forcing America to face all its interrelated flaws—*racism*, where few blacks had not been allowed to register *poverty, militarism, and materialism*. . . . It reveals systemic rather than superficial flaws and suggests that radical reconstruction of society itself is the real issue to be faced.[65]

(In 1967, King was one of the first to speak out against the Vietnam War, which angered most whites.) King's major adviser, Bayard Rustin, had long insisted that the freedom movement would be truly successful only by generating "radical programs for full employment, the abolition of slums, the reconstruction of our educational system, new definitions of work and leisure."[66] For King and Rustin, this lack of major structural changes in the economy, politics, education, and policing made civil rights victories only partial. Given King's dramatic, often forgotten stance against the country's systemic racism and exploitative capitalism, the contemporary intellectual, Cornel West, has aptly described King as the "most significant and successful organic intellectual in American history." No previous American who did not hold public office had "linked the life of the mind to social change with such moral persuasiveness and political effectiveness."[67] West has also reminded us that at the time of his assassination, King was viewed unfavorably by a *large majority* of the population because of his uphill battle against injustice and militarism; he was not then the sanitized saint of contemporary white memory.[68]

By the mid-1960s, there was a new militancy in much of the black freedom movement in the South, one with an even stronger and more overt accent on black consciousness and pride. In 1965, a major organizer of voting efforts who acknowledged his debt to Malcolm X, Stokely Carmichael, together with other SNCC activists and leaders in Lowndes County (Alabama), established a new political organization, the Lowndes County Freedom Organization (LCFO). Pressing for real political power in an area with Klan-type violence, LCFO members carried guns to protect themselves. By 1970, the new LCFO was electing local black officials.[69]

Hidden Aspects of the Movement: Armed Self-Defense

The commonplace image of the civil rights movement is one of black nonviolence and passive resistance to oppression. However, over the decades of white violence from the 1910s to the 1960s, the *armed* self-defense of black individuals and groups was often essential to the success of local civil rights efforts—because local, state, and federal officials regularly failed to protect legitimate nonviolent demonstrations.

During the 1950s and 1960s, a fiercely segregationist Ku Klux Klan and other Klan-type supremacist groups engaged in assaults and murders of blacks throughout the South in attempts to stop the civil rights movement and implementation of new civil rights laws. One Klan group in the Monroe, North Carolina area periodically held large anti-black rallies. Thousands gathered, burned crosses, and raided black areas shooting guns. Robert Williams, a military veteran, militant NAACP leader, and National Rifle Association member, organized armed resistance. After a huge 1957 rally, armed Klan members drove again into black communities, but this time found armed black men who fired back at the Klan members, who quickly fled. A black nationalist strongly committed to black self-determination and power, Williams became famous in the 1950s and 1960s for asserting publicly that black Americans must counter violence with armed resistance. He published a fearless book, *Negroes with Guns*. Williams's brave philosophy brought him national and international attention, including support from other black nationalists such as Malcolm X.[70] However, fearing that armed self-defense would alienate white supporters, the NAACP leadership forced him out of the organization. Williams was harassed with FBI surveillance and other government repression, including trumped-up felony charges (later dismissed), so he fled to Cuba, where he set up a black liberation radio station called "Radio Free Dixie."[71] Understandably, he became a hero in many black communities, including many active in nonviolent protests. Thus, citing his courage, nonviolent civil rights hero Rosa Parks gave a moving eulogy at his 1996 funeral.

Most armed self-defense groups got little attention. Especially in the states of Louisiana, Mississippi, and Alabama, the voter registration and other desegregation activists of the NAACP, CORE, and SNCC were often quietly protected by armed black men. Many of these men were veterans, and most were experienced in keeping firearms to protect their homes from white terrorism. Some civil rights leaders or their bodyguards had hidden firearms. As Dr. Martin Luther King, Jr., once put it, "the right to defend one's home and one's person when attacked has been guaranteed through the ages by common law."[72]

The scholar Akinyele Umoja has emphasized that such armed black resistance became a "complement to self-proclaimed nonviolent organizers and organizations."[73] This remained true throughout the 1950s and 1960s. One important self-defense group was the Deacons for Defense and Justice, based mostly in Louisiana and Mississippi. In 1964, a group of working-class men in Jonesboro, Louisiana organized secretly to resist Klan-type terroristic violence against black demonstrators and their communities. By the time the organization got into the news media, there were twenty-one chapters across Louisiana and Mississippi. As Lance Hill summarizes, these Deacons for Defense and Justice quietly guarded demonstrations and "patrolled the black community to ward off night riders, engaged in shoot-outs with Klansmen, and even defied local police in armed confrontations."[74] When federal officials feared alienating supposedly moderate white southerners and abdicated their federal law enforcement responsibilities, well-armed Deacons periodically appeared to protect black protesters and communities. Indeed, in one major confrontation with the Klan in Bogalusa, Louisiana, the Deacons forced the federal government to enforce the civil rights laws against the actions of white supremacist officials. The

Deacons had a much broader significance, too, for they represented critical themes in the emerging "black power" movement of the 1960s. They clearly emphasized black agency and self-reliance, black pride and a reinvigorated black consciousness, and an unwavering commitment to the use of force where necessary to protect anti-segregation demonstrators and their own communities from recurring white terrorism.[75]

Ironically, the armed self-defense organizations such as those of Robert Williams and the Deacons for Defense not only protected, and thus made possible, numerous successful nonviolent demonstrations but, when they did get publicity, helped to make the publicly nonviolent orientation of the major civil rights organizations more welcome among many whites.

Violent Revolts, North and South

Violent black protest against oppression also took the form of hundreds of more-or-less spontaneous urban uprisings in the South, North, and West. These took place from the 1960s to the early 1970s. Thus, several times in May 1963 in Birmingham, Alabama, from a few hundred to several thousand blacks protested violently in the streets against Klan violence and police brutality. They battled police, who doubtless were surprised by this forceful resistance to oppression. In 1963 and 1965, more violent confrontations between blacks and white supremacists and/or white officers took place in numerous southern and border state towns and cities, including Savannah, Charleston, Cambridge (Maryland), St. Augustine, Natchez, McComb, Jackson, Jacksonville, Henderson, Lexington, Princess Anne, and Bogalusa. These uprisings not only generated federal intervention in several areas but frequently led to local government action to reduce racial segregation.[76] Even the famous 1963 nonviolent March on Washington had a greater effect than it might otherwise have had because officials in the Kennedy administration feared violence and mobilized several thousand soldiers for the demonstration.

In hundreds of unplanned southern and northern uprisings, thousands of black urbanites, mostly working-class men, revolted aggressively, using some violence against central city targets to demonstrate their anger over continuing poverty, unemployment, police brutality, and other institutional racism. Urban uprisings in major cities outside the South—especially those in Los Angeles (1965), Detroit (1967), and Washington, DC (1968)—had major impacts inside and outside black communities. As in the southern uprisings, the common targets of the violent protesters were the police and business establishments considered very exploitative. Significantly, school, church, and government buildings were generally not targeted. These unplanned revolts both reflected and accelerated black consciousness and spurred efforts at increasing black political power and community control.[77]

Both the assertive nonviolent demonstrations and the dramatic urban uprisings were central to precipitating important federal action to reduce racial segregation in several areas of the country.

Well-publicized black uprisings in northern and western cities did not mark a shift in black efforts for justice away from the "righteous" nonviolence of southern civil rights efforts, as is often pictured in popular histories. The nonviolent and violent black protests against and resistance to the country's extensive white oppression had already been part of the same black freedom struggle for quite some time. Racial segregation and other overt racism had long been part of white mistreatment of black northerners, and urban uprisings and other northern black protests against oppression had numerous precedents in similar protests against white oppression from decades well before the 1960s. As I noted previously, while officials in northern cities typically did not officially segregate schools and other institutions, most northern whites were opposed to substantial racial desegregation there, and white decision makers routinely, and often informally, took action to maintain racially segregated patterns in neighborhoods, employment settings, and public schools.[78]

The Black Power Movement

Stokely Carmichael and Malcolm X

As I suggested earlier, black organizations working against racial oppression have taken two somewhat different but regularly overlapping and interacting tracks—one primarily accenting civil rights and nonviolent strategies, the other primarily emphasizing broader issues of black power, community control, and self-determination and a greater array of protest strategies. The latter organizations' leaders have often been critical of civil rights leaders for not being bolder about openly critiquing white racism and supporting community control. However, this is only a rough typology, for organizations such as the Lowndes County Freedom Organization (LCFO) discussed earlier did actually blend perspectives from the civil rights and black power traditions. Moreover, soon after LCFO's political efforts, other important black community control organizations, influenced by or interacting with SNCC organizers, developed in the North (the Revolutionary Action Movement) and West (the Black Panther Party).[79] These black nationalist groups worked with mainstream civil rights groups in particular protests. As Peniel Joseph notes, although they often had different perspectives, the two movements "grew organically out of the same era and thus they simultaneously inspired, critiqued, and antagonized each other."[80]

Soon after his LCFO work, the young civil rights activist Stokely Carmichael enunciated a strong "black power" theme, explicitly using that term in a 1966 Greenwood, Mississippi speech before voting rights marchers. He soon was giving speeches around the country explaining that the phrase meant "a call for black people in this country to begin to define their own goals, to lead their own organizations."[81] He called for a dramatic increase in political power and emphasized a positive framing of black culture and strong black control of all black organizations and communities. In an influential 1967 book, *Black Power*, Carmichael and historian Charles Hamilton emphasized the concept of *institutional* racism. They contrasted their counter-framed view of institutional racism with tepid mainstream approaches just accenting prejudice and individual discrimination.[82] In addition, black power activists did much to increase overt black pride and a more public black counter-framing, as could be seen in the then-common term *Negro* being replaced with *black* or *African American*, in natural hair being more acceptable ("black is beautiful"), and in expanding black Americans' interest in Africa.

Carmichael and certain other civil rights leaders, including some in Europe and Africa, emphasized that they had been influenced by the brilliant Malcolm X, one of the great anti-racist analysts and activists of the last century. Numerous leaders in an array of organizations that increasingly accented themes of community control and self-determination cited his influence. Malcolm X was a central figure in the black power movement of the 1950s and 1960s, and his confrontational speeches emphasizing power themes frightened much of white America. Often drawn from the working class, Malcolm X and his associates attracted many African Americans of all class backgrounds to a more radical vision of black action than that of civil rights leaders who emphasized cooperation and integration with whites. Unlike some middle-class civil rights leaders, Malcolm X stayed very close to his roots in the black community and its home culture, including its inherently resistance-oriented music. Cornel West has described him as black "music in motion; he was jazz in motion . . . . The way he spoke had a swing to it, had a rhythm to it; it was a call and response with the audience that you get with jazz musicians. And he was the blues."[83]

In his bold speeches and commentaries, Malcolm X sought to put whites on the defensive in regard to white racism. For a time a leading minister of the Nation of Islam, he emphasized positive black consciousness, appreciation of black culture, and commitment to aggressive resistance to oppression.[84] As Manning Marable noted, Malcolm X saw himself "as a black man, a person of African descent who happened to be a United States citizen. This was a crucial difference from . . . civil rights leaders." He tied a strong black consciousness "to the ideological imperative of self-determination, the concept that all people have a natural right to decide for themselves their own destiny."[85] His forceful perspective sought to pressure whites to deal with institutional racism, whose structures he gradually came to view as possible to destroy and replace. White fears of his militancy benefitted the actions of nonviolent civil rights leaders, even as it built up his own organizational following in black America.[86]

Over the 1960s, the ever-insightful Malcolm X gave many speeches calling for the U.S. government to reign in white-racist attacks on African Americans and for an expansion of *real* democracy, as well as speeches criticizing the integration perspective of mainstream black leaders. Over time, however, and especially in speeches after he departed from the Nation of Islam in 1964, Malcolm X more often noted that the country's old liberty-and-justice ideals were worth emphasizing and implementing. In his last year of life, he made clear that he was more open to multiracial coalitions and called himself a "Pan-Africanist" rather than a "black nationalist," even as he still stressed black political-economic power and self-determination.[87]

Among the more important of the 1960s black power organizations were the Black Panthers, organized in fall 1966 by Huey P. Newton and Bobby Seale. The Party engaged in important community welfare programs and espoused a strong black counter-framing of U.S. society as institutionally racist, one influenced by the black power and self-determination ideas of Malcolm X. Mostly operating in northern and western cities, Panther organizations pressed hard for significant improvements in everyday conditions faced by modest-income black Americans—for better schools, lunch programs, housing, and job opportunities, particularly in central cities such as of those of Detroit, Chicago, and New York. The *Black Panther* newspaper had an impact in communities across the country. Their sharply counter-framed concepts of institutional racism and significant racial change raised there and in Black Panther leaders' speeches have been resurrected in recent years and still play "prominent roles in the sociopolitical movement that continues to work toward racial equality in this country today."[88]

Black Power: Expanding Individual and Collective Action

Black power perspectives did not just arise in the late 1950s and 1960s and decline with no subsequent influence. They reflected older black nationalist perspectives. Beginning in the colonial period, black leaders have long accented black power and nationalist themes as a response to oppression and as part of a very positive framing of black America. This was certainly true in earlier decades of the twentieth century. Numerous more militant black leaders—such as Paul Robeson and Lorraine Hansberry—had early on rejected the gradual integration perspective of mainstream civil rights leaders for a more aggressive accent on black self-determination and community control.

Over the course of the 1960s, the black self-determination, black pride, and community control ideas of black nationalists were spreading among black Americans in many walks of life. To take a major example, black athletes played an important role in this resurgence of black nationalist ideas. As noted previously, one was the preeminent boxer, Muhammad Ali. Intensely proud of being African American, Muhammad Ali not only was a great boxer but took very courageous stands on behalf of equality for African Americans and for his religion-based (Nation of Islam) right to refuse to fight in what he saw as the imperialistic Vietnam War. This principled stance precipitated widespread white-racist attacks and cost him his heavyweight boxing title. Ali's actions demonstrated, yet again, how centrally involved African Americans of many backgrounds have been in insisting on meaningful liberty-and-justice reforms. Not surprisingly, Ali's antiwar stance and pointed comments such as "I am not going ten thousand miles from here to help murder and kill and burn another poor people simply to help continue the domination of white America" got favorable attention across the globe and in headlines in newspapers from Paris to Hong Kong.[89] Similarly, black sprinters John Carlos and Tommie Smith won gold and silver track medals in the 1968 Olympics but became more famous for raising their fists in black power salutes during the playing of the U.S. national anthem. They were ejected from the Olympic village for their courageous protest, which they did in support of the 1960s black struggles for legal rights, unity, and power.[90] Their bold symbolic protest underscored the recurring importance of athletes in the efforts of African Americans to make the United States a freer country and in increasing the global support for the African American freedom movements. This important role in freedom movements continues to the present day.

As sociologist Joyce Bell has demonstrated, the black power movement's significant expressions included new organizations such as the National Association of Black Social Workers (NABSW). Inspired by the growing black power movement and directly by lectures from Charles Hamilton, the co-author of *Black Power*, the NABSW was created near the end of the 1960s by dissenting social workers at a white-dominated National Conference on Social Welfare. They protested in conference meetings, accented an anti-racist framing, split off to focus on issues particularly facing black communities, and created a black-oriented social work organization (NABSW). Since then, the NABSW has accented black community control efforts and worked hard to improve government social service programs for black communities.[91] Additionally, the founding documents of *dozens* of black professional associations created in this era made much use of black power terminology and arguments. These groups included the Association of Black Psychologists, Caucus of Black Sociologists, Black Caucus of the American Library Association, Association of Black Anthropologists, and the Congressional Black Caucus.[92]

Another important aspect, and continuing impact, of the 1960s black freedom movements was the creation of new African American courses in various academic disciplines and new African American studies programs at colleges and universities. Hundreds of thousands of black student activists and supporters, together with other sympathetic students, at nearly 1,000 historically white and black colleges and universities protested vigorously for African American cultural centers, support programs, academic studies programs, faculty hiring, and changes in racist campus climates. On one key day, February 13, 1969, they protested at colleges and universities in the Midwest, the Northeast, the upper and lower South, and on the West Coast. As Ibram Rogers has emphasized, "It was a day that emitted the anger, determination, and agency of a generation that stood on the cutting edge of educational progression. . . . and changed the course of higher education." These activists did not secure their most revolutionary aims, but did push "to the center a series of historically marginalized academic ideas, questions, frames, methods, perspectives, subjects, and pursuits."[93]

The resulting organizational reforms, especially new African American studies programs and black student unions, brought pressures to increase African American staff and to change many aspects of traditional campus life at historically white institutions, including the previously exclusive white framing of higher education goals. (At historically black institutions, there was also pressure to make them much more oriented to issues of large-scale societal change.) Nearly 200 new African American studies programs facilitated the scholarly analysis of issues rarely analyzed, especially in historically white institutions, and brought the black anti-racist counter-framing of society to the center of many academic and public discussions. These campus movements forced some significant changes in centuries-old implicit and explicit rules at historically white institutions that kept faculties and staffs white, marginalized African American research, and made white-framed perspectives on campus matters the norm.[94]

Even at formerly Jim Crow educational institutions "diversity" is now an official goal, and "multiculturalism" is everywhere demonstrated, at least to a modest degree, in everyday practice. As Fabio Rojas puts it, black studies programs and historically white institutions have coevolved:

Although the academy rejected demands for black-only education and community control, it did accept black studies. This allowed black studies to further influence academia and made possible future developments such as Afrocentrism, black studies Ph.D. programs, and a stronger acceptance of the African American community as a topic worthy of academic attention.

Additionally, black studies programs and their professors have often managed to create oppositional spaces where black counter-framing is freely developed and, most importantly, substantially institutionalized. These programs are thus

> key players in an academic movement that has had a strong impact on current scholarship, classroom teaching, and education policy. . . . This . . . has allowed black studies to influence the academy. If black studies programs had never been established, it is hard to imagine that the modern academy would have engaged with multiculturalism and related issues with the same intensity.[95]

Today, the white backlash against these academic innovations has resulted in some retrogression. Whites have often appropriated the language of (reverse) discrimination, and black student activists and black studies faculty now have to fight cutbacks in programs led by college officials arguing from a colorblind framing. Quiet battles continue, as many blacks on historically white campuses often hold off on directly discussing systemic racism there out of fear of a greater white backlash. Thus, much progress remains for black studies educational and research programs to have the desired long-term effects. Most remain small, and fewer than one in ten four-year colleges and universities have a well-developed, degree-linked black studies curriculum. So far, these black studies programs represent an important but limited intrusion of black-generated issues and knowledge into historically white institutions.[96]

Broad Ramifications of Freedom Movements

The national (white) collective memory of this era often accents the activists in student, antiwar, and women's movements as the major progressive forces, yet it was black activists in the various types of black freedom movements who most consistently pressed for much greater social justice, equality, and democracy *for all Americans*. In addition, their efforts often had broad effects benefitting all Americans. One important strategist of the civil rights movement was Bayard Rustin, a pacifist who exchanged ideas with India's Mahatma Gandhi on nonviolent strategies against oppression. During the 1960s, Rustin asserted that black rights movements were revolutionary because they raised demands beyond just getting the fruits of society to changing major political and economic structures that were institutionally racist and classist. In his view, this long black struggle

> may have done more to democratize life for whites than for Negroes. Clearly, it was the sit-in movement of young Southern Negroes

which, as it galvanized white students, banished the ugliest features of McCarthyism from the American campus and resurrected political debate. It was not until Negroes assaulted de facto school segregation in the urban centers that the issue of quality education for all children stirred into motion.[97]

Rustin's conclusions were borne out by events. The civil rights movement did improve black and white lives by helping to end the political censorship of McCarthyism, making debate about societal problems more acceptable, focusing on improving education for all, and helping generate government social programs (for example, Medicare) improving the lives of all Americans.

As sociologist Aldon Morris and other researchers have demonstrated, the black freedom movement of this era catalyzed numerous others, including antiwar movements, student movements, farm workers movements, gay/lesbian movements, environmental movements, disability rights movements, and unionization efforts. The black freedom movement demonstrated that "oppression is not inevitable and that collective action can generate change" in the direction of much greater democracy.[98] Additionally, civil rights activists honed change strategies later employed by others, such as sit-ins, economic boycotts, large-scale marches, freedom schools, and inventive media strategies. African American activists drew on and extended the nonviolent tactics of Mahatma Gandhi and generated major protest innovations.

Black nationalists and other black activists renewed their connections and collaborations with anti-colonial movements in Asia and Africa (see Chapter 7). With political repression in decline, they worked more openly with anti-colonial movements and decolonized nations overseas. Their protest strategies spread:

> Nonviolent direct action has enabled oppressed groups as diverse as Black South Africans, Arabs of the Middle East, and pro-democracy demonstrators in China to engage in collective action. Leaders of these movements have acknowledged the valuable lessons they have learned from the civil rights movement.[99]

Even in Europe, democratic movements, such as in Ireland and Poland, have involved nonviolent protests influenced by the black freedom movement— sometimes with placards with pictures of Dr. King. Thus, significant global changes have resulted, at least in part, from the impact of the black freedom movement.

From at least the early decades of the twentieth century, as can be seen in the writings of great leaders such as Du Bois and Robeson, many black activists have been globally oriented, with a strong concern with European colonialism. As Nikhil Singh has underscored, this orientation could be observed not only in the communism of Du Bois and Robeson but in the "Christian pacifism of King and the revolutionary, black nationalism of Malcolm X and the Black Panther Party." Black activists have regularly related "their own aspirations to national liberation struggles across the world, including India, Ghana, Cuba, Congo, Vietnam, South Africa, and Palestine."[100]

Conclusion

Much was indeed accomplished by the large-scale civil rights and black power movements from the 1950s to the 1970s, including an end to legal segregation. This movement generated significantly improved economic, educational, and political opportunities for many African Americans, especially those in the growing black middle class—including leader-activists in the black freedom movement. Many became relatively well-paid public and private sector employees, which provided resources to move out of impoverished central cities. In all regions, whites grudgingly accepted more desegregation of employment, housing, and schools, and the publicly professed goals of many historically white organizations shifted in the direction of accenting racial diversity in their operations.[101]

Significantly, most major changes in racial segregation that took place were not so much the result of whites' racial views becoming more progressive but rather because of the major societal disruptions created by the persistent and assertive anti-segregation activism of African Americans (and other Americans of color) over these decades. For a time, black activism pressured many in the white elite who were concerned about the international reputation and position of the United States to take action against official segregation—a situation of clear interest convergence.[102]

However, when the activist civil rights movements began to ebb in the 1970s, this white support for racial change was often replaced by stagnation or retrogression. While some black Americans—usually with great effort—maintained or increased their employment, housing, and political gains, the forward progress of black America slowed considerably because of the reinvigoration of white opposition to racial change. Indeed, even the average new black middle-class family was not nearly as well-off—especially in terms of debt, net worth, and employment networks—as the average white middle-class family. By the late 1960s, officials in the Richard Nixon presidential campaign had devised an aggressive white "southern strategy" to garner support there for conservative Republican candidates and political initiatives. This white-oriented effort encompassed northern whites as well and was substantially successful. The Nixon administration rolled back some civil rights gains, usually with racially conservative Supreme Court appointments and cutbacks in enforcing civil rights laws.[103] Across the country, most whites were unwilling for governments to aggressively eradicate racial discrimination and inequalities that were well institutionalized in employment, housing, educational, or political institutions.

Much speculation has centered on likely reasons for the decline of the civil rights movement after the early 1970s. Some have noted the peddling of a "post-racial" framing of society by influential commentators in light of the ending of Jim Crow. Many have pointed to the demoralization of many black Americans after key civil rights leaders were assassinated. Yet others have noted the movement of many black Americans, including potential civil rights leaders, into better jobs in desegregated settings. A factor cited by some is that too many African Americans had been conned by mainstream individualism and consumerism. Together, these latter factors had created a shift from the age-old we-consciousness of African Americans to a problematical I-consciousness.[104] However, we should emphasize that the substantial white backlash just noted was a major factor. This took the form of the Republican white "southern strategy" in elections, police killings of militant activists in groups such as the Black Panther Party, police crackdowns on large demonstrations, and major Supreme Court and congressional backtracking on civil rights issues from the 1970s to the present.

This white backlash was so strong by the 1970s that established civil rights organizations found themselves constantly on the defensive, defending some gains that had been made—such as school desegregation and affirmative action programs—and trying to move forward on a few poverty and employment issues. Without the pressure of hundreds of organized black protests such as those of the 1960s, efforts at major new programs were mostly doomed. Moreover, numerous black church, community, and civil rights organizations, from the National Council of Negro Women to the NAACP, were losing significant numbers of members. The Black Panthers had been significantly weakened, with internal strife and intentional police harassment. Black talk-radio and music programs increased, but once-powerful newspapers were mostly in decline. In spring 1972, several thousand delegates from civil rights and black nationalist organizations met at a National Black Political Convention in Indiana and hammered out a National Black Political Agenda with strong goals for major political-economic changes. Yet, this Agenda was rejected by some civil rights leaders and militant activists, and it was generally ignored by the black public.[105]

Furthermore, by the 1980s and 1990s, large-scale changes in the U.S. economy were making it harder for many, especially working-class, black workers, to move into better-paying employment areas that were now officially desegregated. Unions were mostly in decline, and workers with a high school education were having a difficult time finding decently paying jobs once available because of unionization. Corporate employers were more aggressively moving well-paying jobs to lower-wage areas overseas. At the same time, neoliberal Republican and Democratic presidential administrations and Congresses were cutting taxes for very well-off, disproportionately white Americans. Such actions reduced the ability of the federal government to provide programs facilitating black workers' and families' recovery from generations of only recently ended Jim Crow oppression.[106] Nonetheless, as we see in Chapter 7, the African American quest for racial justice and equality by no means ended in this era. That quest has remained evident in an array of manifestations.

7
Contemporary Global Impacts
Freedom, Justice, and Democracy

One is hard-pressed to name another group in U.S. history that has had more positive impact in pressing this country toward *real* social justice, equality, and democracy than African Americans, yet has at the same time been so negatively demonized in whites' racial framing of this society. In the 1950s, the distinguished African American author, Richard Wright, insisted that African Americans were "the only group in our nation that consistently and passionately raises the question of freedom. . . . This is a service to America and to the world."[1] Indeed, thinking broadly, European colonizers were the immoral exploiters who spread systems of genocidal oppression all across the globe for the first time in human history. In great contrast, indigenous peoples, African-descent peoples, and other people of color have had to spend much of their blood, treasure, and lives in trying to counter and replace the extraordinarily oppressive practices of European imperialism and associated racial oppression.

Repeatedly over this long history of racial oppression, the resistance efforts and authentic freedom counter-framing of African Americans have forced white elites to take action that, however hesitantly, put the country on a path to expanded social justice. Indeed, African Americans have regularly saved this country from moving toward even worse racial oppression. In recent decades, African Americans and their organizations have continued to lead the charge to win the last great battle of the United States—the one for implementation of real freedom, justice, and democracy.

Continuing White Resistance to Change

From the beginning of the United States, most members of the white elite and rank-and-file whites have not been committed in practice to the famous liberty-and-justice framing of this society. A central reason for the revolutionary revolt against Britain was the desire in much of the elite, northern and southern, to protect their interest in a slavery system central to their economic prosperity and social status. From the seventeenth century onward, they and other whites also feared African American uprisings and revolts. The U.S. Constitution made their concerns and propertied interests evident, as did many other political and legal decisions over two-plus centuries of the slavery system. Once this system was destroyed—substantially because of efforts of black abolitionists, soldiers, and support troops—it was soon replaced by the near-slavery of Jim Crow. Again, decades of organized efforts by African Americans to bring down that oppressive system were critical to ending it, too. Repeatedly, the actions of most in the white elite and most ordinary whites have made it conspicuously clear that there was no serious commitment to fully implementing the country's rhetorical liberty-and-justice ideals.

Previously, I raised the issue of why the civil rights movement ended and why racial change was soon mostly replaced by stagnation and white backlash in many areas. The scale of the pushback against attempts to eradicate racial discrimination and inequality has been large-scale and substantially successful. A majority of the elite has worked hard to make that so. In the late 1960s and early 1970s, white political leaders such as President Richard Nixon and his allies began to roll back some of the civil rights progress, such as by weakening enforcement of civil rights laws. This weakening continued in later Republican administrations, and in the Democratic administrations of Jimmy Carter and Bill Clinton, the rollbacks were mostly not restored. During Clinton's terms in the 1990s, there were great pressures from a Congress often dominated by white conservatives for more cutbacks in reparative and other support programs assisting Americans of color. The Clinton administration and other Democrats periodically colluded in cutbacks in such areas as affirmative action and social welfare programs. In addition, a Supreme Court that had been moved in a very conservative direction by the appointments made by Republican presidents played a key role in moving the country backward on numerous civil rights and inequality issues.

Given this backlash and resistance to change, it is unsurprising that the old racial hierarchy still remains very much at the center of U.S. society. A half century ago, Dr. Martin Luther King, Jr. summarized the black Jim Crow condition in a way that still fits today's racial inequalities:

> When the Constitution was written, a strange formula to determine taxes and representation declared that the Negro was 60 percent of a person. Today another curious formula seems to declare he is 50 percent of a person. Of the good things in life he has approximately one-half of those of whites. . . .[2]

Today, black median household income is still only 59 percent of white median income. Median wealth of white households is thirteen times that of black households. In addition, the black unemployment rate remains twice that of whites, as it has been for decades.[3] This unequal employment situation persists even though in recent decades African Americans have worked hard and increased their high school completion rate to a figure nearing that of whites.

Under pressure from the civil rights movement and laws spurred by it, the black job situation did improve significantly in the late 1960s and 1970s. Many firms and government agencies finally hired significant numbers of black applicants into historically white jobs. By the 1980s, however, with the decline in the civil rights movement and rise of conservative Republican control of government branches, enforcement of anti-discrimination laws sharply declined. Aggregate progress by African American workers slowed dramatically. Since the late 1980s, relatively few white-run firms have ensured or significantly increased their employment diversity. Job segregation remains very high. As one recent social science study concludes, "To produce integrated private-sector workplaces today would require that more than half of all workers switch jobs. ... Little or no national aggregate progress is being made in either [job] desegregation or access to good jobs."[4]

Much interview research shows that African Americans are far more conscious of this country's racialized past and its continuing negative impacts than most white and many other nonblack Americans. In recent surveys, 90 percent or so of African American respondents report continuing discrimination in its blatant, subtle, covert forms. Yet the white-controlled media and white political leaders usually ignore the implications of this important information about contemporary racism. Even though there are now more middle-class African Americans than in the 1960s, there is still racial discrimination facing them and African Americans at other class levels. (Indeed, contemporary research demonstrates that the black middle class is not nearly as well-off as the white middle class in terms of net worth and other economic measures.) Most African Americans still face significant discrimination in an array of employment, housing, policing, and other public settings.[5]

Over the last decade or two, African American scholars have provided much of the research documentation of anti-black discrimination and other aspects of systemic racism. Consider the path-breaking research of Louwanda Evans, who has demonstrated the extensive discrimination faced by African American airline pilots and flight attendants, the type of well-educated professionals whom most whites would likely view as examples of a "postracial society" with little discrimination. However, this is not the reality of most black professionals such as these. All of Evans's numerous respondents report facing substantial blatant and subtle discrimination in their job settings. Recently, one African American pilot explained the current reality thus: Today racism is "subtle, it's underneath, and it's sneaky.

. . . We no longer have to worry about Jim Crow. Now we have to worry about *James Crow Jr. Esquire!*"[6]

Today, deep and persisting racial inequalities are the result both of this type of extensive James Crow, Jr. Esquire discrimination and, at least as important, of the enrichment of most contemporary white families that comes from inheriting some or a lot of unjustly gained income, wealth, or social capital (e.g., networks) of their ancestors. Recall Mueller's research that found huge racial differences in the acquisition and intergenerational transfer of wealth and social capital over several generations. This large differential in socioeconomic inheritances accounts for much of continuing racial inequality today. This is not some abstract and causeless inequality but involves knowingly inherited unjust enrichments and impoverishments from centuries of racial oppression. Yet few whites will admit to this reality. What they ignore, often intentionally, is that the unjust enrichment of parents, grandparents, and more distant ancestors under slavery, Jim Crow, and more recent discrimination carries into the lives of white Americans today. Similarly, the extensive and unjust impoverishment of African Americans' ancestors carries into most African American lives today.

Today, most whites, and indeed many others, have accepted the mythological framing of this society as colorblind, meritocratic, and post-racial. The associated myth of white innocence in regard to past and current racial inequalities has regularly appeared in public discussions and decisions, including those of the U.S. Supreme Court.[7] Many whites, including conservatives on that Court, have viewed even modest remedial programs designed to redress some effects of past and present discrimination as harming whites whom they consider to be largely blameless.

Continuing Battles against Systemic Racism

Black Community Movements

Today, African Americans often lead the overt battles against systemic racism, including that manifested in this government backtracking. While the 1960s civil rights and black power movements have not been followed by similarly numerous protest movements in more recent decades, black communities have continued to be major generators of progressive efforts and organizations. One sees evidence in the

activities of thousands of grassroots organizations, community development corporations, churches, and protest groups—some delivering social services, some acting as gadflies to state and local governments, others still working against the odds for a revolution that seemed more and more distant by the day.[8]

African Americans have long accented collective goals and efforts. Recall the point made in previous chapters that there has always been a common core to the African American perspective on freedom that is communally oriented, both because of the African culture background and everyday necessity. Unlike with a majority of whites for whom freedom has usually been about individual freedom without bureaucratic interference, African American conceptions of freedom have generally been more communal.[9] Historically, we see this in the efforts of abolitionists such as Harriet Tubman who, contrary to many portraits, did not work alone. She was part of an extensive black support network that made possible the large-scale flight from slavery. Moreover, researchers working on the history of African American organizations have found that before the Civil War, there were many African-influenced voluntary associations in free black communities in addition to churches. These laid the foundation for the development and expansion of African American communities and culture to the present day. As Craig Wilder has emphasized, the

universality of the voluntary tradition suggests that African American community has its basis in collectivism: a behavioral and rhetorical tendency to privilege the group over the individual. Collective cultures arose as enslaved Africans unleashed the potential for group action and mass resistance in familiar West African relationships.[10]

African American scholar Manning Marable has argued that the historically different black and white perspectives on freedom continue to be in tension. For most whites, freedom still means an absence of bureaucratic limits on their individual activities whereas, for most blacks, freedom continues to be much more about community action and capacity building without racially discriminatory barriers. For most African Americans and many other Americans of color, the counter-frame accenting true freedom and democracy has been principally about the "eradication of all structural barriers to full citizenship and full participation in all aspects of public life and economic relations" and, even more important, about group self-determination, "the ability to decide, on our own terms, what our future as a community with a unique history and culture might be."[11]

Today, many community efforts are directed at the serious discrimination that confronts black youths. These efforts include organizations for and of black prisoners and families that have been severely affected by the government's "drug wars," including by the high level of black incarceration over recent decades.[12] In addition, many of these and other recent local, state, and national organizational efforts have involved black youth activists. Examples include numerous criminal justice reform movements, the Free

South Africa Movement against apartheid, the 1980s New Haven youth movement, and the Black Student Leadership Network.[13]

Yet other community efforts have focused on organizing lower-wage workers against exploitative employers, organizing communities against attempts to locate toxic waste dumps near them, and organizing voters to fight conservative white legislators trying to make voting difficult and to cut funding for crucial educational and other social programs, especially in sunbelt and Midwestern states. Notice, too, how these community organizations' endeavors usually involve seeking more transparent and democratic government decision making—and thus more authentic democracy for this country.

These contemporary organizational labors have regularly involved much institutional leveraging. This creates a complex contemporary reality. As Sekou Franklin stresses, often the "networks of activists that cultivate movement-building activities and supply activist groups with resources and legitimacy—are channeled into established bureaucratic and political institutions."[14] While such establishment channeling does typically signal significant political and funding successes at the local and national level, it also frequently limits the development of national, broader-based social justice movements.

We should note, too, that since the 1960s, there have been periodic, large-scale demonstrations against particular types of racial discrimination in numerous black communities. For instance, frequent local protests have targeted the recurring incidents of anti-black violence involving white police officers—for example, in the 2009 protests in Oakland, California; the 2014 protests in Ferguson, Missouri; the 2014 protests in New York City; and similar 2014–2015 protests in nearly 200 cities across the country over the continued killing of unarmed black men by white police officers. Significantly, African Americans from all walks of life, together with significant numbers of nonblacks, have participated in these very assertive protests, sometimes including prominent black athletes and other celebrities speaking out as they did in the 1960s.

Increasing Democracy: Black Voters and Officials

Over the decades since the 1960s, one area where African Americans have had important effects on extending this country's democracy and social justice has been in the political arena. Recall our discussion of the impact of southerners' northward migration on progressive movements. Because of that large-scale migration, black voters had a very significant impact on local and national elections. Without them, Democratic presidential candidates such as Truman and Kennedy likely would have lost. This impact of black voters, in the North and the South, has continued. The 1964 and 1965 Civil Rights Acts were some of the most game-changing pieces of legislation ever passed, and they would not have passed without the efforts of many thousands of black southerners and northerners in the black freedom movements. Once that right to vote was legally protected, black voters increasingly participated in local, state, and national elections, mostly voting for Democratic Party candidates. One result is that the Democratic Party is now the most racially diverse major party in U.S. history, with large groups of African Americans and other Americans of color as key voters.[15]

Because of the involvement of the federal government in bringing down massive voting barriers and other Jim Crow segregation and the successful election of many black candidates to political offices since the migration to the North, African Americans have put substantial faith in electoral strategies for change. In the 1980s, thus, civil rights leader Jessie Jackson developed a strong political campaign and was the first black man to get substantial votes for the presidency in major party primaries, thereby helping to prepare a foundation for the election of Barack Obama as president decades later.

At the national level, one now sees dramatic differentials in black and white voter patterns. For example, in the 1972 presidential election, the percentage of black voters opting for the Democratic candidate minus the percentage of white voters opting for that candidate reached 57 percent, up significantly from just 23 percent in 1960. That differential has remained high since the 1970s, exceeding 50 percent in Barack Obama's presidential elections. Since the 1960s, black voters have been critical to numerous Democratic Party victories, including Obama's dramatic wins. Significantly, over this recent period, black voters have tended to cast disproportionate numbers of votes for Democratic candidates in local, state, and federal elections. Given this pattern at all government levels, the great importance of African American voters has pressured Democratic leaders to make democratizing reforms in numerous party rules and organizational efforts. Generally, African Americans have become the most loyal part of the Party's voter base.[16]

Not only is the makeup of U.S. voters more diverse than ever before, so too is the makeup of political officials. Thanks to the black freedom movement's successes in bringing the 1965 Voting Rights Act and other voting reforms, elected officials form a more diverse and representative group now than ever before. Since the 1970s, there has been a dramatic growth in African American political officials, including several dozen members of Congress, hundreds of state legislators, and thousands of other state and local officials. This represents significant and institutionalized political power that did not exist before the 1960s.[17]

Created in 1971 with a small number of House members, the Congressional Black Caucus (CBC) had grown to forty-two members by

2014. By then, the Caucus made up a fifth of all Democratic members. The Caucus has been successful in numerous public policy areas, especially those dealing with recurring civil rights and socioeconomic justice issues. The Caucus Web site accurately summarizes:

> For more than 40 years, the CBC has consistently been the voice for people of color and vulnerable communities in Congress and has been committed to utilizing the full Constitutional power, statutory authority, and financial resources of the Government of the United States of America to ensure that everyone in the United States has an opportunity to achieve their version of the American Dream.[18]

Notably, over a half century, the CBC has persistently pressed the mostly white male congressional leadership and presidents for major anti-discrimination, social justice, and other progressive legislation benefitting all Americans—carrying on such efforts begun by the first African Americans to Congress during Reconstruction. Caucus member Major Owens has described how the Caucus has played crucial roles in getting federal legislation protecting homeless veterans, extending voting rights, providing substantial support for the unemployed, and guaranteeing computer access for schools and libraries. Moreover, like earlier African American political leaders in various legislative bodies, the CBC members have viewed themselves as representing all African Americans, not just those in their districts.[19] They were successful in their long-term effort to get the national Martin Luther King holiday approved by Congress and, since the 1980s, they have been effective in getting presidents and the Congress to increase funding for historically impoverished black colleges and universities. Representative Eddie Bernice Johnson (Texas) has summed up its broad, even global impact:

> The Congressional Black Caucus is one of the world's most esteemed bodies, with a history of positive activism unparalleled in our nation's history. Whether the issue is popular or unpopular, simple or complex, the CBC has fought for thirty years to protect the fundamentals of democracy. Its impact is recognized throughout the world. . . . We work together almost incessantly, we are friends and, more importantly, a family of freedom-fighters.[20]

For many decades, in the North and South, African American voters have labored hard to get and keep the right to vote, including today in the face of extensive white conservative attempts to again restrict their ability to vote. African American voters have frequently been the chief voting bloc responsible for electing legislators who represent the best of this country's social justice and democratic ideals. If it were not for African Americans protesting over the centuries for these ideals, finally getting the right to vote in the 1960s, and then being very politically active since then, a range of very important public policies—such as those expanding civil rights, resisting nativism, improving unemployment and antipoverty programs, implementing progressive health care programs, and meeting numerous important societal welfare needs—would likely not have been as well developed and implemented.

Fighting Racism: Individual and Group Resistance

Facing "James Crow, Jr., Esquire" discrimination in contemporary society, the majority of African Americans as individuals and in family or other groups hone the centuries-old black counter-frame for dealing with present-day racism. This anti-racist frame encompasses a strong critique of white oppression and its everyday operation, as well as an intensive countering of negative framing of African Americans and an emphatic accent on creating real social justice. This anti-oppression counter-frame typically draws on a traditional home-culture frame that African Americans have also developed since the first century of enslavement. They have maintained a substantial home culture with important features stemming from their African backgrounds and aspects imported from the dominant culture, all shaped significantly by their adaptations to the U.S. settings of racial oppression.

One major source of everyday resistance to racial oppression lies in this centuries-old background with its long history of resistance strategies, its strong religion, and its supportive music and many other cultural elements. Today, as in the past, major elements of this African American history and cultural creativity are recounted in black churches and families as training in coping with and resistance to white oppression, especially for youths. Much has been made of black family "problems," especially in much commonplace white framing, yet it is the black family that has long been the main setting where most get regular instruction in the home-culture frame and the resistance counter-frame. Most youths learn at least some significant aspects of the counter-frame from family and friends, including lessons about the history and reality of racism and how African Americans have dealt with it. For example, as *Africana: The Encyclopedia of the African and African American Experience* puts it, for African Americans who participated in the migration out of the South, together with their children and grandchildren, that courageous migration "continues to resonate as one of the most powerful stories of African-American struggle and opportunity" and resistance to oppression.[21]

Parents and other socializers of black children typically fit teachings about discrimination to a child's capacities, age, and gender. Thus, given the especially aggressive white targeting of black males for everyday discrimination, they often provide stronger lessons about being cautious around white authorities, such as police officers, for sons than for daughters. In contrast, girls are frequently taught a somewhat different array of strategies, some gendered, for dealing with other aspects of white racism. In one research study, a savvy college student explained her intergenerational socialization in counter-framing thus:

> My parents tried to tell me one thing, they tried to instill in me that I was a beautiful person, that my blackness was a beautiful thing, that the fact that I braided my hair was fine. . . . But when you're like, nine, ten, eleven, you tend not to listen to your parents, and you tend to listen to everything else, which is white people, in my case white people . . . .[22]

Here we find a significant affirmation of black beauty and humanity.

The primary socialization and transmission of the home-culture frame and the anti-racist counter-frame regularly take place in friendship and kinship groups and community organizations. The latter include black-owned beauty shops, barber shops, and taverns. These provide relatively safe spaces for black Americans. Indeed, in the early 1900s, Madam C. J. Walker, a savvy black entrepreneur (the first woman self-made millionaire) and civil rights activist, created hair care products specifically for black women. Sociologist Adia Wingfield interviewed the black owners of beauty salons. The latter had usually become beauty shop owners to make black women feel beautiful and supported. Their

> efforts to value their work, to create safe spaces for black women, and to help other women achieve the financial and social benefits of entrepreneurship are a counter-frame to the systemic gendered racist ideology that black women and the work that they do are unappreciated and worthless.[23]

Developed understandings of how gendered racial oppression works and about the strategies that counter that oppression are passed along in these important community settings.

Among black youths, critical understandings of how white racial framing, hostility, and discrimination operate can in many circumstances increase positive outcomes for them, including self-esteem. Like other black Americans, youths spend much time trying to make sense of and deal with subtle and blatant discrimination in their everyday lives—what sociologist Louwanda Evans has analyzed well as their required *emotional and cognitive labor*.[24] Black youths often continue to face challenges from white peers in historically white schools and colleges. Consider the account of this savvy young college student at a historically white college on the West Coast, who speaks of recent sad and angry nights because white students periodically call him the N-word:

> At first I used to wonder where they actually take the time in their heads to separate me from everyone else by the color of my skin. I used to just blame alcohol consumption for their obvious ignorance and racist attitudes, but I have since stopped trying to make excuses for them. . . . I don't understand how such a system of hate could exist. . . . Sometimes it seems that if I am around all white people, then I become nothing more then a token black "exhibit" for their amusement. I guess that even I have to be careful not to judge all based on a few bad examples, which more often then not is the fate of many in the black community today. The saddest thing, however, is that . . . these college students are supposed to be the supposed crème de la crème, the future business and political leaders.[25]

The level of great emotional and cognitive labor is high in such examples, of which we have hundreds in this large field study. This teenage college student not only reacts emotionally to recurring racist epithets but carefully sorts out his thoughts in a journal entry. He used to explain whites' racist actions in terms of ignorance and drunkenness but has stopped, implying that he now accents their racism. Much effort and reflection must go into blacks' assessments of white-racist behaviors. This is a very important type of everyday resistance, as it helps to shape strategies for dealing with such events. Though his cognitive labor seems to have strengthened his self-respect, there are negative impacts from the events. A considered awareness of discrimination usually links to some negative effects, including substantial emotional or cognitive labor and personal stress. The white-racist worlds faced by African Americans of all backgrounds constantly generate negative health consequences, even as they often create a stronger will to fight back.[26]

For centuries to the present day, African Americans have paid a significant price for actively resisting racial oppression. Those who have spoken out frequently get labeled as "difficult" people. One police officer with long service put it this way:

> Some people used to say I was a troublemaker, I said, "Troublemaker, how? What have I done to cause trouble? Because I won't let you say 'nigger' in front of me? That's a troublemaker? Because I won't let you treat people wrong, that's a troublemaker?"[27]

Everyday resistance can be costly in terms of losing work rewards and in terms of this emotional and cognitive labor.

The prominent scholar, bell hooks, has reported on a painful racist event that she and a black female companion faced with a white cab driver. He

> wanted us to leave his taxi and take another; he did not want to drive to the airport. When I said I would willingly leave but also report him, he agreed to take us. . . . We faced similar hostility when we stood in the first-class line at the airport.[28]

Observe again how African Americans resist everyday racist actions. Calling for the supervisor, they finally got the necessary counter service. Yet, on the plane, her friend was accused by white attendants of trying to sit in a seat not assigned to her, although she was in her correct seat but had an incorrect boarding pass. They demonstrated strong resistance, yet the impact generated some "killing rage." Unmistakably, African Americans today must use significant resources and labor in confronting this discrimination. In our interviews many, like this black psychologist, emphasize the deep family resources that help to sustain them:

> Black people are more spiritual. . . . We believe in relationships. I don't know whether it was African tradition, all I know is what happened in America you had a lot of extended families, where there was a lot of love and concern and helping and working with, and trying to do for each other, and not for ourselves. And see the white man's situation is very selfish, everything for him, whatever it takes for that one person to have power.[29]

Yet again, we observe that the white framing of African American families as weak is usually far off the mark. Like those of other Americans, African American communities do have significant family problems, many of which come from unjust economic circumstances. Even so, in some ways, African Americans have stronger family values than do whites, and a substantial majority have strong family networks they can use in dealing with white racism.[30]

Currently, much white racial framing of the United States accents the erroneous notion that this is a "post-racial" society in which black Americans already have rough equality with whites. From this perspective, government remedial action is not necessary. One Gallup poll found that, though a significant majority of black respondents still saw a major need for government action to improve black socioeconomic conditions, a very small percentage of whites felt the same. Strikingly, too, the majority of black respondents said there was a need for more enforcement of civil rights laws, whereas few whites agreed. Even among younger Americans, another survey found that only 19 percent of whites thought there was a need for affirmative action programs to redress past discrimination, as compared with three-fourths of blacks. Recent surveys do not indicate that younger whites are more understanding about racism and its impacts than their parents.[31]

Scholar-Activists: Realistic Analyses for Building Real Democracy

One of the great contributions that African Americans have made to this society are many incisive, realistic, and honest analyses of systemic racism. The previous accounts fully demonstrate how such analysis is critical to successfully fighting everyday racism. As black demonstrators said during the 1960s freedom movements, it is necessary to "tell it like it is." In recent decades, as in the distant past, African American scholars and activists have been on the cutting edge of research on and public analysis of systemic racism, including how to change it. More than a century ago, W. E. B. Du Bois assessed the reality constantly faced by African Americans—"How does it feel to be a problem?" Like African Americans before him, Du Bois forthrightly named and evaluated white Americans as the *real* racial problem. In fact, in his pioneering book, *Darkwater*, he was the first to develop what is now called "whiteness studies," a field of study that has emerged prominently since the 1970s.[32]

Today, this realistic approach to well-institutionalized racism is still central to thought and action of most African American scholars and scholar-activists. For example, in a famous recent (2012) example of realistic truth telling about U.S. racial matters, Dr. Jeremiah Wright gave a sermon at the centennial celebration of a Washington, DC, Baptist church. Wright was President Barack Obama's former pastor, who in the 2008 election had become a target of fierce white attacks for honest sermons about racism. Wright assertively criticized the long history of U.S. racial oppression and underscored the pushback that black truth-tellers have endured, quoting lines from a Fourth of July speech by the leading activist-intellectual of the nineteenth century, Frederick Douglass:

> Had I the ability, and could I reach the nation's ear, I would, today, pour out a fiery stream of biting ridicule, blasting reproach, withering sarcasm, and stern rebuke. For it is not light that is needed, but fire; it is not the gentle shower, but thunder. . . . the hypocrisy of the nation must be exposed; and its crimes against God and man must be proclaimed and denounced.[33]

Articulating a strong African American counter-framing and the importance of African American collective memory over generations, Wright accented the gross injustices of centuries-old oppression and, especially, the need for assertive and aggressive anti-racist action in the present day.

This same sense of racial realism and urgency is clear in Dr. Wright's other recent sermons condemning the U.S. government's history of racialized oppression globally. In one earlier 2003 sermon, he ended with strongly worded language condemning continuing U.S. government oppression. The U.S. government

> . . . when it came to treating her citizens of Indian descent fairly, she failed. She put them on reservations. When it came to treating her citizens of Japanese descent fairly, she failed. She put them in internment prison camps. When it came to treating citizens of African descent fairly. . . . The government put them on slave quarters, put them on auction blocks, put them in cotton fields, put them in inferior schools, put them in substandard housing, put them in scientific experiments, put them in the lowest paying jobs, put them outside the equal protection of the law. . . . and then wants us to sing God bless America? . . . Not God bless America; God damn America! That's in the Bible, for killing innocent people. God damn America for treating her citizen as less than human. . . . as long as she keeps trying to act like she is God. . . .[34]

Ministers in many denominations regularly make such prophet-like statements about this, the country's sins. In this case, Dr. Wright, the recipient of many awards and university honorary degrees, placed his biblically phrased and prophetic words at the end of an honest and mostly accurate sermon on societal injustice. Operating out of the astute black counter-framing of racial oppression, he argued that even the powerful U.S. government is fallible and a failure in guaranteeing that all its citizens are treated fairly. His forthright words eventually created so much critical discussion that presidential candidate Obama had to break openly with his pastor.[35]

Rooted for centuries in black institutions such as the church, this black counter-frame has critically assessed the white responsibility for oppression and demanded actions implementing social justice ideals. In a 2008 National Press Club speech, Dr. Wright further noted that the black church's role in fighting for justice was central from the eighteenth century to the present. The church

> has always had as its core the non-negotiable doctrine of reconciliation . . . . Reconciliation means we embrace our individual rich histories, all of them. We retain who we are, as persons of different cultures, while acknowledging that those of other cultures are not superior or inferior to us; they are just different from us. We root out any teaching of superiority, inferiority, hatred or prejudice.[36]

Contemporary versions of this black counter-framing reject notions of racial inferiority and superiority and envision real progress to social justice and reconciliation. Note, too, that throughout this book, we have seen how central African American ministers, civil rights leaders, cultural artists, and scholars have been to honing and foregrounding this extraordinarily important anti-racist counter-framing.

In the past and present, most African Americans, both leaders and average citizens, have asserted and utilized at least some important aspects of this black counter-framing, with its strong ideals of justice and democratic progress. Of course, in their everyday framing, some African Americans fall between a more aggressive expression of this counter-frame and the other end of the continuum where some make little use of its anti-racist framing. Moreover, one needs to avoid essentialism in thinking about how these frames operate in the United States today. Neither the black counter-frame nor the dominant white racial frame it tries to counter is utilized just by members of one racial group. African Americans do have to operate out of the white frame at least some of the time, if only to accommodate whites who control aspects of their lives, while some do operate aggressively out of it and thereby greatly help to sustain this racist society. Additionally, some whites, albeit to varying degrees, come to understand some or many insights from the black counter-frame and act to help destroy elements of systemic racism.

From the slavery era through Jim Crow segregation to present-day discrimination, African Americans of all backgrounds have emphasized and acted on major elements of the black counter-frame, and this black resistance has regularly improved their lives and made this a better country. In effect, African Americans have frequently been an authentic *moral* conscience for a country with an immoral racist foundation. Many speeches, books, and articles of African American activists, organizational leaders, and scholars, as well as ordinary citizens constantly signal their continuing insights about and pressures for truly expanded social justice and real U.S. democracy.[37]

Contemporary African American intellectuals and scholar-activists have contributed numerous other critical analytical tools necessary to better understand and to change this highly racist society. Let us consider briefly two of these essential contributions, the Afrocentric perspective and the womanist (gendered-racism) perspective. Working in the tradition of W. E. B. Du Bois, Marcus Garvey, and Malcolm X, numerous contemporary African American scholars and community leaders have continued to emphasize and extend the importance of African values and traditions. Contemporary manifestations of this include a comprehensive Afrocentric perspective, one aggressively critical of continuing white cultural imperialism.

Drawing on earlier African-oriented analysts, scholar-activists such as Molefi Kete Asante, Maulana Karenga, and Marimba Ani have forcefully developed an influential concept of Afrocentricity to counter the dominance of a white-centered Eurocentric culture and educational system. These scholar-activists are particularly concerned with the absorption of Eurocentric culture by African Americans, young and old, and with countering it with a heavy and creative emphasis on African origins and African and African American history, values, and concepts. A scholar-activist, Molefi Kete Asante has published many books advocating black cultural liberation and fleshing out a critical Afrocentric perspective; he founded the first PhD program in African American studies (Temple University). A 1960s black power activist and Africana studies scholar, Maulana Karenga originated a holiday (Kwanzaa) designed to assertively celebrate African and African American heritages of contemporary African Americans. Marimba Ani, an anthropologist, has developed an Afrocentric framing that problematizes white sociocultural imperialism for projecting its European ideology in all historically white institutions. In her detailed assessments, including in her path-breaking book, *Yurugu*, a realistic recognition of Eurocentric cultural imperialism means that African Americans must direct their "energies toward the recreation of cultural alternatives informed by ancestral visions of a future that celebrates Africanness."[38]

Over recent decades, African American scholars and scholar-activists have also done innovative work to demonstrate the gendered-racism aspects of oppression in three racist regimes—slavery, legal segregation, and contemporary systemic racism. To take a major example, the scholar-activist Angela Davis has examined how enslaved black women faced both racialized oppression and gendered oppression. They were exploited for their labor and as breeders of enslaved children who would become yet more highly exploited workers. Focusing on the contemporary scene, social scientist Philomena Essed has examined and named the "gendered racism" faced by black women in both the United States and Europe. She was one of the first to assess *intersectionality* issues—specifically, how the experiences of women of color with racial discrimination are distinctively gendered in numerous ways. Moreover, in a series of path-breaking articles and books, sociologist Patricia Hill Collins has honed a black feminist counter-framing of society, including deeply critical assessments of prevailing negative stereotypes and imagery of black women. These commonplace gendered-racist framings of black women are still regularly fostered by the mostly white-controlled mainstream media. Numerous contemporary African American researchers have emphasized the importance of liberating women of color from racial, gender, and gendered-racist framing and discrimination.[39]

Significantly, as we have seen in earlier chapters, early black female analysts did much to lay the groundwork for this recent analysis and naming of the concept of gendered racism. Thus, in the late nineteenth and early twentieth centuries, a few pioneering African American activist-scholars such as Ida B. Wells-Barnett were the first to do a sociological analysis of rape and lynching and of the sexual violence regularly used by white men on black women. She was part of a larger movement of African American women who protested rape and violence issues a century ago. As one recent scholarly analysis has underscored, long before the contemporary white feminist movement accented rape issues, these public protests by African American women had "galvanized local, national, and even international outrage and sparked larger campaigns for racial justice and human dignity."[40]

Global Contexts and Impacts of Black Freedom Movements

Going back to the enslavement era, numerous African Americans, especially freedom rights leaders, have had a strong international orientation and significant international linkages. This international tradition has long been a central aspect of African American history, and its meaning can be clearly seen in numerous areas, including in supportive African American reactions to the "organized Black struggle in overseas lands, as this process has supported the historic struggle against racism."[41] Note, too, that African Americans have created international linkages without getting the support of the U.S. government, indeed, often against its directives.

International Linkages: A Two-Way Street

The international linkages have long been a two-way street. In a 1950s lecture in Europe, Richard Wright emphasized the impact of African American writers and activists on global freedom and justice efforts: "The voice of the American Negro is rapidly becoming the most representative voice of America and of oppressed people anywhere in the world today."[42] Indeed, African American resistance movements have often inspired movements against oppression across the globe, even in Europe. For instance, in 1945, the influential German theologian, Dietrich Bonhoeffer, was hanged by the German Nazis for organizing anti-Nazi resistance among church leaders. In his writings, Bonhoeffer made clear he was greatly influenced by African American resistance to oppression, including songs that were important in black freedom movements. In the 1930s, he had studied at New York's Union Theological Seminary, during which time he was influenced by Harlem Renaissance intellectuals and activists and attended New York's Abyssinian Baptist Church. There he learned of a black Jesus committed to resistance to oppression.[43]

There is also a mostly forgotten history of interactions between Asian peoples and African Americans. In the early twentieth century, both African American leaders and political leaders in Japan were looking for support outside the racist sociopolitical spheres then controlled by Europeans and European Americans. In the 1910s–1930s era, white U.S. government officials attempted to reign in, eventually successfully, an expanding Japanese empire that was viewed as a threat to the U.S. empire in the Pacific. One response by Japanese officials was to seek a trans-Pacific alliance of the Japanese and African Americans. Indeed, black civil rights leaders and intellectuals had significantly influenced Japanese leaders, including the latter's attempts to throw off the white-racist framing of Asian "racial inferiority." In the view of Japanese leaders, African Americans were "colored yet modern and westernized" and a model for the young country of Japan "in its endeavors to reach a 'higher' level of civilization and become a member of the Western world."[44] Prior to World War II, there was extensive correspondence, travel, and other interaction between Japanese officials and African American leaders, including W. E. B. Du Bois and James Weldon Johnson.

By 1940, this important interaction had ended as the United States and Japan moved toward a war footing. Even then, many African American leaders made it clear that whites' racist views of the Japanese accounted in part for the early U.S. underestimation of the Japanese military. Soon, too, the African American leaders' approach during this war was to accent a "Double V" strategy. Thus, African Americans were in a war against fascism overseas and also against white racism facing them at home. Indeed, among some African Americans, there was significant ambivalence about the war in its first years, because of a feeling that if Japan won, African Americans might well be better off. In this view, Japan would show the white world that a "colored" nation could actually stand up to white-racist supremacy. Interestingly, even today, Japanese students read excerpts from important African American writers such as Booker T. Washington, Richard Wright, Martin Luther King, Jr., and Marian Anderson—probably more often than do most white American students.[45]

In addition, before and after World War II, there were many international linkages between major anti-colonialism activists in southern Asia (especially India) and African American activist-leaders such as W. E. B. Du Bois, Paul Robeson, and Bayard Rustin. As Nico Slate has underscored, there was a global

> constellation of connections in which nonviolent activists, Black and South Asian Muslims, Hindu reformers, Christian missionaries, followers of Marcus Garvey, African American soldiers, Indian immigrants, labor organizers, and many others forged links across

freedom struggles. . . . African Americans and South Asians together imagined a colored cosmopolitanism, a "dark" or "colored" world united in the struggle against racism, imperialism, and other forms of oppression.[46]

For example, influenced by Gandhi's nonviolent resistance ideas, Bayard Rustin, Martin Luther King's brilliant colleague, pressed these nonviolent ideas successfully on leaders of the black civil rights movement. Later on, after Gandhi's assassination, Rustin gave numerous lectures in India and Africa on how these nonviolent resistance strategies had been used in the United States and elsewhere. Many gave Rustin credit for helping to reduce nationalistic violence in India after Gandhi's death and for stimulating nonviolent efforts in African decolonization movements.[47]

For more than a century, African American leaders have interacted with, and often influenced, African leaders and other Africans. Since the 1890s, there have been numerous mutual interconnections and influences between African Americans and black South Africans. Early on, these included interactions between the South Africans and W. E. B. Du Bois, Paul Robeson, Booker T. Washington, Marcus Garvey, and numerous African American musicians. African American intellectuals and activists were early advocates of black liberation in South Africa, including the 1930s organization of the U.S. Council on African Affairs, whose task was informing the U.S. public and policymakers on intelligent policies for Africa. This organization set the foundation for later African American efforts in the 1940s–1960s, including the American Committee on Africa and the Organization of Afro-American Unity, to bring down South Africa's racist apartheid regime. During the 1950s, leaders of the African National Congress in South Africa and key leaders of the U.S. civil rights movement corresponded, thereby building up resistance movements in both countries. During and after the 1960s, numerous U.S. black intellectuals and civil rights activists migrated to African countries— for example, W. E. B. Du Bois and Shirley Graham Du Bois, Kwame Ture (Stokely Carmichael), and Maya Angelou. Some became advisors to political leaders or faculty members at universities. One goal was to assist African nation-building and emergence from colonialism; another was building up a pan-African identity.[48] The importance of this international linkage has rarely been publicly noted, and central to it were activist African Americans. One Howard University project summarizes thus: "African Americans became a metaphor for progress and success. Africans saw them as survivors of slavery who were now advancing themselves in an industrialized and westernized society similar to their own."[49]

Moreover, in the 1970s, the CBC helped to establish TransAfrica, one of the oldest African American organizations established to advocate for, as their Web site underscores, a "just US foreign policy for Africa and

Africans in the Diaspora." One function of this important organization is to disseminate accurate information about African countries and about socioeconomic and human rights issues facing Africans in the global African Diaspora.[50] In the 1980s, the Caucus worked with TransAfrica and others to spur on the U.S. anti-apartheid movement and to get a reluctant, Republican-led government to back economic sanctions against the violently racist white South African government. They were eventually successful in getting the 1986 Comprehensive Anti-Apartheid Act passed, over conservative President Ronald Reagan's veto. On another democratic rights matter, the Caucus also effectively pressured Presidents George H. W. Bush and Bill Clinton to back the legally elected president in Haiti.[51]

In an acceptance speech for the Liberty Medal in 1993, Nelson Mandela, the formerly imprisoned activist and soon-to-be president of South Africa, cited Frederick Douglass numerous times, thereby indicating the great impact of African American liberty-and-justice framing on South African revolutionaries. Indeed, at a major speech to the NAACP's 1993 convention, Mandela explained that the NAACP was an important example of anti-racist efforts that the African National Congress had also drawn on in its struggle against South African apartheid.[52]

More recently, there have been major conferences on global racism issues that again demonstrate the international impact of African American rights movements. One important example was the 2001 World Conference against Racism, Racial Discrimination, Xenophobia and Related Intolerance, which convened in Durban, South Africa. African American delegates were important in the African Descendants Caucus, which aggressively pressed for the leaders of Western countries to apologize for long years of racialized imperialism and to implement programs of reparations. After expected opposition from European and U.S. delegates, a watered-down Durban Declaration and Programme of Action included a recognition of the immorality of colonialism and slavery but without a call for meaningful reparations.[53]

In addition, we should note the fact that many African Americans have actively critiqued and resisted U.S. imperialism overseas, including imperialistic wars, now for more than a century. These included U.S. invasions of the Philippines and Cuba in the 1890s. One dramatic aspect of these U.S. wars and those since World War II is that the enemy soldiers have mostly been people of color—especially Asian (Korean, Vietnamese) and Middle Eastern peoples. The U.S. military intervention in these areas has regularly involved a white racial framing of the enemies that is in some ways similar to that of African Americans. This framing centers on the white elite's insistence that they have the right to judge and control the politics and economies of countries deemed problematical, including those well beyond U.S. borders.

As African American scholar Ron Walters has underscored, many African Americans have been quite aware of, and have opposed, U.S. wars aimed at global white dominance, even as many have also still served in U.S. armed forces for loyalty reasons.[54] Indeed, African American activists and intellectuals have often worked with anti-racist and other human rights activists in other countries against U.S. and European imperialism, whatever its form. Michael Clemons notes that historical circumstances of oppression have "rendered African Americans more likely than other racial groups to formulate and/or evolve foreign affairs interpretations and positions that are antithetical to the stance maintained by the American foreign policy establishment."[55] More frequently than whites, African American civil rights leaders, elected politicians, and appointed officials have raised questions about the imperialistic character of much U.S. involvement in military and other interventions overseas.

Not surprisingly, too, African Americans have probably been the most pacifistic of the large U.S. racial groups. Several African American civil rights activists have been prominent international pacifists—for example, Bayard Rustin, who was imprisoned for resisting the U.S. draft and played a role in the development of international anti-nuclear movements. Indeed, as Joan Lipkin puts it, he was "a model for what it means to be not just an African American citizen and an LGBT citizen, but also a global citizen. He worked on behalf of Soviet Jewry, refugees in Thailand and Cambodia, nuclear disarmament."[56]

Worldwide Response to the Black Freedom Movement

The long African American struggle for social justice has had major global impacts for centuries, to the present day. In the minds of many across the globe, African Americans, and especially civil rights leaders, have become synonymous with great resistance to oppression. One can see this impact today in a thousand places.

For example, in Belfast, Northern Ireland, there is a prominent wall mural celebrating African American freedom-fighters, with images of abolitionists Frederick Douglass, Sojourner Truth, and Harriet Tubman. In the 1840s, Douglass made an important trip to Ireland to build support for slavery's abolition in the United States. He visited during the movement to separate Ireland from the United Kingdom. He and Irish nationalists saw their liberation efforts as similar. Historian Leigh Fought has summarized the mural's layout:

> Douglass is central but connected to a broader struggle for rights for oppressed people of color. The artists trace this history from the origins of the slave trade through resistance to slavery in the U.S.,

the U.S. Civil Rights movement, resistance to apartheid in South Africa, opposition to South American dictatorships, and even—with Muhammad Ali—resistance to wars of imperialism in Southeast Asia, and all the way to the election of the first black American president.[57]

She adds that in the United States, this mural would seem to be a celebration only of black history, but the fact that it is in Belfast near other Irish Catholic murals and nationalist organization offices makes it appear as a strong declaration of "ongoing resistance." Several key points about the global impact of the African American freedom movement are clear in this mural. There is an understanding of U.S. racial history, and the Irish artists connect U.S. rights movements to other people's movements across the globe. Indeed, Irish nationalists have often cited U.S. civil rights struggles as inspirations for rebellions in Ireland. Ironically, these overseas significant understandings of U.S. civil rights movements seem more widespread and sharper than one finds today in most U.S. schools.

Recently, thousands of copies of a civil-rights-era comic book, titled "Martin Luther King and the Montgomery Story," were translated into Arabic and circulated among the Arab Spring protesters in Egypt by those seeking to generate nonviolent protests. In Hiroshima, Japan, Dr. King's birthday is celebrated as a message of peace to the world. Social movements of ordinary people in Poland, India, China, Czechoslovakia, and Romania have used documentaries on, and songs and themes from, the U.S. civil rights movement. Overseas, many have studied King's writings on nonviolent themes and strategies. His famous "Letter from Birmingham City Jail" (in response to white clergy criticizing the nonviolent movement) has been cited and used thousands of times by people in a broad array of liberation movements across the globe. Eastern European dissidents used it in protesting Communist dictatorships, as did African dissidents in numerous colonized African countries, Argentinean dissidents against a dictatorship there, and Palestinian dissidents protesting Israeli dominance. When Nelson Mandela won the presidency in South Africa, he again cited King and his perspective on freedom.[58] In all of these examples, Dr. King's name and message are used as shorthand representations of the larger African American communities' global lessons on freedom, justice, and equality. Unmistakably, many people across the globe have read the writings and speeches of African American black civil rights leaders and modeled their protests on these African American perspectives and actions.

Dr. King is also celebrated in thousands of geographical places. For example, in 1978, a large bust of King was put in the front of a historic church in a major Hungarian city. There are celebratory statues of him not only in Washington, DC but in numerous other countries, including in England's Westminster Abbey. National forests in Israel are named after King and his wife, Coretta Scott King, and many schools, streets, bridges, and other local facilities on all continents are named after Dr. King. In New Delhi, India, the Gandhi-King Plaza garden is named after the major advocates of nonviolent rights struggles. In 1989, a nonviolent study center named for King was established in Johannesburg, South Africa. Across the globe, many other research centers, organizations, educational programs, and achievement awards are named after King and earlier freedom movement leaders such as Frederick Douglass, Harriet Tubman, and W. E. B. Du Bois.[59] Indeed, Cornel West has suggested that Martin Luther King's social justice legacy seems better protected

> in Brazil, in Africa, in Asia, than in America, since that Martin is really a prophetic figure . . . . I think he is too much for America. He is too honest; he is too truthful; he is too loving for a culture that is fearful of the truth and is fearful of a genuine love especially of poor people.[60]

More recently, and in spite of his backing of Western neoliberal interventions overseas, President Barak Obama and his family have become inspirations, heroes, or role models for many people across the globe, especially men, women, and children of color. For example, numerous Africans came to one or both of Obama's inaugurations.[61] A Pew Center review of overseas polls found that Obama was popular with people of all backgrounds in countries in Africa, Europe, and Asia. A 2014 report summarized his popularity: "Half or more of the public in 27 of 43 countries surveyed by the Pew Research Center in 2014 said they had confidence in him to do the right thing in world affairs. . . ."[62] Over his two terms, huge crowds turned out to hear him speak in numerous African, Asian, and European countries that he visited, including 200,000 in one visit to Germany. He has been especially celebrated in African countries where, at one stop at a slave house in Senegal, he explained that being African American made him more committed to human rights causes. In surveys, many African men and women remain strongly impressed by and supportive of Obama's presidency. In contrast to this dramatic overseas welcoming, however, a majority of Americans in a national poll erroneously believed that Obama was not respected overseas.[63]

Additionally, First Lady Michelle Obama has become an influential role model for women of color in Africa, Europe, and Asia. Much U.S. media coverage has accented her impact on U.S. women. Yet few have recognized her consequential international impacts, especially as a woman of color who regularly expresses elements of a black counter-framing of global society—including her emphasis on the humanity and equality of women, and especially women of color. Large enthusiastic crowds have turned out in cities where she has spoken, often calling on youths to get educations so they can become leaders of the future. She has won over prominent leaders in various countries. In one event, a Buckingham Palace reception with the Queen of England, who almost never shows affection in public, the Queen put her arm around Obama's waist, and the latter reciprocated. Clearly, Barack and Michelle Obama's international influence and impact have grown over the course of their tenure as the first ever black "first family" in the U.S. White House.[64]

Conclusion

For centuries, African American activists and intellectuals have insisted on a broad collective view of this society, including an emphasis on genuine liberty and justice for all. Accenting a broad global view, Dr. Martin Luther King, Jr. described all human beings as part of a "great world house," where we must develop a collective humanistic perspective for long-term survival:

> From time immemorial human beings have lived by the principle that "self-preservation is the first law of life." But this is a false assumption. I would say that *other-preservation is the first law of life* precisely because we cannot preserve self without being concerned about preserving other selves.[65]

Present-day societies exist because of major contributions to human knowledge that diverse people within them have made and because of contributions by people in other societies and eras. Persisting and unjust major inequalities severely disrupt this process and eventually destroy all societies.

As human beings, we do have a major say about changing unjust contemporary arrangements, yet we do not choose the historical circumstances in which we act. In the case of systemic racism, those circumstances are substantially transmitted from our racialized past. The scope of racial oppression in this country's past and present is such that only *radical* solutions have any chance of bringing real liberty and justice for all. As the courageous and prophetic civil rights activist, Ella Baker, put it during the 1960s rights revolution,

> In order for . . . oppressed people to become part of a society that is meaningful, the system under which we now exist has to be radically changed. This means we have to learn to think in radical terms. I use the word radical in its original meaning—*getting down to and understanding the root cause.*[66]

Getting most whites to recognize this root cause and accept responsibility for contemporary racism is, of course, very difficult. One reason is the threat that major change would bring to whites' unjust material standing and their framing of whites as especially moral, civilized, entitled, and virtuous. In a major documentary by Lee Mun Wah, "The Color of Fear," he asks a white male participant in a racially mixed group why he cannot accept what men of color in the group are saying about harsh experiences with white racism. The white participant says that would require admitting to a horrific human reality, a "travesty of life."[67] Other teachers who deal explicitly with white-racism issues regularly get similar responses from whites. Undeniably, full acceptance of this white-racist reality would conflict with the dominant framing of white-group virtuousness and thus should require the dramatic actions to eradicate systemic racism insisted upon by African American thinkers and activists throughout this book. It would also mean whites' recognizing the massive material and nonmaterial debts (including compensatory reparations) that the white majority owes to African Americans as a group for their great labor, cultural genius, and huge sacrifices over nearly four centuries.

Given that a majority of white Americans, and many Americans of color, have explicitly or implicitly supported the continuing betrayal by this country's dominant leaders of the ideals of authentic liberty, justice, and democracy for all, it is hard to be optimistic about future positive change. Nonetheless, African Americans have faced the horrors of white oppression over centuries, and many still operate out of an assertive counter-frame and press hard for societal and global changes implementing social justice. In activist-scholar Cornel West's view, this black prophetic framing is still

> fundamentally committed to the priority of poor and working people, thus pitting it against the neoliberal regime, capitalist system, and imperial policies of the US government. The Black prophetic tradition has never been confined to the interests and situations of Black people. It is rooted in principles and visions that embrace these interests and confront the situations, but its message is for the country and world. . . . The Black prophetic tradition has tried to redeem the soul of our fragile democratic experiment.[68]

Recall that constitutional scholar Derrick Bell argued that the liberal idea of thorough racial integration has turned out to be a pipedream, for most whites have been unwilling to allow such major societal transformation. No living American is likely to see comprehensive racial integration and meaningful social justice for all. In Bell's admittedly pessimistic view, however, African Americans—and, by implication, others truly committed to social justice—must nonetheless continue their active struggles against white racism to keep gains from being rolled back, even while they must maintain a hard-nosed "racial realism" about continuing white oppression. Bell insists that "We must realize, as our slave forebears, that the struggle for freedom is, at bottom, *a manifestation of our humanity* that survives and grows stronger through resistance to oppression, even if that oppression is never overcome." To conclude his argument, he makes clear what this courageous human strategy means with a personal story from the 1960s civil rights era, one where he was once walking with a resident of the African American community of Harmony, Mississippi:

> Some Harmony residents, in the face of increasing white hostility, were organizing to ensure implementation of a court order mandating desegregation of their schools the next September. Walking with Mrs. Biona MacDonald, one of the organizers, up a dusty, unpaved road toward her modest home, I asked where she found the courage to continue working for civil rights in the face of intimidation that included her son losing his job in town, the local bank trying to foreclose on her mortgage, and shots fired through her living room window. "Derrick," she said slowly, seriously, "I am an old woman. I lives to harass white folks."[69]

Notes

Preface

1 W. E. B. Du Bois, *The Souls of Black Folk* (New York: Bantam Classic Books, 1989 [1903]), pp. 186–187.
2 W. E. B. Du Bois, *The Gift of Black Folk: The Negroes in the Making of America* (Garden City Park, NY: Square One Publishers, 2009 [1924]), p. 57. See also pp. 22–23.
3 Ralph Ellison, "What America Would Be Like without Blacks," *Time*, April 6, 1970, p. 109.
4 Angela Y. Davis, *The Meaning of Freedom: And Other Difficult Dialogues* (San Francisco, CA: City Lights Open Media, 2012), Kindle loc. 2321–2324, 2394–2395.

1 White Racism, Black Resistance

1 John Winthrop, "A Model of Christian Charity (1630)," *Collections of the Massachusetts Historical Society (Boston, 1838)*, 3rd series 7: 31–48, http://history.hanover.edu/texts/winthmod.html (accessed November 30, 2010). I have modernized the spelling. See Richard Howland Maxwell, "Pilgrim and Puritan: A Delicate Distinction," Pilgrim Society Note, Series Two, March 2003, www.pilgrimhall.org (accessed November 18, 2010).
2 A. Leon Higginbotham, Jr., *Shades of Freedom: Racial Politics and the Presumptions of the American Legal Process* (New York: Oxford University Press, 1996), pp. 14–51.
3 Ralph Ellison, "What America Would Be Like without Blacks," *Time*, April 6, 1970, p. 110.
4 Kristin Collins, "Plantation Tours Downplay Slavery: Study," *Chicago Sun-Times*, February 11, 2009, www.suntimes.com/news/nation/1424984,w-plantations-slavery-joellane-museum021109. article (accessed March 13, 2009).
5 "Torture," Google.com (accessed December 11, 2014).
6 Werner Heisenberg, *Physics and Philosophy: The Revolution in Modern Science* (London: Penguin Books, 1989 [1958]), p. 46.
7 Even savvy white scholars of racial matters fail to provide in-depth discussions of systemic racism as such. For example, Ira Berlin, *The Making of African America: The Four Great Migrations* (New York: Viking, 2010), pp. 217–219.
8 Seth Rockman, *Scraping By: Wage Labor, Slavery, and Survival in Early Baltimore* (Baltimore, MD: Johns Hopkins University Press, 2011), p. 262. See David R. Roediger, *The Wages of Whiteness: Race and the Making of the American Working Class* (New York: Verso, 1991), pp. 44 ff.
9 Herbert Aptheker, *American Negro Slave Revolts* (New York: International Publishers, 1943), pp. 12–18, 162, and passim. Current estimates are even larger than the 250 he counted.
10 Ralph Ellison, "*An American Dilemma*: A Review," in *The Collected Essays of Ralph Ellison*, ed. J. F. Callahan (New York: Random House, 2011), p. 328.
11 Joe R. Feagin, *Systemic Racism: A Theory of Oppression* (New York: Routledge, 2006), pp. 16–45. See also Joe R. Feagin and Sean Elias, "Rethinking Racial Formation Theory: A Systemic Racism Critique," *Ethnic and Racial Studies* 36 (2012): 1–30.

12 Maurice Halbwachs, *On Collective Memory*, ed. and trans. by Lewis Coser (Chicago, IL: University of Chicago Press, 1992), pp. 38, 52.

13 Nilanjana Dasgupta, Debbie E. McGhee, Anthony G. Greenwald, and Mahzarin R. Banaji, "Automatic Preference for White Americans: Eliminating the Familiarity Explanation," *Journal of Experimental Social Psychology* 36 (2000): 316–328.

14 Kristen Lavelle, *Whitewashing the South: White Memories of Segregation and Civil Rights* (Lanham, MD: Rowman & Littlefield, 2015), especially Chapter 7.

15 Gunnar Myrdal, *An American Dilemma* (New York: McGraw Hill, 1964 [1944]), vol. 2, pp. 959–960.

16 Joyce Ladner, "Introduction," in *The Death of White Sociology*, ed. Joyce Ladner (New York: Vintage Books, 1973), p. xxi. See also Lawrence W. Levine, *Black Culture and Black Consciousness: Afro-American Folk Thought from Slavery to Freedom* (New York: Oxford University Press, 2007 [1977]), Kindle loc. 6396–6399.

17 For instance, Michael Omi and Howard Winant, *Racial Formation in the United States*, 2nd ed. (New York: Routledge, 1994), p. 22.

18 William Dillon Piersen, *Black Legacy: America's Hidden Heritage* (Amherst, MA: University of Massachusetts Press, 1993), p. ix. Italics added.

19 W. E. B. Du Bois, *Black Reconstruction in America 1860–1880* (New York: Harcourt, Brace and Company, 1935), Kindle loc. 16676.

20 Frederick Douglass, "The United States Cannot Remain Half-Slave and Half-Free," in *Frederick Douglass: Selected Speeches and Writings*, eds. P. S. Foner and Y. Taylor (Chicago, IL: Lawrence Hall Books, 1999), pp. 657–658.

21 James Baldwin, *The Fire Next Time* (New York: Dell, 1962–1963), p. 20.

22 Ellison, "What America Would Be Like without Blacks," p. 109.

23 Cheryl Harris, "Whiteness as Property," in *Critical Race Theory: The Key Writings that Formed the Movement*, eds. K. Crenshaw et al. (New York: The New Press, 1995), p. 282.

24 Toni Morrison, *Playing in the Dark: Whiteness and the Literary Imagination* (New York: Vintage Books, 1992), p. 65.

25 For example, Nick Mrozinske, "Derivational Thinking and Racism," unpublished research paper, University of Florida, 1998. My recent Google searches have replicated his findings.

26 Quoted in Richard S. Newman and Roy E. Finkenbine, "Black Founders in the New Republic: Introduction," *The William and Mary Quarterly* 64 (January 2007): p. 89.

27 I am indebted here to conversations with Glenn Bracey, including this quotation.

28 "Shrinking Majority of Americans Support Death Penalty," http://www.pewforum.org/2014/03/28/shrinking-majority-of-americans-support-death-penalty/ (accessed October 27, 2014).

29 "The Death Penalty in Black and White: Who Lives, Who Dies, Who Decides," http://www.deathpenaltyinfo.org/death-penalty-black-and-white-who-lives-who-dies-who-decides (accessed October 27, 2014). I am indebted here to insights from and discussion with Adia Harvey Wingfield.

30 Gerald Horne, *The Counter-Revolution of 1776: Slave Resistance and the Origins of the United States of America* (New York: New York University Press, 2014), pp. 250–251.

31 Du Bois, *Black Reconstruction*, Kindle loc. 16956.

2 Black Labor: Building The Economy

1 "Inaugural Poem," *New York Times*, January 20, 2009, http://www.nytimes.com/2009/01/20/us/politics/20text-poem.html?ref=books (accessed May 8, 2011).

2 Frederick Douglass, *Narrative of the Life of Frederick Douglass, an American Slave : Written by Himself*, Entered, According to Act of Congress, in the Year 1845 (Clerk's Office of the District Court of Massachusetts, 1845), http://www.pinkmonkey.com/dl/library1/digi009.pdf (accessed March 10, 2002), pp. 60-61.

3 Claud Anderson, *Black Labor, White Wealth* (Edgewood, MD: Duncan & Duncan, 1994), p. 97.

4   I am indebted to discussions with Holly Hanson and draw on John Thornton, *Africa and Africans in the Making of the Atlantic World, 1400–1680* (New York: Cambridge University Press, 1992), pp. 5–9; and Howard Dodson, *Jubilee: The Emergence of African American Culture* (Washington, DC: National Geographic, 2002), p. 105.

5   Quoted in J. H. Parry and P. M. Sherlock, *A Short History of the West Indies*, 3rd ed. (New York: St. Martin's Press, 1971), pp. 110–111. Italics added.

6   See David R. Roediger and Elizabeth D. Esch, *The Production of Difference: Race and the Management of Labor in U.S. History* (New York: Oxford University Press, 2012).

7   W. E. B. Du Bois, *The Gift of Black Folk: The Negroes in the Making of America* (Garden City Park, NY: Square One Publishers, 2009 [1924]), Kindle loc. 2173.

8   George Fitzhugh, *Cannibals All! or, Slaves Without Masters* (Richmond, VA: A. Morris, Publisher, 1857), pp. 332–334. Italics added.

9   David R. Roediger, *The Wages of Whiteness: Race and the Making of the American Working Class* (rev. ed.; London: Verso, 2007), p. 144. I am indebted to research assistance from Rachel Feinstein.

10 Douglass C. North, *The Economic Growth of the United States, 1790–1860* (Englewood Cliffs, NJ: Prentice-Hall, 1961), pp. 38–45; Herbert Aptheker, *The Unfolding Drama: Studies in U.S. History*, ed. Bettina Aptheker (New York: International Publishers, 1978), p. 84 ff.

11 Fritz Hirschfeld, *George Washington and Slavery: A Documentary Portrayal* (Columbia, MO: University of Missouri Press, 1997), p. 236. See also pp. 16, 37, 68–69.

12 Ronald T. Takaki, *Iron Cages: Race and Culture in 19th Century America* (New York: Oxford University Press, 1990), pp. 43–55.

13 Carole E. Scott, "America's Colonial Period," http://freepages.history.rootsweb. com/~cescott/colonial.html (accessed December 19, 2003).

14 North, *The Economic Growth of the United States*, pp. 38–45; Takaki, *Iron Cages*, p. 77.

15 W. E. B. Du Bois, *Black Reconstruction in America, 1860–1880* (New York, Harcourt: Brace and Company, 1935), pp. 98–100 and passim.

16 Ibid.

17 The estimates are in James Marketti, "Estimated Present Value of Income Diverted During Slavery," in *The Wealth of Races: The Present Value of Benefits from Past Injustices*, ed. Richard F. America (New York: Greenwood, 1990), p. 118. I have updated Marketti's estimates to 2013 dollars. See Richard F. America, *Paying the Social Debt: What White America Owes Black America* (Westport, CT: Praeger, 1993).

18 One estimate is $100 trillion, including compounded interest. "Making the Case for Racial Reparations," *Harper's*, November 2000, http://harpers.org/archive/2000/11/making-the-case-for-racial-reparations/ (accessed January 23, 2015).

19 Samuel H. Williamson and Louis P. Cain, "Measuring Slavery in 2011," http://www. measuringworth.com/slavery.php#foot9 (accessed December 20, 2013). Italics added.

20 Sven Beckert and Seth Rockman, "How Slavery Led to Modern Capitalism," *Bloomberg News*, January 24, 2012, http://www.bloomberg.com/news/2012-01-24/how-slavery-led-to-modern-capitalism-echoes.html (accessed September 17, 2013).

21 Seth Rockman, *Scraping By: Wage Labor, Slavery, and Survival in Early Baltimore* (Baltimore, MD: Johns Hopkins University Press, 2009), Kindle loc. 231–235.

22 Peter J. Parish, *Slavery: History and Historians* (New York: Harper and Row, 1989), pp. 126–132.

23 See Du Bois, *The Gift of Black Folk*, p. 13; and Rockman, *Scraping By*, Kindle loc. 213–230.

24 Fitzhugh, *Cannibals All!* pp. 334–336.

25 Ibid.

26 Lorenzo J. Greene, *The Negro in Colonial New England* (New York: Atheneum, 1969), pp. 68–69; Ronald Bailey, "The Other Side of Slavery," *Agricultural History* 68 (Spring 1994): 36.

27 Beckert and Rockman, "How Slavery Led to Modern Capitalism." On Wall Street, see "Slave Market," http://maap.columbia.edu/place/22.html (accessed November 1, 2013); "15 Major Corporations You Never Knew Profited from Slavery," http://atlantablackstar.

com/2013/08/26/17-major-companies-never-knew-benefited-slavery/2/ (accessed January 22, 2015).

28 See Steven Deyle, *Carry Me Back: The Domestic Slave Trade in American Life* (New York: Oxford University Press, 2006), passim.

29 Rockman, *Scraping By*, Kindle loc. 213–230. Italics added.

30 See W. E. B. Du Bois, *The World and Africa: An Inquiry into the Part that Africa Played in World History* (New York: International Publishers, 1965), p. 58–80.

31 Letter to Pavel V. Annenkov, December 28,1846, as quoted in Kevin Anderson, *Marx at the Margins: On Nationalism, Ethnicity, and Non-Western Societies* (Chicago, IL: University of Chicago Press, 2010), Kindle loc. 1157–1158. Italics added.

32 Du Bois, *Black Reconstruction*, Kindle loc. 342–345.

33 Craig Steven Wilder, *Ebony and Ivy: Race, Slavery, and the Troubled History of America's Universities* (New York: Bloomsbury Press, 2013), Kindle loc. 67, 135, 161.

34 Ibid., Kindle loc. 236, 475.

35 See Joe R. Feagin, *The White Racial Frame: Centuries of Racial Framing and Counter-Framing*, 2nd ed. (New York: Routledge, 2013), pp. 3–45.

36 Wilder, *Ebony and Ivy*, Kindle loc 3572–3574.

37 Joe R. Feagin, *Racist America: Roots, Current Realities, and Future Reparations*, 3rd. ed. (New York: Routledge, 2014), pp. 73–79.

38 "Jackson City Hall," http://www2.historyarchives.org/Marker.asp?Marker=49682 (accessed February 3, 2014); "Old Arkansas State House," http://www.u-s-history.com/pages/h2132.html (accessed February 3, 2014).

39 J. A. Rogers, *Africa's Gift to America* (St. Petersburg, FL: H. M. Rogers, 1961), p. 216; "U.S. Capitol," http://www.britannica.com/EBchecked/topic/94002/United-States-Capitol (accessed November 1, 2013).

40 Theodore Kornweibel, Jr., "Railroads, Race, and Reparations," *Souls: A Critical Journal of Black Politics, Culture, and Society* 5 (2003): 23.

41 Ibid.

42 Wilder, *Ebony and Ivy*, Kindle loc. 4407. For a white conservative example, Patrick J. Buchanan, "A Brief for Whitey," March 21, 2008, www.buchanan.org (accessed January 12, 2014).

43 *Dred Scott v. John F. A. Sandford*, 60 U.S. 393, 403–408 (1857).

44 Robin L. Einhorn, "Slavery," *Enterprise & Society*, 9 (September 2008): pp. 494–495, 500.

45 Joe R. Feagin, *White Party, White Government: Race, Class, and U.S. Politics* (New York: Routledge, 2012), pp. 16–26 and passim.

46 Sally Hadden, *Slave Patrols* (Boston: Harvard University Press, 2003); Tom Kennedy, *Houston Blue: The Story of the Houston Police Department* (Denton, TX: University of North Texas Press, 2012).

47 Marcus Anthony Hunter, *Black Citymakers: How the Philadelphia Negro Challenged Urban America* (New York: Oxford University Press, 2013), p. 33. I also draw on pp. 27–30. Douglass's views are quoted by Hunter.

48 Ellis Tallman, "Some Unanswered Questions about Bank Panics," *Federal Research Bank of Atlanta Economic Review* (November/December 1988): pp. 2–10; Hunter, *Black Citymakers*, passim.

49 Frederick Douglass, "The Color Line," *North American Review* (June 1881), as excerpted in *Jones et ux. v. Alfred H. Mayer Co.*, 392 U.S. 409, 446–447 (1968). Emphasis added.

50 Gerald Jaynes, *Branches Without Roots: Genesis of the Black Working Class in the American South, 1862–1882* (New York: Oxford University Press, 1986).

51 Frederick Douglass, "I Denounce the So-Called Emancipation as a Stupendous Fraud" Speech on the occasion of the Twenty-Sixth Anniversary of Emancipation in the District of Columbia, Washington, DC, April 16, 1888, http://vi.uh.edu (accessed January 24, 2014).

52 Ibid.

53 Ibid.

54 Ida B. Wells-Barnett, *The Red Record: Tabulated Statistics and Alleged Causes of Lynching in the United States* (Published by author, 1895), Kindle loc. 1361–1364 passim.

55 Anonymous, "White People of State will Never Let Negroes rule," *Greensboro Daily News*, July 20, 1921, p. 1.

56 Ronald L. Lewis, *Black Coal Miners in America* (Lexington, KY: University Press of Kentucky, 1987).

57 See Yanick St. Jean and Joe R. Feagin, *Double Burden: Black Women and Everyday Racism* (Armonk: M. E. Sharpe, 1998), especially Chapters 3–4.

58 Harvard Sitkoff, *A New Deal for Blacks: The Emergence of Civil Rights as a National Issue* (New York: Oxford, 1978), pp. 37–38.

59 Terence Fitzgerald, *Black Males and Racism: Improving the Schooling and Life Chances of African Americans* (Boulder, CO: Paradigm Publishers, 2013), pp. 30–32; John M. Brackett, "Cutting Costs by Cutting Lives: Prisoner Health and the Abolishment of Florida's Convict-Lease System," *Southern Studies* 14 (2007): 69–83; Douglas A. Blackmon, *Slavery by Another Name: The Re-Enslavement of Black Americans from the Civil War to World War II* (New York: Anchor Books, 2009), p. 185 ff; Alex Lichtenstein, *Twice the Work of Free Labor: The Political Economy of Convict Labor in the New South* (New York: Verso, 1996).

60 Dwight T. Farnham, "Negroes a Source of Industrial Labor," *Industrial Management* 56 (1918): 123–129. See David R. Roediger and Elizabeth D. Esch, *The Production of Difference: Race and the Management of Labor in U.S. History* (New York: Oxford University Press, 2012).

61 Elizabeth Esch and David Roediger, "One Symptom of Originality: Race and the Management of Labour in the History of the United States," *Historical Materialism* 17 (2009): 1. I also draw on pp. 19, 31, 38–39. See Feagin, *White Party, White Government.*

62 Esch and Roediger, "One Symptom of Originality," pp. 1, 19, 31, 38–39.

63 Roediger and Esch, *The Production of Difference,* passim.

64 Rudi Williams, "African Americans Gain Fame as World War II Red Ball Express Drivers," *American Forces Press Service,* http://www.defense.gov/News/NewsArticle. aspx?ID=43934 (accessed February 20, 2014).

65 "A Brief History of the Tuskegee Airmen," http://www.redtail.org/the-airmen-a-brief-history/ (accessed February 20, 2014).

66 Ibid.

67 See Philip A. Klinkner and Rogers M. Smith, *The Unsteady March: The Rise and Decline of Racial Equality in America* (Chicago, IL: University of Chicago Press, 2002), pp. 3 ff; and Feagin, *White Party, White Government,* especially Chapter 5.

68 Paul T. Murray, "Blacks and the Draft: A History of Institutional Racism," *Journal of Black Studies* 2 (September 1971): 57–76.

69 Oliver C. Cox, *Caste, Class, and Race* (Garden City, NY: Doubleday, 1948), p. 332.

70 I have updated the data in David H. Swinton, "Racial Inequality and Reparations," in *The Wealth of Races,* p. 156. See also Roger L. Ransom and Richard Sutch, "Growth and Welfare in the American South in the 19th Century," in *Market Institutions and Economic Progress in the New South 1865–1900,* eds. Gary Walton and James Shepherd (New York: Academic Press, 1981), pp. 150–151.

71 Melvin L. Oliver and Thomas M. Shapiro, *Black Wealth/White Wealth: A New Perspective on Racial Equality* (New York: Routledge, 1995), pp. 51–52.

72 Derrick Bell, "Property Rights in Whiteness—their Legal Legacy, their Economic Costs," in *Critical Race Theory: the Cutting Edge,* ed. Richard Delgado (Philadelphia: Temple University Press, 1995), p. 75.

73 Feagin, *Racist America,* pp. 178–189.

74 Sidney M. Willhelm, *Who Needs the Negro?* (Cambridge, MA: Schenkman, 1970); Sidney M. Willhelm, *Black in a White America* (Cambridge, MA: Schenkman, 1983).

75 Thomas J. Sugrue, *The Origins of the Urban Crisis: Race and Inequality in Postwar Detroit* (rev. ed.; Princeton, NJ: Princeton University Press, 2005), Kindle loc. 270–290.

76 Willhelm, *Who Needs the Negro?*

77 Michelle Alexander, *The New Jim Crow: Mass Incarceration in the Age of Colorblindness* (New York: The New Press, 2010), pp. 49, 186.
78 Ibid., pp. 53, 186; and Verna M. Weaver, "Frontlash: Race and the Development of Punitive Crime Policy," *Studies in American Political Development* 21 (Fall 2007): 242–243. See also Feagin, *White Party, White Government*, pp. 105–111.
79 "Criminal Justice Fact Sheet," NAACP, http://www.naacp.org/pages/criminal-justice-fact-sheet (accessed December 30, 2013); Feagin, *Racist America*, pp. 158–161.
80 Fitzgerald, *Black Males and Racism;* and Angela Y. Davis, "Masked Racism: Reflections on the Prison Industrial Complex," in *Race and Resistance: African Americans in the 21st Century,* ed. Herb Boyd (Cambridge, MA: South End Press, 2002), p. 57.
81 Caitlin Seandel, "Prison Labor: Three Strikes and You're Hired," June 27, 2013, http://ellabakercenter.org/blog/2013/06/prison-labor-is-the-new-slave-labor (accessed December 29, 2013).
82 Zatz is quoted in Rania Khalek, "21st-Century Slaves: How Corporations Exploit Prison Labor," http://www.alternet.org/story/151732/21st-century_slaves%3A_how_corporations_exploit_prison_labor?paging=off&current_page=1#bookmark (accessed December 30, 2013).
83 Fitzgerald, *Black Males and Racism,* p. 31.
84 Khalek, "21st-Century Slaves"; and Seandel, "Prison Labor".
85 William A. Darity, Jr., "Forty Acres and a Mule: Placing the Price Tag on Oppression," in *The Wealth of Races,* p. 11. Several scholars have put the total figures, including lost interest, in the trillions.
86 Trina Williams, "The Homestead Act—Our Earliest National Asset Policy," paper presented at the Center for Social Development's symposium, Inclusion in Asset Building, St. Louis, Missouri, September 21–23, 2000.
87 *Pigford v. Veneman*: Consent Decree in Class Action Suit by African American Farmers, Background and Current Status, Federation of Southern Cooperatives Land Assistance Fund, available at http://www.usda.gov/da/consentsum.htm. See also Jennifer Myers, "Rough Terrain," *Legal Times* (November 18, 2002), p. 1, and Joe Feagin, Clairece Feagin, and David Baker, *Social Problems,* 6th ed. (Upper Saddle River, NJ: Prentice-Hall, 2005), p. 49.
88 Trevor Delaney, "Subprime Lenders Under Fire," *Black Enterprise* (October 2007): 31–32; Vikas Bajaj and Ford Fessenden, "What's Behind the Race Gap?" *New York Times,* November 4, 2007, p. 18.
89 Amaad Rivera, Brenda Cotto-Escalera, Anisha Desai, Jeannette Huezo, and Dedrick Muhammad, *Foreclosed: State of the Dream 2008* (Boston: United for a Fair Economy, 2008).
90 Stephen Jay Gould, *The Panda's Thumb: More Reflections in Natural History* (New York: W. W. Norton, 1922), p. 151. See Ruth Thompson-Miller, Joe R. Feagin, and Leslie H. Picca, *Jim Crow's Legacy: The Segregation Stress Syndrome* (Lanham, MD: Rowman & Littlefield, 2015).
91 Jennifer C. Mueller, personal e-mail communication, July 11, 2013. See also Jennifer Mueller, "The Social Reproduction of Systemic Racial Inequality" unpublished PhD dissertation, Texas A&M University, 2013.
92 Kwame Ture [Stokely Carmichael] and Charles V. Hamilton, *Black Power: The Politics of Liberation in America* (New York: Vintage Books, 1967).
93 Angela Davis, "Reflections on the Black Woman's Role in the Community of Slaves," *Black Scholar* 3 (December 1971): 2–15; Philomena Essed, *Understanding Everyday Racism* (Newbury Park, CA: Sage, 1991).

3 Black Genius Shaping U.S. Culture

1 See Joe R. Feagin, *Systemic Racism: A Theory of Oppression* (New York: Routledge, 2006), Chapter 2, and Thomas Jefferson, *Notes on the State of Virginia,* ed. F. Shuffleton (New York: Penguin Books, 1999 [1785]).

2 See Stanford Lyman, *The Black American in Sociological Thought* (New York: Putnam, 1972), and Lawrence W. Levine, *Black Culture and Black Consciousness: Afro-American Folk Thought from Slavery to Freedom* (New York: Oxford University Press, 2007), Kindle loc. 6396–6399. See also Gunnar Myrdal, *An American Dilemma* (New York: McGraw-Hill, 1964 [1994]), vol. 2, pp. 928–929.
3 Ralph Ellison, *Shadow and Act* (New York: Random House, 1995), pp. 315–316.
4 Ibid.
5 Adrian Miller, *Soul Food* (Chapel Hill, NC: University of North Carolina Press, 2013), Kindle loc. 195–196.
6 W. E. B. Du Bois, *The Souls of Black Folk* (Mineola, NY: Dover, 1994), Kindle loc. 74–80.
7 Akinyele Omowale Umoja, *We Will Shoot Back: Armed Resistance in the Mississippi Freedom Movement* (New York: New York University Press, 2013), Kindle loc. 191–197.
8 Craig Wilder, *In the Company of Black Men: The African Influence on African American Culture in New York City* (New York: New York University Press, 2001), p. 13.
9 Ibid., pp. 10–11. Wilder is summarizing research in Sylviane A. Diouf, *Servants of Allah: African Muslims Enslaved in the Americas*, 15th anniversary ed. (New York: New York University Press, 2013).
10 I am indebted here to suggestions from Glenn Bracey.
11 Patricia Hill Collins, "Learning from the Outsider Within: The Sociological Significance of Black Feminist Thought," *Social Problems* 33 (October–December, 1986): S22.
12 Child Development Institute, *Achieving Cultural Competence: Children's Mental Health* (Toronto: Child Development Institute, 2007), p. 4.
13 William Dillon Piersen, *Black Legacy: America's Hidden Heritage* (Amherst, MA: University of Massachusetts Press, 1993), p. ix.
14 "Recognizing the Importance of African-American Music to Global Culture and Calling on the People of the United States to Study, Reflect On, and Celebrate African-American music," 106th CONGRESS, 2d Session, H. RES. 509, https://www.govtrack.us/congress/bills/106/hres509/text/ih (accessed November 17, 2014).
15 Cornel West and Christa Buschendorf, *Black Prophetic Fire* (Boston: Beacon Press, 2014), Kindle loc. 1757–1761.
16 Howard Dodson, "America's Cultural Roots Traced to Enslaved African Ancestors," *National Geographic*, February 5, 2003, http://news.nationalgeographic.com/news/2003/02/0205_030205_jubilee4.html (accessed June 30, 2014).
17 Sterling Stuckey, *Slave Culture: Nationalist Theory and the Foundations of Black America*, 2nd ed. (New York: Oxford University Press, 2013), Kindle loc. 535–541. I draw here on John Stauffer, "Foreword," in Stuckey, *Slave Culture*, Kindle loc. 160.
18 Charles Keil, *Urban Blues* (Chicago, IL: University of Chicago Press, 1966), p. 16. See also Tamara Moffett, "The History of African-American Music," http://www.ehow.com/about_5212464_history-african_american-music.html (accessed January 16, 2015).
19 Mel Watkins, *On the Real Side: A History of African American Comedy*, 2nd ed. (Chicago, IL: Chicago Review Press, 1999), pp. 58–62.
20 Kevin Phinney, *Souled American: How Black Music Transformed White Culture* (New York: Billboard Books, 2005), p. 25. Italics added.
21 Piersen, *Black Legacy*, p. 183.
22 Eric Lott, *Love and Theft: Blackface Minstrelsy and the American Working Class* (New York: Oxford University Press, 1993), pp. 3–4.
23 Robert C. Toll, *Blacking Up: The Minstrel Show in Nineteenth Century America* (New York: Oxford University Press, 1974), passim; and Lott, *Love and Theft*, pp. 3–4.
24 Lott, *Love and Theft*, pp. 8–13; and David Roediger, *The Wages of Whiteness: Race and the Making of the American Working Class*, 2nd ed. (New York: Verso, 2007), passim.
25 See examples in "Minstrel Show," wikipedia, http://en.wikipedia.org/wiki/Minstrel_show#cite_ref-105 (accessed May 16, 2014).
26 James Oliver Horton and Lois E. Horton, *In Hope of Liberty: Culture, Community and Protest among Northern Free Blacks, 1700–1860* (New York: Oxford University Press, 1998), Kindle loc. 3655.
27 Lott, *Love and Theft*, pp. 3–5.

28 Ibid., pp. 4–5; Joe Feagin, *The White Racial Frame: Centuries of Racial Framing and Counter Framing*, 2nd ed. (New York: Routledge, 2013), pp. 127–128 and passim. See the BET series on white celebrities like Billy Crystal at 2012 Oscars doing blackface stunts at, for example, http://www.bet.com/celebrities/photos/2013/05/celebrities-in-blackface.html#!052813-celebs-in-blackface-Billy-Crystal-oscars (accessed July 3, 2014).

29 Du Bois, *The Souls of Black Folk*, p. 119.

30 Levine, *Black Culture and Black Consciousness*, Kindle loc. 631, 1284.

31 Herbert Marcuse, *The Aesthetic Dimension* (Boston, MA: Beacon Press, 1977 [2003]), p. 9. Italics added.

32 Melville J. Herskovits, *The Myth of the Negro Past* (New York: Harper & Brothers, 1941), p. 261.

33 This is taken from an RCA Victor record cover for the New World Symphony, 1953. Some have questioned whether Dvořák made this exact comment or whether it was a paraphrase by a journalist. Italics are added.

34 Michael Beckerman, "The Real Value of Yellow Journalism: James Creelman and Antonin Dvořák," *The Musical Quarterly*, 77 (Winter 1993): 749–768. See also John Edward Philips, "The African Heritage of White America," in *Africanisms in American Culture*, J. E. Holloway, ed. (Bloomington, IN: Indiana University Press, 1990), p. 236 ff.

35 Stuckey, *Slave Culture*, Kindle loc. 213–220.

36 Frederick Douglass, *From Narrative of the Life of Frederick Douglass, Written by Himself*, ed. David W. Blight (Boston: St. Martin's Press, 1993), pp. 46–47, as quoted at http://www.kansasheritage.org/crossingboundaries/narrative.html (accessed May 30, 2014). Italics added.

37 Marcuse, *The Aesthetic Dimension*, p. 14.

38 Angela Y. Davis, *Blues Legacies and Black Feminism: Gertrude Ma Rainey, Bessie Smith, and Billie Holiday* (New York: Knopf Doubleday, 1998), Kindle loc. 442–444.

39 Daphne Duval Harrison, *Black Pearls: Blues Queens of the 1920s* (New Brunswick, NJ: Rutgers University Press, 1990), p. 10. See "Sister Rosetta Tharpe," http://www.biography.com (accessed January 20, 2015).

40 Davis, *Blues Legacies and Black Feminism*, Kindle loc. 236–241.

41 West and Buschendorf, *Black Prophetic Fire*, Kindle loc. 764–770.

42 Ibid., Kindle loc. 726–728, 742–745.

43 James Weldon Johnson, "Preface," in *The Book of American Negro Poetry*, ed. James Weldon Johnson (New York: Harcourt, Brace and Company, 1922), Kindle loc. 159–163.

44 Ibid., Kindle loc. 132–136.

45 Herskovits, *The Myth of the Negro Past*, p. 261.

46 James M. Gregory, *The Southern Diaspora: How the Great Migrations of Black and White Southerners Transformed America* (Chapel Hill, NC: University of North Carolina Press, 2005), p. 326.

47 Davarian L. Baldwin, "Our Newcomers to the City," in *Beyond Blackface: African Americans and the Creation of American Popular Culture, 1890–1930*, ed. W. F. Brundage (Chapel Hill, NC: University of North Carolina Press, 2011), p. 180.

48 Peter M. Rutkoff and Willima B. Scott, *Fly Away: The Great African American Cultural Migrations* (Baltimore, MD: Johns Hopkins University Press, 2010), pp. 12–13; Gregory, *The Southern Diaspora*, p. 326.

49 B. Lee Cooper, "Review of Hidden in the Mix: The African-American Presence in Country Music," *Popular Music and Society*, (October 14, 2013), published online at DOI: 10.1080/03007766.2013.844911 (accessed July 3, 2014). See Diane Pecknold (ed.), *Hidden in the Mix: The African-American Presence in Country Music* (Durham, NC: Duke University Press, 2013).

50 Patrick Huber, "Black Hillbillies: African American Musicians on Old-Time Records, 1924–1932," in *Hidden in the Mix: The African American Presence in Country Music* (Durham, NC: Duke University Press, 2013), Kindle loc. 549–553.

51 Ibid., Kindle loc. 452–499; Piersen, *Black Legacy*, pp. 184–185.
52 "Whites, Blacks, and the Blues," PBS.org, ww.pbs.org/theblues/classroom/intwhitesblacks.html (accessed April 13, 2014).
53 Ibid.
54 John Hope Franklin and Evelyn Brooks Higginbotham, *From Slavery to Freedom* (New York: McGraw-Hill, 2010), pp. 381–390.
55 Gordon Hancock papers, box 2, Duke University Library, n.d. (ca. 1950s).
56 "Whites, Blacks, and the Blues." Other cultural impacts included distinctive types of hand-slapping and hair styling and shifts in clothing fashions.
57 Keil, *Urban Blues*, p. 16.
58 Marian Mair, "Black Rhythm and British Reserve: Interpretations of Black Musicality in Racist Ideology Since 1750," unpublished dissertation, University of London, 1987. This is from the summary.
59 Mair, "Black Rhythm and British Reserve."
60 Tricia Rose, *The Hip-hop Wars: What We Talk about When We Talk about Hip-hop – and Why It Matters* (New York: Basic Books, 2008), pp. 1–2. I am indebted here to comments from Wally Hart.
61 Jay-Z, "Introduction," in Michael E. Dyson, *Know What I Mean? Reflections on Hip-Hop* (New York: Basic Books, 2007), p. ii.
62 Rose, *The Hip-hop Wars*, pp. 1–2. I am indebted here to comments from Wally Hart.
63 Dyson, *Know What I Mean?*, Kindle loc. 173.
64 Ibid., pp. 66, 86.
65 "Whites, Blacks, and the Blues."
66 Ibid.
67 Rose, *The Hip-hop Wars*, p. 139; Walter Edward Hart, "The Culture Industry, Hip-hop Music and the White Perspective: How One-Dimensional Representation of Hip-hop Music Has Influenced White Racial Attitudes," unpublished master's thesis, University of Texas at Arlington, 2009.
68 I am indebted here to suggestions from Kimberley Ducey and Wally Hart.
69 Ian Condry, "Yellow B-Boys, Black Culture, and Hip-Hop in Japan: Toward a Transnational Cultural Politics of Race," *Positions* 15 (2007): 638. See also West and Buschendorf, *Black Prophetic Fire*, Kindle loc. 1209–1211.
70 Condry, "Yellow B-Boys, Black Culture, and Hip-Hop in Japan," p. 663.
71 Joseph E. Holloway, "African Contributions to American Culture," http://slaverebellion.org/index.php?page=african-contribution-to-american-culture (accessed June 29, 2014).
72 Eileen Southern, *The Music of Black Americans*, 3rd ed. (New York: W. W. Norton, 1997), pp. 409–416.
73 Ibid., pp. 514–586.
74 Ibid., pp. 431–434.
75 Hunter Havelin Adams, III, "African and African-American Contributions to Science and Technology," Portland Public Schools Geocultural Baseline Essay Series, Portland, Oregon, 1986, p. 65.
76 Ibid., p. 71.
77 Piersen, *Black Legacy*, p. 99.
78 George W. Williams, *History of the Negro Race in America from 1619 to 1880*, (New York: G. P. Putnam's Sons, 1883), vol. 2, Kindle loc. 9275.
79 John H. Lienhard, "Black Inventors," *University of Houston Engineering Series*, http://www.uh.edu/engines/epi127.htm (accessed March 12, 2014).
80 Jeffrey C. Stewart, *1001 Things Everyone Should Know about African American History* (New York: Doubleday, 1996), pp. 321–337.
81 Ibid., pp. 337–352.
82 John T. Barber, *The Black Digital Elite* (New York: Praeger, 2006), p. xiii.
83 Ibid., pp. 1–29.
84 Judith A. Carney and Richard M. Rosomoff, *In the Shadow of Slavery: Africa's Botanical Legacy in the Atlantic World* (Berkeley: University of California Press, 2009), Kindle loc. 119–120.

85 Ibid., Kindle loc. 100–111. See also Melville Herskovits, "What has Africa Given America?" *New Republic* 84 (1935): 92–94.
86 Miller, *Soul Food*, Kindle loc. 330–333; Piersen, *Black Legacy*, p. 171. See also Psyche A. Williams-Forson, *Building Houses out of Chicken Legs: Black Women, Food, and Power* (Chapel Hill, NC: University of North Carolina Press, 2006), Kindle loc. 81–82.
87 Judith Ann Carney, *Black Rice* (Cambridge, MA: Harvard University Press, 2002), Kindle loc. 120–121. See also Walter Hawthorne, "African Foods and the Making of the Americas," http://www.common-place.org/vol-11/no-03/reviews/hawthorne.shtml (accessed March 14, 2014).
88 Peter A. Coclanis, "White Rice: The Midwestern Origins of the Modern Rice Industry in the United States," http://www.history.upenn.edu/economichistoryforum/docs/coclanis_13a.pdf (accessed March 14, 2014); and Clifford D. Conner, *A People's History of Science* (New York: Nation Books, 2005), pp. 89–93.
89 Carney, *Black Rice*, Kindle loc. 30-31.
90 Philips, "The African Heritage of White America," p. 232. I also draw from Holloway, "African Contributions to American Culture."
91 See Philips, "The African Heritage of White America."
92 Johnson, *The Book of American Negro Poetry*, Kindle loc. 159–166.
93 Jupiter Hammon, "An Address to the Negroes in the State of New-York," 1787, http://digitalcommons.unl.edu/cgi/viewcontent.cgi?article=1011&context=etas (accessed January 7, 2015). I am using information from an abstract by Paul Royster at http://digitalcommons.unl.edu/etas/12/ (accessed January 7, 2015). See also Mola Lenghi, "UTA Student Discovers Forgotten Poem by Nation's First African-American Writer," http://www.nbcdfw.com/news/local/UTA-Student-Discovers-Forgotten-Poem-by-Nations-First-African-American-Writer-190931171.html (accessed January 7, 2015).
94 Johnson, *The Book of American Negro Poetry*, Kindle loc. 187–193.
95 Phillis Wheatley to Samson Occum, February 11, 1774. See *The Poems of Phillis Wheatley*, ed. Julian D. Mason, Jr. (Chapel Hill, NC: University of North Carolina Press, 1989), pp. 203–204. See also Peter A. Dorsey, 'To Corroborate Our Own Claims': Public Positioning and the Slavery Metaphor in Revolutionary America," *American Quarterly* 55 (September 2003), pp. 366–367.
96 Absalom Jones and Richard Allen, "A Narrative of the Proceedings of the Black People During the Late Awful Calamity in Philadelphia," in *Pamphlets of Protest*, eds. Richard Newman, Patrick Rael, and Philip Lapsansky (New York: Routledge, 2001), p. 42.
97 Henry Bibb, "Narrative of the Life and Adventures of Henry Bibb," as quoted in William Andrews, *To Tell a Free Story: The First Century of Afro-American Autobiography* (Urbana, IL: University of Illinois Press, 1886), p. 10.
98 See their writings in Patricia Madoo Lengermann and Jill Niebrugge-Brantley, eds., *The Women Founders: Sociology and Social Theory, 1830–1930* (New York: McGraw-Hill, 1998), passim.
99 "Harlem Renaissance," http://www.britannica.com/EBchecked/topic/255397/Harlem-Renaissance/272831/The-legacy (accessed March 14, 2014).
100 Ibid.
101 Ibid.
102 Ibid.
103 Davarian L. Baldwin and Minkah Makalani, eds., *Escape from New York: The New Negro Renaissance beyond Harlem* (Minneapolis, MN: University of Minnesota Press, 2013), as quoted at http://www.upress.umn.edu/book-division/books/escape-from-new-york (accessed November 20, 2014).
104 W. E. B. Du Bois, *The Gift of Black Folk: The Negroes in the Making of America* (Garden City Park, NY: Square One Publishers, 2009 [1924]), p. 139.
105 Toni Morrison, *Playing in the Dark: Whiteness and the Literary Imagination* (New York: Vintage Books, 1992), p. 63.
106 Samuel Sewall, *The Selling of Joseph, A Memorial* (Boston: Bartholomew Green and John Allen, 1700), as reprinted at http://www.pbs.org/wgbh/aia/part1/1h301t.html (accessed May 11, 2008). See also John Saffin, "A Brief, Candid Answer to a Late Printed Sheet,

Entitled, 'The Selling of Joseph,'" in *A House Divided: The Antebellum Slavery Debates in America, 1776–1865*, ed. by Mason I. Lowance, Jr. (Princeton, NJ: Princeton University Press, 2003), at http://press.princeton.edu/chapters/ s7553.html (retrieved May 11, 2008).

107 Du Bois, *The Gift*, p. 139.

108 Morrison, *Playing in the Dark*, p. 17.

109 Franklin and Higginbotham, *From Slavery to Freedom*, pp. 381–390.

110 Ralph Ellison, "What America Would Be Like without Blacks," *Time*, April 6, 1970, p. 109.

111 Watkins, *On the Real Side*, p. 69.

112 Ibid., p. 79.

113 Holloway, "African Contributions To American Culture."

114 Stuckey, *Slave Culture*, Kindle loc. 272–274.

115 Watkins, *On the Real Side*, pp. 69, 79. I am influenced by Robin Bernstein, *Racial Innocence: Performing American Childhood from Slavery to Civil Rights* (New York: New York University Press, 2011), Kindle loc. 528–530.

116 Trudier Harris, "The Trickster in African American Literature," National Humanities Center, http://nationalhumanitiescenter.org/tserve/freedom/1865-1917/essays/trickster.htm (accessed May 29, 2014).

117 Ellison, "What America Would Be Like without Blacks," p. 109. See Ralph Ellison, *Going to the Territory* (New York: Random House, 1986), pp. 111–112.

118 Quoted in Piersen, *Black Legacy*, p. 157.

119 Shelley Fisher Fiskhin, "Reclaiming the Black Presence in Mainstream Culture," in *African Roots/American Cultures*, ed. Sheila S. Walker (Lanham, MD: Rowman & Littlefield, 2001), p. 85. See Horton and Horton, *In Hope of Liberty*, Kindle loc. 3583.

120 Du Bois, *The Gift*, p. 154.

121 Du Bois, *The Souls of Black Folk*, p. 93.

122 Du Bois, *The Gift*, p. 154.

123 See list in Wikipedia, at http://en.wikipedia.org/wiki/List_of_slaves. I am indebted here to discussions with Jennifer Harvey.

124 Du Bois, *The Gift*, p. 162.

125 Herskovits, "What has Africa Given America?" pp. 92–94; Philips, "The African Heritage of White America," p. 231.

126 I am indebted here to discussions with Glenn Bracey. See Charles H. Long, *Significations: Signs, Symbols, and Images in the Interpretation of Religion*, ed. (Aurora, CO: Davies Group Publishers, 2004).

127 Piersen, *Black Legacy*, p. x.

128 David Wiggins, "Climbing the Racial Mountain: A History of the African American Experience in Sport," in *Diversity and Social Justice of College Sports: Sport Management and the Student Athlete*, eds D. Brooks and R. Althouse (Morgantown, WV: Fitness Information Technology, 2007), pp. 21–47. I am indebted to discussions with Michael Regan. See Shaun Powell, *Souled Out? How Blacks are Winning and Losing in Sports* (Champaign, IL: Human Kinetics, 2008); Russell T. Wigginton, *The Strange Career of the Black Athlete: African Americans and Sports* (Westport, CT: Praeger Publishers, 2006; Dave Zirin, *A People's History of Sports in the United States: 250 Years of Politics, Protest, People, and Play* (New York, NY: The New Press, 2008).

129 Stewart, *1001 Things Everyone Should Know About African American History*, p. 356.

130 Ibid., pp. 353–361.

131 Ibid., pp. 381–382. I am indebted here to discussion with Michael Regan.

132 Stewart, *1001 Things Everyone Should Know About African American History*, p. 383.

133 Gerald L. Early, *A Level Playing Field: African American Athletes and the Republic of Sports* (Cambridge, MA: Harvard University Press, 2011), pp. 50–51, 69; Wiggins, "Climbing the Racial Mountain," pp. 32–34.

134 Interview with Rachel Robinson, http://articles.latimes.com/1997-03-31/news/ss-43970_1_rachel-robinson (accessed August 19, 2014); Interview with Rachel Robinson, http://www.thirteen.org/metrofocus/2014/02/rachel-robinson-on-her-late-husband-jackies-legacy-race-and-baseball/ (accessed August 19, 2014).

135 Dave Zirin, "Whitewash: How The NY Times Just Rewrote The History of Sports," http://www.edgeofsports.com/2014-05-03-924/index.html (accessed May 11, 2014).
136 Wiggins, "Climbing the Racial Mountain," p. 37.
137 Earl Smith, *Race, Sport, and the American Dream*, 3rd ed. (Durham, NC: Carolina Academic Press, 2013), p. 22.
138 I am indebted here to discussions with Michael Regan.
139 See Corey Nachman, "12 Pro Athletes Who Became Successful Politicians," *Business Insider*, May 13, 2011, http://www.businessinsider.com/12-professional-athletes-turned-politicians-2011-5 (accessed July 4, 2014).
140 Philips, "The African Heritage of White America," p. 236.

4 Black Counter-Framing: Real Freedom, Justice, and Democracy (1600s–1910s)

1 Gordon S. Wood, *The Radicalism of the American Revolution* (New York: Vintage, 1993), p. 7.
2 Ralph Ellison, "What America Would Be Like without Blacks," *Time*, April 6, 1970, p. 109.
3 W. E. B. Du Bois, *The Gift of Black Folk: The Negroes in the Making of America* (Garden City Park, NY: Square One Publishers, 2009 [1924]), Kindle loc. 60, 753
4 Joe Feagin, *The White Racial Frame: Centuries of Racial Framing and Counter Framing*, 2nd ed. (New York: Routledge, 2013), passim; Jane J. Mansbridge, "The Making of Oppositional Consciousness," in *Oppositional Consciousness: The Subjective Roots of Social Protest*, eds. Jane J. Mansbridge and Aldon Morris (Chicago, IL: University of Chicago Press, 2001), pp. 1–16.
5 Francis D. Adams and Barry Sanders, *Alienable Rights: The Exclusion of African Americans in a White Man's Land, 1619–2000* (New York: HarperCollins, 2003).
6 Carter G. Woodson, *The Mind of the Negro* (Washington, DC: Association for the Study of Negro Life and History, 1926).
7 Rusticus is quoted in Richard Newman, Patrick Rael, and Phillip Lapsansky, "Introduction" in *Pamphlets of Protest: An Anthology of Early African American Protest Literature, 1790–1860*, eds. Richard Newman, Patrick Rael, and Phillip Lapsansky (New York: Routledge, 2001), p. 5.
8 The quotes are in "Letters from Africanus," *The United States Gazette*, March-April, 1790.
9 "Banneker's letter to Jefferson, 1791," *PBS Resource Bank*, http://www.pbs.org/wgbh/aia/part2/2h71.html (accessed November 28, 2010). Italics added.
10 Ibid.
11 Ibid.
12 Alexander Hamilton, James Madison, and John Jay, *The Federalist Papers*, http://www.gutenberg.org/ebooks/22788 (accessed July 5, 2011). I draw on Joe R. Feagin, *White Party, White Government: Race, Class, and U.S. Politics* (New York: Routledge, 2012), passim.
13 Alfred F. Young, Ray Raphael, and Gary Nash, "Introduction," in *Revolutionary Founders: Rebels, Radicals, and Reformers in the Making of the Nation*, eds. Alfred F. Young, Ray Raphael, and Gary Nash (New York: Vintage Books, 2012), Kindle loc. 127–130. I am influenced here by Peter A. Dorsey, *Common Bondage: Slavery as Metaphor in Revolutionary America* (Knoxville, TN: University of Tennessee Press, 2009), pp. 2–49.
14 Quoted in Richard S. Newman and Roy E. Finkenbine, "Black Founders in the New Republic: Introduction," *The William and Mary Quarterly* 64 (January 2007): 89.
15 Richard S. Newman, "Prince Hall, Richard Allen, and Daniel Coker: Revolutionary Black Founders, Revolutionary Black Communities," in *Revolutionary Founders*, p. 305.
16 Absalom Jones and Richard Allen, "A Narrative of the Proceedings of the Black People During the Late Awful Calamity in Philadelphia," in *Pamphlets of Protest*, eds. Richard Newman, Patrick Rael, and Phillip Lapsansky (New York: Routledge, 2001), pp. 41–42.
17 Coker and Forten are quoted and discussed in Newman, Rael, and Lapsansky, "Introduction," in *Pamphlets of Protest*, pp. 10–11.

18 Gary B. Nash, *The Forgotten Fifth: African Americans in the Age of Revolution* (Cambridge, MA: Harvard University Press, 2009), p. 132.

19 Ibid.

20 Robert S. Levine, "Circulating the Nation: David Walker, the Missouri Compromise, and the Rise of the Black Press," in *The Black Press: New Literary and Historical Essays*, ed. Todd Vogel (New Brunswick, NJ: Rutgers University Press, 2001), Kindle loc. 31–37, 281–282. I also draw on Todd Vogel, "Introduction," in Ibid., Kindle loc. 31–37.

21 Todd Vogel, "The New Face of Black Labor," in Ibid., Kindle loc. 495.

22 David Walker, *Appeal to the Coloured Citizens of the World*, ed. Charles M. Wiltse (New York: Hill and Wang, 1965), pp. 7, 16, and 56.

23 Opcit., p. 75. Walker's italics and punctuation.

24 David S. Cecelski, *Fire of Freedom: Abraham Galloway and the Slaves' Civil War* (Chapel Hill, NC: University of North Carolina Press, 2012), Kindle loc. 393, 410.

25 On Walker's integration orientation, see Peter Hicks, *To Awaken My Afflicted Brethren: David Walker and the Problem of Antebellum Slave Resistance* (State College, PA: Penn State University Press, 1996), pp. 237–258.

26 James Oliver Horton and Lois E. Horton, *In Hope of Liberty: Culture, Community and Protest among Northern Free Blacks, 1700–1860* (New York: Oxford University Press, 1998), pp. 174–176.

27 Ibid.

28 Henry Highland Garnet, "An Address to the Slaves of the United States of America," Buffalo, New York, 1848, in *Electronic Texts in American Studies*, University of Nebraska, Lincoln, Nebraska, pp. 2, 4, 7, 9.

29 James M. McPherson, *The Negro's Civil War: How American Blacks Felt and Acted During the War for the Union* (New York: Knopf Doubleday, 2008), Kindle loc. 4702.

30 Martin R. Delany, *The Condition, Elevation, Emigration, and Destiny of the Colored People of the United States* (Project Gutenberg ebook, 2005 [1852]), Kindle loc. 111, 361.

31 Ibid., Kindle loc. 202, 695, 492.

32 "The Reverend Alexander Crummell, 1819–1898," Episcopal Archives, http://www. episcopalarchives.org/Afro-Anglican_history/exhibit/leadership/crummell.php (accessed January 12, 2015).

33 John S. Rock, "Address to a Meeting in Boston, 1858," in *Afro-American History: Primary Sources*, ed. Thomas R. Frazier (New York: Harcourt Brace Jovanovich, 1971), pp. 71–73; and Newman, Rael, and Lapsansky, "Introduction" in *Pamphlets of Protest*, p. 13.

34 "Journal of Charlotte Forten Grimké, Free Woman of Color, Selections from 1854 to 1859," *National Humanities Center Resource Toolbox: The Making of African American Identity: vol. I, 1500–1865*, p. 7.

35 Elizabeth F. Chittenden, *Profiles in Black and White: Stories of Men and Women Who Fought Against Slavery* (New York: Atheneum, 1973), p. 112. See also "Charlotte Forten Grimke," http://voices.cla.umn.edu/artistpages/grimkeCharlotte.php (accessed July 23, 2014).

36 Jane Rhodes, *Mary Ann Shadd Cary: The Black Press and Protest In The 19th Century* (Bloomington, IN: Indiana University Press, 1998), pp. x–xviii; and Adrienne Shadd, "Mary Ann Shadd Cary: Abolitionist," Library and Archives Canada, http://www. collectionscanada.gc.ca/northern-star/033005-2201-e.html (accessed July 23, 2014).

37 Mary A. Shadd, *A Plea for Emigration* (Detroit, MI: George W. Pattison, 1852), p. 44.

38 Frederick Douglass, *Narrative of the Life of Frederick Douglass* (Boston: Anti-Slavery Office, 1845); Frederick Douglass, *My Bondage and My Freedom* (New York: Miller, Orton, and Mulligan, 1855).

39 Harriet Jacobs, *Incidents in the Life of a Slave Girl* (Boston: Thayer and Eldridge, 1861).

40 Frederick Douglass, "The Meaning of July Fourth for the Negro," July 5, 1852, http:// www.pbs.org/wgbh/aia/part4/4h2927.html (accessed August 21, 2013).

41 Shelley Fisher Fishkin and Carla L. Peterson, "'We Hold These Truths to Be Self-Evident': The Rhetoric of Frederick Douglas's Journalism," in *The Black Press: New Literary and Historical Essays*, ed. Todd Vogel (New Brunswick, NJ: Rutgers University Press, 2001), Kindle loc., 1063–1064.

42 Frederick Douglas, "West India Emancipation," August 3, 1857, http://www.blackpast.org/?q=1857-frederick-douglass-if-there-no-struggle-there-no-progress (accessed January 13, 2015).

43 Ibid.

44 W. E. B. Du Bois, *John Brown* (New York: Random House, [1909] 2001), p. 252.

45 Frederick Douglass, "The Proclamation and the Negro Army," speech at Cooper Institute, New York, February 6, 1863, http://www.sethkaller.com/about/educational/douglass/ (accessed July 14, 2014).

46 Quoted in John Stauffer, *Giants: The Parallel Lives of Frederick Douglass and Abraham Lincoln* (New York: Hachette Books, 2008), Kindle loc. 3592.

47 Quoted in Ibid., Kindle loc. 4868.

48 Frederick Douglass, "The United States Cannot Remain Half-Slave and Half-Free," in *Frederick Douglass: Selected Speeches and Writings*, eds. P. S. Foner and Y. Taylor (Chicago, IL: Lawrence Hall Books, 1999), pp. 657–658.

49 Frederick Douglass, "I Denounce the So-Called Emancipation as a Stupendous Fraud," Speech on the Occasion of the Twenty-Sixth Anniversary of Emancipation in the District of Columbia, Washington, DC, April 16, 1888, http://vi.uh.edu (accessed January 24, 2014).

50 See Stauffer, *Giants*, Kindle loc. 400, 4463.

51 Cornel West and Christa Buschendorf, *Black Prophetic Fire* (Boston: Beacon Press, 2014), Kindle loc. 201–205.

52 Albion W. Tourgée, "A Memorial of Frederick Douglass from the City of Boston (1895)," in *Undaunted Radical: The Selected Writings and Speeches of Albion W. Tourgée*, ed. Mark Elliott (Baton Rouge, LA: Louisiana State University Press, 2010), Kindle loc. 4049–4091.

53 Carolyn Karcher, "Introduction," in Albion W Tourgée, *Bricks without Straw: A Novel* (Durham, NC: Duke University Press, 2009), p. 2.

54 See Anna Julia Cooper, *The Voice of Anna Julia Cooper*, eds. Charles Lemert and Esme Bhan (Lanham, MD: Rowman & Littlefield, 1998); Ida B. Wells-Barnett, *The Red Record: Tabulated Statistics and Alleged Causes of Lynching in the United States* (Chicago, IL: Donohue and Henneberry, 1895).

55 *Crusade for Justice: The Autobiography of Ida B. Wells*, ed. A. M. Duster (Chicago, IL: University of Chicago Press, 1970); Joe R. Feagin, *The White Racial Frame: Centuries of Racial Framing and Counter-Framing*, 2nd ed. (New York: Routledge, 2013), pp. 173–174; West and Buschendorf, *Black Prophetic Fire*, Kindle loc. 2221–2210.

56 Wells-Barnett, *The Red Record*, Kindle loc. 1483; see also Paula J. Giddings, *When and Where I Enter*, 2nd ed. (New York: HarperCollins, 2009), Kindle loc. 220–233.

57 Tommy J. Curry, "The Fortune of Wells: Ida B. Wells-Barnett's Use of T. Thomas Fortune's Philosophy of Social Agitation as a Prolegomenon to Militant Civil Rights Activism," *Transactions of the Charles S. Peirce Society*, 48 (2012): 456–482.

58 Ida B. Wells, "The Lyncher Winces," *New York Age*, September 19, 1891, as quoted in Curry, "The Fortune of Wells," p. 465. Italics added.

59 Wells-Barnett, *The Red Record*, Kindle loc. 1474–1479.

60 Curry, "The Fortune of Wells," pp. 466–467; Emma Lou Thornbrough, *T. Thomas Fortune: Militant Journalist* (Chicago, IL: University of Chicago, 1972); Emma Lou Thornbrough, "The National Afro-American League, 1887–1908," in *Journal of Southern History* 27, No. 4 (November 1961): 494–512.

61 "William Monroe Trotter," http://www.britannica.com/EBchecked/topic/973555/William-Monroe-Trotter (accessed January 14, 2015).

62 C. Eric Lincoln and Lawrence H. Mamiya, *The Black Church in the African American Experience* (Durham, NC: Duke University Press, 1990), Kindle loc. 410–416 424–428.

5 Black Action: Accelerating Freedom, Justice, and Democracy (1700s–1800s)

1 See John Hope Franklin and Loren Schweninger, *Runaway Slaves: Rebels on the Plantation* (New York: Oxford University Press, 2000), Kindle loc. 232–243.
2 Henry Louis Gates, Jr., "Did African-American Slaves Rebel?" pbs.org, http://www.pbs.org/wnet/african-americans-many-rivers-to-cross/history/did-african-american-slaves-rebel/ (accessed July 28, 2014).
3 Gary B. Nash, *The Forgotten Fifth: African Americans in the Age of Revolution* (Cambridge, MA: Harvard University Press, 2006), pp. 3–6, 18, 23. See also Alfred F. Young, Ray Raphael, and Gary Nash, *Revolutionary Founders: Rebels, Radicals, and Reformers in the Making of the Nation* (New York: Random House, 2011), Kindle loc. 216–220.
4 "Black Sailors and Soldiers in the War of 1812," http://www.pbs.org/wned/war-of-1812/essays/black-soldier-and-sailors-war (accessed July 31, 2014).
5 Seth Rockman, *Scraping By: Wage Labor, Slavery, and Survival in Early Baltimore* (Baltimore, MD: Johns Hopkins University Press, 2011), p. 262. See David R. Roediger, *The Wages of Whiteness: Race and the Making of the American Working Class* (New York: Verso, 1991), pp. 44 ff.
6 Nash, *The Forgotten Fifth*, p. 18.
7 "Petition of Absalom Jones and Others," December 30, 1799, *Records of the U. S. House of Representatives*, Record Group 233 (4~HR6A-F4.2. Jan. 2, 1800), National Archives, Washington, DC, as reprinted at Roy Rosenzweig Center for History and New Media, George Mason University, http://chnm.gmu.edu/fairfaxtah/documents/absalomjones.doc (accessed July 8, 2014).
8 Richard S. Newman, "Prince Hall, Richard Allen, and Daniel Coker: Revolutionary Black Founders, Revolutionary Black Communities," in *Revolutionary Founders*, pp. 319–320. See also Stephen Kantrowitz, *More Than Freedom: Fighting for Black Citizenship in a White Republic, 1829–1889* (New York: Penguin Press, 2012), Kindle loc. 176.
9 John Wood Sweet, *Bodies Politic: Negotiating Race in the American North, 1730–1830* (College Park, PA: University of Pennsylvania Press, 2006), pp. 351–352.
10 Newman, "Prince Hall, Richard Allen, and Daniel Coker," p. 306.
11 Frederick Douglass, *Narrative of the Life of Frederick Douglass, an American Slave. Written by Himself*, Entered according to Act of Congress, in the Year 1845 (Clerk's Office of the District Court of Massachusetts, 1845), http://www.pinkmonkey.com/dl/library1/digi009.pdf (accessed March 10, 2002), p. 68.
12 Frederick Douglass, *My Bondage and My Freedom* (New York: Humanity Books, 2002 [1855]), p. 282.
13 Declaration of Independence, "Original Rough Draught," June 1776, http://www.pbs.org/jefferson/archives/documents/frame_ih198038.htm (accessed July 30, 2014).
14 Walter C. Rucker, "Westmoreland Slave plot of 1687," *Encyclopedia Virginia*, online at http://www.encyclopediavirginia.org/Westmoreland_Slave_Plot_1687 (accessed December 13, 2012).
15 James Oliver Horton and Lois E. Horton, *In Hope of Liberty: Culture, Community and Protest among Northern Free Blacks, 1700–1860* (New York: Oxford University Press, 1998), Kindle loc. 1155.
16 I draw on summaries by Henry Louis Gates, Jr., "Did African-American Slaves Rebel?" pbs.org, http://www.pbs.org/wnet/african-americans-many-rivers-to-cross/history/did-african-american-slaves-rebel/ (accessed July 28, 2014); and Joe R. Feagin and Clairece B. Feagin, *Racial and Ethnic Relations*, 8th ed. (Upper Saddle River, NJ: Prentice-Hall, 2008), pp. 197–198.
17 Steven Hahn, *The Political Worlds of Slavery and Freedom* (Cambridge, MA: Harvard University Press, 2009), Kindle loc. 209.
18 Gates, "Did African-American Slaves Rebel?"; Feagin and Feagin, *Racial and Ethnic Relations*, pp. 197–198.

19 Alan Gilbert, *Black Patriots and Loyalists: Fighting for Emancipation in the War for Independence* (Chicago, IL: University of Chicago Press, 2012), p. 257.
20 Daniel Rasmussen, *American Uprising: The Untold Story of America's Largest Slave Revolt* (New York: HarperCollins, 2011), Kindle loc. 1170–1178.
21 Ibid., Kindle loc. 1323–1563.
22 Ibid., Kindle loc. 1653, 1848.
23 Ibid., Kindle loc. 1848–1873.
24 Ibid., Kindle loc. 1991.
25 Sterling Stuckey, *Slave Culture* (New York: Oxford University Press, 1987), pp. 27–43; Nat Turner, http://en.wikipedia.org/wiki/Nat_Turner (accessed June 6, 2008); and Feagin and Feagin, *Racial and Ethnic Relations*, pp. 197–198.
26 Manning Marable, *Living Black History: How Reimagining the African-American Past Can Remake America's Racial Future* (New York: Basic Books, 2011), p. 4.
27 Fergus Bordewich, *Bound for Canaan: The Epic Story of the Underground Railroad* (New York: HarperCollins, 2007), passim.
28 Ibid., Kindle loc. 274.
29 Ibid., Kindle loc. 288. Italics added.
30 "Declaration of the Immediate Causes Which Induce and Justify the Secession of South Carolina from the Federal Union," Yale Avalon Project, http://avalon.law.yale.edu/19th_century/csa_scarsec.asp (accessed August 24, 2014).
31 Kantrowitz, *More than Freedom*, Kindle loc. 2933, 4420; Mark A. Lause, *Race and Radicalism in the Union Army* (Champaign, IL: University of Illinois Press, 2009), Kindle loc. 379.
32 W. E. B. Du Bois, *John Brown* (New York: International Publishers, 1962), pp. 263–265; W. E. B. Du Bois, *The Gift of Black Folk: The Negroes in the Making of America* (Garden City Park, NY: Square One Publishers, 2009 [1924]), Kindle loc. 1705.
33 Osborne P. Anderson, "A Voice from Harper's Ferry," http://www.historyisaweapon.com/defcon1/andersonvoiceharpersferry.html (accessed July 24, 2014). See also Osborne P. Anderson, "A Voice from Harper's Ferry: A Narrative of Events at Harper's Ferry; With, Incidents Prior and Subsequent to its Capture by Captain Brown and His Men," (Boston: Printed for the author, 1861), in Jean Libby, *Black Voices from Harper's Ferry: Osborne Anderson and the John Brown Raid* (Palo Alto, CA: Jean Libby, 1979), pp. 59–62.
34 Anderson, "A Voice from Harper's Ferry."
35 Hannah N. Geffert, "John Brown and His Black Allies: An Ignored Alliance," *The Pennsylvania Magazine of History and Biography* 126 (October 2002): 601–607.
36 Anderson, "A Voice from Harper's Ferry." See also Geffert, "John Brown and His Black Allies," pp. 601–607.
37 Geffert, "John Brown and His Black Allies," p. 607.
38 Kantrowitz, *More Than Freedom*, Kindle loc. 4197.
39 Judkin Browning, "Visions of Freedom and Civilization Opening before Them: African Americans Search for Autonomy During Military Occupation in North Carolina," in *North Carolinians in the Era of the Civil War and Reconstruction*, ed. P. D. Escott (Chapel Hill, NC: University of North Carolina Press, 2008), p. 70.
40 See Browning, "Visions of Freedom and Civilization Opening before Them," p. 72 ff.
41 Alys Eve Weinbaum, "Gendering the General Strike: W. E. B. Du Bois's Black Reconstruction and Black Feminism's 'Propaganda of History,'" *South Atlantic Quarterly* 112 (2013): 437–463.
42 Bordewich, *Bound for Canaan*, Kindle loc. 292.
43 William Loren Katz, "Lincoln, the Movie," portside.com, http://lists.portside.org/cgi-bin/listserv/wa?A2=PORTSIDE;89ff2d2b.1212c (accessed July 27, 2014); Hahn, *The Political Worlds of Slavery and Freedom*, Kindle loc. 453.
44 Quoted in James M. McPherson, *The Negro's Civil War: How American Blacks Felt and Acted During the War for the Union*, 2nd ed. (New York: Anchor Books, 1991), Kindle loc. 762.
45 David S. Cecelski, *Fire of Freedom: Abraham Galloway and the Slaves' Civil War* (Chapel Hill, NC: University of North Carolina Press, 2012), Kindle loc. 106. See also "The

Emancipation Declaration," http://www.historylearningsite.co.uk/emancipation-declaration.htm (accessed August 15, 2014).
46 Cecelski, *Fire of Freedom*, Kindle loc. 106.
47 Kantrowitz, *More Than Freedom*, Kindle loc. 4917–4940.
48 McPherson, *The Negro's Civil War*, Kindle loc. 3648.
49 Katz, "Lincoln, the Movie."
50 Abraham Lincoln, "Public Letter to James Conkling," August 26, 1863, http://millercenter.org/president/lincoln/speeches/speech-3510 (accessed August 25, 2014).
51 Lause, *Race and Radicalism in the Union Army*, Kindle loc. 1693.
52 *John Washington's Civil War*, ed. Crandall Shifflett (Baton Rouge, LA: Louisiana State University Press, 2008), p. 49. I removed a little capitalization and clarified two words.
53 Quoted in David W. Blight, *A Slave No More: Two Men Who Escaped to Freedom* (Orlando: Harcourt, Inc, 2007), p. 257
54 Cecelski, *Fire of Freedom*, Kindle loc. 2787, 2967–2985. The quotes are at loc. 2994 and 4399.
55 Ibid., Kindle loc. 142. See Deborah Beckel, *Radical Reform: Interracial Politics in Post-Emancipation North Carolina* (Charlottesville, VA: University of Virginia Press, 2010), pp. 39–40.
56 Quoted in David E. Swift, *Black Prophets of Justice: Activist Clergy before the Civil War* (Baton Rouge, LA: Louisiana State University Press, 1989), p. 332.
57 James M. McPherson, *The Negro's Civil War: How American Blacks Felt and Acted During the War for the Union* (New York: Knopf Doubleday, 2008), Kindle loc. 4713–4735.
58 Manning Marable, *Race, Reform, and Rebellion: The Second Reconstruction and Beyond in Black America, 1945–2006*, 3rd ed. (Oxford, MS: University Press of Mississippi, 2007), Kindle loc. 119.
59 Kantrowitz, *More Than Freedom* location 154, 5150–5205
60 Marable, *Race, Reform, and Rebellion*, Kindle loc. 119.
61 Eric Foner, *Freedom's Lawmakers: A Directory of Black Officeholders During Reconstruction* (New York: Oxford, 1993), pp. ix–xxxi.
62 W. E. B. Du Bois, *Black Reconstruction in America, 1860-1880* (New York: Harcourt, Brace and Company, 1935), Kindle loc. 16676.
63 Quoted in Ronald C. White, Jr., *Liberty and Justice for All: Racial Reform and the Social Gospel (1877-1925)* (Louisville, KY: Westminster John Knox Press, 2002), pp. 3–4, 8–9.
64 Mark Elliott, *Undaunted Radical: The Selected Writings and Speeches of Albion W. Tourgée* (Baton Rouge, LA: Louisiana State University Press, 2010), p. 227.

6 Black Counter Framing and Liberatory Action (1900s–1970s)

1 Ralph Ellison, "What America Would Be Like without Blacks," *Time*, April 6, 1970, p. 109.
2 See Ira Katznelson, *When Affirmative Action Was White: An Untold History of Racial Inequality in 20th-Century America* (New York: W. W. Norton, 2006).
3 Ruth Thompson-Miller, Joe R. Feagin, and Leslie H. Picca, *Jim Crow's Legacy: The Lasting Impact of Segregation* (Lanham, MD: Rowman & Littlefield, 2015).
4 Aldon Morris, "A Retrospective on The Civil Rights Movement: Political and Intellectual Landmarks," *Annual Review of Sociology* 25 (1999): 538.
5 Mary Church Terrell, "In Union There is Strength," http://www.blackpast.org/1897-mary-church-terrell-union-there-strength#sthash.XUJXFpcK.dpuf (accessed October 7, 2014).
6 Ibid.
7 Mary Church Terrell, "The Progress of Colored Women, Address Before The National American Women's Suffrage Association," February 18, 1898, ttp://gos.sbc.edu/t/terrellmary.html (accessed July 23, 2014).

8 Mary Church Terrell, "What It Means to be Colored in the Capital of the United States," *The Independent*, January 24, 1907, http://www.americanrhetoric.com/speeches/ marychurchterrellcolored.htm (accessed July 22, 2014).

9 Joe R. Feagin, *Racist America: Roots, Current Realities, and Future Reparations*, 3rd ed. (New York: Routledge, 2014), pp. 30–32.

10 Steven Hahn, *The Political Worlds of Slavery and Freedom* (Cambridge, MA: Harvard University Press, 2009), Kindle loc. 854.

11 Ibid., Kindle loc. 1150–1160.

12 Ibid., Kindle loc. 640–673.

13 W. E. B. Du Bois, *The Philadelphia Negro: A Social Study* (Millwood, NY: Kraus-Thomson, [1899] 1973).

14 Francille Rusan Wilson, *The Segregated Scholars: Black Social Scientists and the Creation of Black Labor Studies, 1890–1950* (Charlottesville, VA: University of Virginia Press, 2006), pp. 249–253; Herman Schwendinger and Julia Schwendinger, *The Sociologists of the Chair: A Radical Analysis of the Formative Years of North American Sociology (1883–1922)* (New York: Basic Books, 1974), p. 506.

15 W. E. B. Du Bois, *Black Reconstruction in America 1860–1880* (New York: Atheneum, 1992 [1935]), p. 715.

16 W. E. B. Du Bois, *Dusk of Dawn: An Essay Toward an Autobiography of a Race Concept* (New Brunswick, NJ: Transaction Books, 1984 [1940]), p. 131.

17 W. E. B. Du Bois, *The Souls of Black Folk* (New York: Bantam Books, 1989 [1903]), p. 3.

18 See W. E. B. Du Bois, "On the Ruling of Men," in *The Oxford W. E. B. Du Bois Reader*, ed. Eric J. Sundquist (New York: Oxford University Press, 1996), pp. 555–557.

19 W. E. B. Du Bois et al., "Appeal to the World: A Statement on the Denial of Human Rights to Minorities in the Case of Citizens of the United States of America and an Appeal to the United Nations for Redress, 1947," quoted in Mary L. Dudziak, *Cold War Civil Rights: Race and the Image of American Democracy* (Princeton, NJ: Princeton University Press, 2011), p. 45.

20 Ibid.

21 "We Charge Genocide," Petition to the United Nations, 1951, http://www.blackpast.org/ (accessed December 31, 2014).

22 See W. E. B. Du Bois, *The World and Africa* (New York: International Publishers, 1965 [1946]), p. 23 ff.

23 Gunnar Myrdal, *An American Dilemma*, (New York: McGraw-Hill, 1964 [1944]), vol. 1, p. 4.

24 Nikhil P. Singh, *Black is a Country: Race and the Unfinished Struggle for Democracy* (Cambridge, MA: Harvard University Press, 2004), Kindle loc. 1916.

25 W. E. B. Du Bois, *The Autobiography of W. E. B. Du Bois* (New York: International Publishers, 1968); Ralph Ellison, *Shadow and Act* (New York: Random House, 1964). I am influenced here by Singh, *Black is a Country*, Kindle loc. 2076–2078.

26 Oliver C. Cox, *Caste, Class, and Race: A Study in Social Dynamics* (New York: Doubleday, 1948), pp. 332, 531.

27 Oliver Cromwell Cox, *Capitalism and American Leadership* (New York: Philosophical Library), p. 288.

28 Eric Foner, *The Story of American Freedom* (New York: W. W. Norton, 1999), p. 245.

29 Devon Carbado and Donald Weiss, eds., *Time on Two Crosses: The Collected Writings of Bayard Rustin* (San Francisco, CA: Cleis Press, 2003), Kindle loc. 107–109.

30 Robert L. Allen, *The Brotherhood of Sleeping Car Porters* (Boulder, CO: Paradigm Publishers, 2014), p. 127.

31 Robert Caro, *The Years of Lyndon Johnson: Master of The Senate* (New York: Knopf, 2002), pp. 97, 100; Benjamin Quarles, *The Negro in the Making of America* (New York: Simon and Schuster, 1996), p. 253 and passim.

32 James N. Gregory, *The Southern Diaspora: How the Great Migrations of Black and White Southerners Transformed America* (Chapel Hill, NC: University of North Carolina Press, 2005), p. 327.

33 Keneshia Grant, "Relocation & Realignment: How the Great Migration Changed the Face of the Democratic Party," unpublished PhD dissertation, Syracuse University, 2014, pp. 58–60.

34 Henry Lee Moon, *Balance of Power: The Negro Vote* (Garden City, NY: Doubleday, 1948), p. 40.

35 Nancy Joan Weiss, *Farewell to the Party of Lincoln: Black Politics in the Age of FDR* (Princeton, NJ: Princeton University Press, 1983), p. 43.

36 David Karol, *Party Position Change in American Politics: Coalition Management* (Cambridge, England: Cambridge University Press, 2009), Kindle loc. 25–30; Moon *Balance of Power*, passim.

37 Grant, "Relocation & Realignment," pp. 51–52, 92–93, 100, 114; Moon, *Balance of Power*, passim.

38 Isabel Wilkerson, *The Warmth of Other Suns: The Epic Story of America's Great Migration* (New York: Knopf Doubleday, 2010), Kindle loc. 362–366.

39 Gregory, *The Southern Diaspora*, p. 326.

40 Ibid., Kindle loc. 362–366.

41 Claudia Jones, "An End to the Neglect of the Problems of the Negro Woman!" in *Let Nobody Turn Us Around: An African American Anthology*, eds. Manning Marable and Leith Mullings (Lanham, MD: Rowman & Littlefield, 2009), pp. 316–317.

42 Robin D. G. Kelley, *Freedom Dreams: The Black Radical Imagination* (Boston: Beacon Press, 2003), p. 57. See also Kenneth Janken, "From Colonial Liberation to Cold War Liberalism: Walter White, the NAACP, and Foreign Affairs, 1941–1955," *Ethnic and Racial Studies* 12 (1998): 1074–1095.

43 James L. Roark, "American Black Leaders: The Response to Colonialism and the Cold War, 1943–1953," *African Historical Studies* 4 (1971): 270.

44 "Southern Regional Council is Organized," *Southern Frontier*, August 1943, n.p. See "Letter to Dr. Hancock from Jessie Daniel Ames," August 1946, Gordon B. Hancock papers, Rubenstein Collection, Duke University Library, Durham, NC.

45 See newspaper clippings in Jessie Daniel Ames papers, Southern Historical Collection, University of North Carolina, Chapel Hill, NC.

46 Joe Feagin, "School Desegregation: A Political-Economic Perspective," in *School Desegregation: Past, Present, and Future*, eds. Walter Stephan and Joe R. Feagin (New York: Plenum Press, 1980), pp. 25, 29–35; Philip A. Klinkner and Rogers M. Smith, *The Unsteady March: The Rise and Decline of Racial Equality in America* (Chicago, IL: University of Chicago Press, 1999), pp. 3–4; and Richard M. Valelly, *The Two Reconstructions* (Chicago, IL: University of Chicago Press, 2004), Kindle loc. 2372.

47 Jo Ann Gibson Robinson, *The Montgomery Bus Boycott and the Women Who Started It*, ed. D. J. Garrow (Knoxville, TN: University of Tennessee Press, 1987), Kindle loc. 61–90.

48 Fannie Lou Hamer, http://www.findagrave.com/cgi-bin/fg.cgi?page=gr&GRid=19859 (accessed January 22, 2015).

49 Barbara Ransby, *Ella Baker and the Black Freedom Movement: A Radical Democratic Vision* (Chapel Hill, NC: University of North Carolina Press, 2003), pp. 13–63, 137–145; and Richard M. Valelly, *The Two Reconstructions: The Struggle for Black Enfranchisement* (Chicago, IL: University of Chicago Press, 2004), Kindle loc. 2382.

50 Ransby, *Ella Baker and the Black Freedom Movement*, pp. 5–6.

51 Stephen Kantrowitz, *More Than Freedom: Fighting for Black Citizenship in a White Republic, 1829–1889* (New York: Penguin Press, 2012), Kindle loc. 7220.

52 Manning Marable, *Living Black History: How Reimagining the African-American Past Can Remake America's Racial Future* (New York: Perseus Books, 2005), Kindle loc. 88.

53 Valelly, *The Two Reconstructions*, Kindle loc. 2573.

54 President Lyndon Johnson, "We Shall Overcome," http://www.historyplace.com/speeches/johnson.htm (accessed September 16, 2014).

55 Thomas J. Sugrue, *Sweet Land of Liberty: The Forgotten Struggle for Civil Rights in the North* (New York: Random House, 2008), Kindle loc. 225.

56 See Alvin B. Tillery, Jr., *Between Homeland and Motherland: Africa, U.S. Foreign Policy, and Black Leadership in America* (Ithaca, NY: Cornell University Press, 2011), p. 5.

57 Dudziak, *Cold War Civil Rights*, p. 11.
58 Moon, *Balance of Power*, p. 40.
59 John H. Franklin, *From Slavery to Freedom*, 4th ed. (New York: Knopf, 1974), p. 421.
60 Derrick Bell, *"Brown v. Board of Education* and the Interest Convergence Dilemma," *Harvard Law Review* 93 (1980): 518.
61 Lyndon B. Johnson, "To Fulfill These Rights," June 4, 1965, http://www.lbjlib.utexas.edu/johnson/archives.hom/speeches.hom/650604.asp (accessed July 9, 2008).
62 Coretta Scott King, ed., *The Words of Martin Luther King, Jr.* (New York: Newmarket Press, 1996), p. 52.
63 James M. Washington, ed., *A Testament of Hope: The Essential Writings and Speeches of Martin Luther King* (New York: HarperCollins, 1991), p. 314. Italics added.
64 "Honoring Dr. Du Bois," in *Black Titan: W. E. B. Du Bois*, ed. John Henrik Clarke et al. (Boston: Beacon Press, 1970), p. 183.
65 Quoted in William Henry Chafe, *The Unfinished Journey: America Since World War II* (New York: Oxford University Press, 2003), p. 354. Italics added.
66 Carbado and Weiss, *Time on Two Crosses*, p. 124.
67 Cornel West and Christa Buschendorf, *Black Prophetic Fire* (Boston: Beacon Press, 2014), Kindle location 994–996.
68 Ibid., Kindle loc. 1076.
69 Charles E. Cobb, Jr., *This Nonviolent Stuff'll Get You Killed: How Guns Made the Civil Rights Movement Possible* (New York: Basic Books, 2014), pp. 233–235.
70 Robert F. Williams, *Negroes with Guns* (New York: Marzani and Munsell Publishers, 1962); Daniel Rasmussen, *American Uprising: The Untold Story of America's Largest Slave Revolt* (New York: HarperCollins, 2011), Kindle loc. 2439–2455; Tommy J. Curry and Max Kelleher, "Robert F. Williams and Militant Civil Rights: The Legacy and Philosophy of Pre-emptive Self-Defense," *Radical Philosophy Review* 18 (2015): forthcoming.
71 Lance Hill, *The Deacons for Defense: Armed Resistance and the Civil Rights Movement* (Chapel Hill, NC: University of North Carolina Press, 2006), Kindle loc. 72–73.
72 Cobb, *This Nonviolent Stuff'll Get You Killed*, Kindle loc. 309-313.
73 Akinyele Omowale Umoja, *We Will Shoot Back: Armed Resistance in the Mississippi Freedom Movement* (New York: New York University Press, 2013), Kindle loc. 122-134.
74 Hill, *The Deacons for Defense* Kindle loc. 45.
75 Ibid., Kindle loc. 149–151.
76 Ibid., Kindle loc. 259.
77 Joe R. Feagin and Harlan Hahn, *Ghetto Revolts: The Politics of Violence in American Cities* (New York: Macmillan, 1973), pp. 167–198, 263–332.
78 Ibid., pp. 57–97; and Jeanne Theoharis, "Alabama on Avalon: Rethinking the Watts Uprising and the Character of Black Protest in Los Angeles," in *The Black Power Movement: Rethinking the Civil Rights-Black Power Era*, ed. Peniel E. Joseph (New York: Routledge, 2006), pp. 29–31.
79 Cobb, *This Nonviolent Stuff'll Get You Killed*, pp. 233–235.
80 Peniel E. Joseph, *Waiting 'Til the Midnight Hour: A Narrative History of Black Power in America* (New York: Holt, 2007), Kindle loc. 42.
81 John J. Goldman, "Stokely Carmichael, Black Activist, Dies," November 16, 1998, http://articles.latimes.com/1998/nov/16/news/mn-43406 (accessed October 9, 2014).
82 Stokely Carmichael (Kwame Ture) and Charles V. Hamilton, *Black Power* (New York: Vintage, 1967).
83 West and Buschendorf, *Black Prophetic Fire*, Kindle loc. 1794–1798.
84 Manning Marable, *Malcolm X: A Life of Reinvention* (New York: Viking, 2011), Kindle loc. 9142 and passim.
85 Ibid., Kindle loc. 9144–9147.
86 Joseph, *Waiting 'Til the Midnight Hour*, p. 14.
87 Marable, *Malcolm X*, Kindle loc. 9207–9209.
88 Todd Vogel, ed., *The Black Press: New Literary and Historical Essays* (New Brunswick, NJ: Rutgers University Press, 2001), Kindle loc. 3008.

89 Jed S. Serrano "The X Factor: How Malcolm X Internationalized the Civil Rights Movement," *Student Pulse*, 2010, http://www.studentpulse.com/articles/231/2/the-x-factor-how-malcolm-x-internationalized-the-civil-rights-movement (accessed July 3, 2014).

90 Jeffrey C. Stewart, *1001 Things Everyone Should Know about African American History* (New York: Doubleday, 1996), p. 383.

91 Joyce M. Bell, *The Black Power Movement and American Social Work* (New York: Columbia University Press, 2014), p. 44; National Association of Black Social Workers, "History," http://nabsw.org/?page=History (accessed September 18, 2014).

92 See Bell, *The Black Power Movement and American Social Work*, Chapter 3.

93 Ibram H. Rogers, *The Black Campus Movement: Black Students and the Racial Reconstitution of Higher Education, 1965–1972* (New York: Palgrave Macmillan, 2012), Kindle loc. 217-222 and 253–258.

94 Ibid., p. 219.

95 Fabio Rojas, *From Black Power to Black Studies How a Radical Social Movement Became an Academic Discipline* (Baltimore, MD: Johns Hopkins University Press, 2007), p. 219.

96 Ibid., pp. 5–15.

97 Carbado and Weiss, *Time on Two Crosses*, pp. 123–124.

98 Morris, "A Retrospective On The Civil Rights Movement," p. 527.

99 Ibid., p. 529. I am indebted here to conversations with Glenn Bracey.

100 Singh, *Black is a Country*, Kindle loc. 716. See Brenda Gayle Plummer, *In Search of Power* (Cambridge, England: Cambridge University Press, 2012), Kindle loc. 351 and passim.

101 Feagin, *Racist America*, pp. 273 ff.

102 Ibid., pp. 83–84. See also Bell, *The Black Power Movement and American Social Work*.

103 Joe R. Feagin, *White Party, White Government: Race, Class, and U.S. Politics* (New York: Routledge, 2012), pp. 86–97.

104 West and Buschendorf, *Black Prophetic Fire*, Kindle loc. 31–32.

105 Sugrue, *Sweet Land of Liberty*, Kindle loc. 8978.

106 Joe R. Feagin, Clairece B. Feagin, and David Baker, *Social Problems*, 6th ed. (Upper Saddle River, NJ: Prentice-Hall, 2005), pp. 128–131, 395–401; Sugrue, *Sweet Land of Liberty*, Kindle loc. 9467.

7 Contemporary Global Impacts: Freedom, Justice, and Democracy

1 Richard Wright, *Black Power: Three Books from Exile: Black Power; The Color Curtain; and White Man, Listen!* (New York: HarperCollins, 2008), p. 769. I am indebted here to conversations with Kimberley Ducey.

2 Martin Luther King, Jr., *Where Do We Go from Here: Chaos or Community*, (New York: Bantam Books, 1967), p. 7.

3 Rakesh Kochhar and Richard Fry, "Wealth Inequality has Widened along Racial, Ethnic Lines since End of Great Recession," Pew Research Center, December 12, 2014, http://www.pewresearch.org/fact-tank/2014/12/12/racial-wealth-gaps-great-recession/ (accessed December 12, 2014); Pew Research Center, "King's Dream Remains an Elusive Goal; Many Americans See Racial Disparities," August 22, 2013, http://www.pewsocialtrends.org/files/2013/08/final_full_report_racial_disparities.pdf (accessed December 12, 2014); Pew Research Center, "Public School Enrollment Disparities Exist 60 Years after Historic Desegregation Ruling," May 16, 2014, http://www.pewresearch.org/fact-tank/2014/05/16/public-school-enrollment-disparities-exist-60-years-after-historic-desegregation-ruling/ (accessed December 12, 2014).

4 Kevin Stainback and Donald Tomaskovic-Devey, *Documenting Desegregation* (New York: Russell Sage Foundation, 2012), pp. 298–299, 320.

5 See Joe R. Feagin, *Racist America: Roots, Current Realities, and Future Reparations*, 3rd edn. (New York: Routledge, 2014), Chapter 7 and passim.

6 Louwanda Evans, *Cabin Pressure* (Lanham, MD: Rowman & Littlefield, 2013), p. 103.

7   Stephen Kantrowitz, *More Than Freedom: Fighting for Black Citizenship in a White Republic, 1829-1889* (New York: Penguin Press, 2012), Kindle loc. 7276-7286. On meritocracy, see Nancy DiTomaso, *The American Non-Dilemma: Racial Inequality without Racism* (New York: Russell Sage Foundation, 2013), pp. 64-66 and passim.

8   Thomas J. Sugrue, *The Origins of the Urban Crisis: Race and Inequality in Postwar Detroit* (rev. ed.; Princeton, NJ: Princeton University Press, 2005), Kindle loc. 8900-9000.

9   See C. Eric Lincoln and Lawrence H. Mamiya, *The Black Church in the African American Experience* (Durham, NC: Duke University Press, 1990), Kindle loc. 410-416 and 424-428.

10 Craig Steven Wilder, *In the Company of Black Men: The African Influence on African American Culture in New York City* (New York: New York University Press, 2001), p. 3.

11 Manning Marable, *The Great Wells of Democracy: The Meaning of Race in American Life* (New York: Basic Books, 2003), pp. 5-6.

12 Marable, *The Great Wells of Democracy*, p. xiv.

13 Sekou M. Franklin, *After the Rebellion: Black Youth, Social Movement Activism, and the Post-Civil Rights Generation* (New York: New York University Press, 2014), Kindle loc. 203-230 and passim.

14 Ibid., Kindle loc. 203-230.

15 See Joe R. Feagin, *White Party, White Government: Race, Class, and U.S. Politics* (New York: Routledge, 2012), especially Chapter 7.

16 Ibid., pp. 54-72. See also Tali Mendelberg, *The Race Card: Campaign Strategy, Implicit Messages, and the Norm of Equality* (Princeton, NJ: Princeton University Press, 2001), p. 13.

17 See Christina R. Rivers, *Congressional Black Caucus, Minority Voting Rights, and the U.S. Supreme Court* (Ann Arbor, MI: University of Michigan Press, 2012), Kindle loc. 53-56.

18 "Congressional Black Caucus," http://cbc.fudge.house.gov/about/our-history/ (accessed October 16, 2014).

19 Major Owens, *The Peacock Elite, A Case Study of the Congressional Black Caucus* (Jonesboro, AK: Grant House Publishers, 2011). I also draw on summaries of the book here: http://www.amazon.com/Peacock-Elite-Study-Congressional-Caucus/dp/1935316419/ref=sr_1_4?s=books&ie=UTF8&qid=1413484544&sr=1-4&keywords=congressional+black+caucus (accessed October 16, 2014). See Alvin B. Tillery, Jr., *Between Homeland and Motherland: Africa, U.S. Foreign Policy, and Black Leadership in America* (Ithaca, NY: Cornell University Press, 2011), p. 7.

20 Quoted at "Congressional Black Caucus," http://www.dkosopedia.com/wiki/Congressional_Black_Caucus (accessed December 28, 2012). I also draw on "Our History," http://thecongressionalblackcaucus.com/about/our-history (accessed December 28, 2012).

21 "Great Migration," *Africana: The Encyclopedia of the African and African American Experience*, eds. Kwame A. Appiah and Henry L. Gates, Jr., vol. 3, 2nd ed. (New York: Oxford University Press, 2005), p. 53.

22 Yanick St. Jean and Joe R. Feagin, *Double Burden: Black Women and Everyday Racism* (Armonk, NY: M. E. Sharpe, 1998), pp. 83-84.

23 Adia Harvey Wingfield, *Doing Business with Beauty: Black Women, Hair Salons, and the Racial Enclave Economy* (Lanham, MD: Rowman & Littlefield, 2008), p. 92.

24 Evans, *Cabin Pressure*, passim.

25 Leslie Houts and Joe R. Feagin, "Backstage Racism," unpublished.

26 Feagin, *Racist America*, pp. 198-199.

27 Ken Bolton and Joe Feagin, *Black in Blue: Black Police Officers in White Departments* (New York: Routledge, 2004), pp. 193-194.

28 bell hooks, *Killing Rage: Ending Racism* (New York: Henry Holt, 1995), pp. -10.

29 St. Jean and Feagin, *Double Burden*, p. 158.

30 See Robert B. Hill, *The Strengths of Black Families: Twenty-Five Years Later* (New York: University Press of America, 1999).

31 "Blacks, Whites Differ on Government's Role in Civil Rights," Gallup.com, August 19, 2011, http://www.gallup.com/poll/149087/Blacks-Whites-Differ-Government-

Role-Civil-Rights.aspx (accessed June 10, 2013); Tyler Kingkade, "Students Split On Affirmative Action for College Admissions Ahead of *Fisher v. University of Texas* at Austin Supreme Court Case," *Huffington Post*, October 5, 2012, http://www.huffingtonpost.com/2012/10/05/affirmative-action-fisher-university-of-texas-at-austin_n_1942720.html (accessed June 11, 2013).

32 W. E. B. Du Bois, *Darkwater: Voices from within the Veil* (New York: Humanity Books, 2003 [1920]). The quotation is from W. E. B. Du Bois, *The Souls of Black Folk* (New York: Bantam Books, 1989 [1903]), p. 10.

33 Quoted in *Bartlett's Familiar Quotations*, 15th ed., ed. Emily M. Beck (Boston: Little, Brown, 1980), p. 556.

34 Jeremiah Wright, "Confusing God and Government," http://en.wikipedia.org/wiki/Jeremiah_Wright_controversy#cite_note-22 (accessed January 29, 2009). I draw here on Joe R. Feagin, *The White Racial Frame: Centuries of Racial Framing and Counter-Framing*, 2nd ed. (New York: Routledge, 2013), pp. 180–189.

35 Feagin, *The White Racial Frame*, pp. 181–183.

36 Jeremiah Wright, "National Press Club Address," April 28, 2008, http:// www.americanrhetoric.com/speeches/jeremiahwrightntlpressclub.htm (accessed November 7, 2008).

37 Ibid.

38 Marimba Ani, *Yurugu: An African-Centered Critique of European Cultural Thought and Behavior* (Trenton, NJ: Africa World Press, 1994), pp 567, 570. See Molefi Kete Asante, *Afrocentricity* (Trenton, NJ: Africa World Press, 1988); Maulana Karenga, *Introduction to Black Studies*, 3rd ed. (Los Angeles: University of Sankore Press, 2002).

39 Angela Davis, "Reflections on the Black Woman's Role in the Community of Slaves," *Black Scholar* 3 (December 1971): 2–15; Philomena Essed, *Understanding Everyday Racism* (Newbury Park, CA: Sage, 1991); Patricia Hill Collins, *Black Feminist Thought: Knowledge, Consciousness, and the Politics of Empowerment* (Boston: Unwin Hyman, 1990).

40 Danielle L. McGuire, *At the Dark End of the Street: Black Women, Rape, and Resistance—A New History of the Civil Rights Movement from Rosa Parks to the Rise of Black Power* (New York: Knopf Doubleday, 2010), p. 227.

41 Henry J. Richardson III, "Two Treaties, and Global Influences of the American Civil Rights Movements, through the Black International Tradition," *Virginia Journal of Social Policy and the Law* 18 (2010): 59.

42 Wright, *Black Power*, p. 769.

43 Reggie L. Williams, *Bonhoeffer's Black Jesus: Harlem Renaissance Theology and an Ethic of Resistance* (Waco, TX: Baylor University Press, 2014); Tiffany Stanley, "The Life of Dietrich Bonhoeffer: An Interview with Charles Marsh," July 30, 2014, http://religionandpolitics.org/2014/07/30/the-life-of-dietrich-bonhoeffer-an-interview-with-charles-marsh/#sthash.p0PMn10I.dpuf (accessed November 9, 2014).

44 Yukiko Koshiro, "Beyond an Alliance of Color: The African American Impact on Modern Japan: Positions-East Asia Cultures Critique," *Positions: East Asia Cultures Critique* 11 (2003): 185.

45 Marc Gallicchio, *The African American Encounter with Japan and China: Black Internationalism in Asia, 1895–1945* (Chapel Hill, NC: University of North Carolina Press, 2000), pp. 110–120.

46 Nico Slate, *Colored Cosmopolitanism* (Cambridge, MA: Harvard University Press, 2012), p. 53.

47 Sebastian C. Galbo, "The 'Roving Ambassador:' Bayard Rustin's Quaker Cosmopolitanism and the Civil Rights Movement," *Student Pulse* 6 (2014): 3.

48 "African-American Linkages with South Africa," Howard University, https://www.howard.edu/library/reference/bob_edgar_site/maintext.html (accessed November 10, 2014); Kevin Gains, *American Africans in Ghana: Black Expatriates and the Civil Rights Era* (Chapel Hill, NC: University of North Carolina Press, 2006), passim.

49 "African-American Linkages with South Africa."

50 See, "Who We Are," http://transafrica.org (accessed October 28, 2014).

51 Owens, *The Peacock Elite, A Case Study of the Congressional Black Caucus.* I draw on summaries here: http://www.amazon.com/Peacock-Elite-Study-Congressional-Caucus/dp/1935316419/ref=sr_1_4?s=books&ie=UTF8&qid=1413484544&sr=1-4&keywords=congressional+black+caucus (accessed October 16, 2014); "Origins of the CBC," A Voice Online, 2006, http://www.avoiceonline.org/cbc/timeline.html (accessed March 16, 2011).

52 Nelson Mandela, "Acceptance Speech," http://constitutioncenter.org/libertymedal/recipient_1993_speecha.html (accessed November 9, 2014); "NAACP Celebrates and Honors the Life and Work of Nelson Mandela," https://s3.amazonaws.com/naacp.3cdn.net/9092bf78c8f594f83c_dlm6iifxz.pdf (accessed November 10, 2014).

53 Ife Williams, "The Looming Quest for Global Reparations: African Americans and the World Conference against Racism," in *African Americans in Global Affairs,* ed. Michael L. Clemons (Boston: Northeastern University Press, 2010), p. 10.

54 Ron Walters, "Racial Justice in Foreign Affairs," in ibid., pp. 3–8.

55 Quoted in ibid., p. 4.

56 Quoted in Mary Edwards and Alex Heuer, "Remembering Bayard Rustin, An Unsung Civil Rights Activist," St. Louis Public Radio, June 22, 2013, http://news.stlpublicradio.org/post/remembering-bayard-rustin-unsung-civil-rights-activist (accessed November 17, 2014). I also draw here on Jean Allman, "Nuclear Imperialism and the Pan-African Struggle for Peace and Freedom: Ghana, 1959–1962," *Souls* 10 (2008), 98. See also 83–102.

57 Leigh Fought, "Douglass in Belfast," November 8, 2011, http://leighfought.blogspot.ca/2011/11/douglass-in-belfast.html (accessed November 3, 2014). I am indebted to suggestions from Kimberley Ducey.

58 Douglas Brinkley, "Martin Luther King's 'Letter from Birmingham City Jail,'" http://iipdigital.usembassy.gov/st/english/article/2005/07/20050713095810pssnikwad0.2951776.html#axzz36Es6pOgt (accessed November 21, 2014); Emily Wax "Martin Luther King Jr. Sites Across the Globe," *Washington Post,* August 23, 2011, http://www.washingtonpost.com/lifestyle/style/martin-luther-king-jr-sites-across-the-globe/2011/08/04/gIQAK4R9YJ_story.html (accessed November 7, 2014); and Emily Wax, "Martin Luther King's Nonviolent Civil Rights Efforts Still Inspire Across Globe," *Washington Post,* August 23, 2011, http://www.washingtonpost.com/lifestyle/style/martin-luther-kings-nonviolent-civil-rights-efforts-still-inspire-across-globe/2011/07/27/gIQA3Nj9YJ_story.html (accessed November 7, 2014).

59 Emily Wax, "Martin Luther King Jr. Sites across the Globe," *Washington Post,* August 23, 2011, http://www.washingtonpost.com/lifestyle/style/martin-luther-king-jr-sites-across-the-globe/2011/08/04/gIQAK4R9YJ_story.html (accessed November 7, 2014); Wax, "Martin Luther King's Nonviolent Civil Rights Efforts Still Inspire Across Globe."

60 Cornel West and Christa Buschendorf, *Black Prophetic Fire* (Boston: Beacon Press, 2014), Kindle loc. 1170–1173.

61 Sean Jacobs, "The United States of Africa," http://africasacountry.com/the-united-states-of-africa/ (accessed November 9, 2014). I am indebted in this section to reference help from Kimberley Ducey.

62 Bruce Stokes, "How the World sees Obama," CNN, July 16, 2014, http://globalpublicsquare.blogs.cnn.com/2014/07/16/how-the-world-sees-obama/ (accessed November 9, 2014). See also "Global Opinion of Barack Obama," Pew Research Center, July 18, 2013, http://www.pewglobal.org/2013/07/18/chapter-2-global-opinion-of-barack-obama/ (accessed November 9, 2014).

63 Jeffrey M. Jones, "Fewer Americans Think Obama Respected on World Stage," http://www.gallup.com/poll/167534/fewer-americans-think-obama-respected-world-stage.aspx?version=print (accessed November 9, 2014); Jeff Mason, "Obama Brings Out the African in the American," http://articles.chicagotribune.com/2013-07-02/news/sns-rt-obama-africa-pix-tv-20130702_1_barack-obama-nelson-mandela-cape-town (accessed November 10, 2014).

64 John Blake, "Why Michelle Obama Inspires Women Around the Globe," CNN, April 28, 2009, http://www.cnn.com/2009/POLITICS/04/28/first.lady/index.html?iref=24hours (accessed November 10, 2014); "Michelle Obama Hits Her Stride as First Lady," *Mail*

and Guardian, June 27, 2011, http://mg.co.za/article/2011-06-27-michelle-obama-hits-her-stride-as-first-lady (accessed December 17, 2014).

65 King, *Where Do We Go from Here*, pp. 209–210. Italics added.

66 Quoted in Charles E Cobb, Jr., *This Nonviolent Stuff'll Get You Killed: How Guns Made the Civil Rights Movement Possible* (New York: Basic Books, 2014), p. 246. Italics added.

67 Lee Mun Wah, *The Color of Fear*, DVD. (Oakland, CA: Stir-Fry Seminars & Consulting, 1994). I am indebted to suggestions by Cherise Harris. Also see Kristen Lavelle, *Whitewashing the South: White Memories of Segregation and Civil Rights* (Lanham, MD: Rowman & Littlefield, 2014).

68 West and Buschendorf, *Black Prophetic Fire*, Kindle loc. 2497–2505.

69 Derrick Bell, "Racial Realism," *Connecticut Law Review* 24 (Winter 1992), p. 379. Italics added.

Index

Acuff, Roy 63
abolitionists 95, 102, 105–6, 109–10, 130–1, 135, 140, 178; *see also* slavery system
abolitionist newspapers 102–3, 108, 111
Adams, Francis 95
Adams, Hunter 69
Adventures of Huckleberry Finn, The (novel) 57
affirmative action 143, 161, 178
Africa 167, 172, 199; migration 195
African American *see* black Americans
Afric-American Female Intelligence Society 105
African American Studies programs 88, 170, 192; black studies 170–1
African Americans *see* black Americans
African and African American agricultural contributions: black-eyed pea 72; bulldogging 74; cattle raising 74; Coca-Cola 72; coffee 72; collard greens 72; cornbread 72; cotton gin 72; deep fat frying 72; "doggies" 74; eggplants 72; fried chicken 72; gumbos 72; hibiscus 72; kola nut 72; millet 72; okra 72; paddy-rice system 73; palm oil 72; Palmolive soap 72; red zinger tea 72; rice 72; rice industry 73–4; Snapple and other soft drinks 72; sorghum 72; soul food 72; Southern cooking 72; tamarind 72; watermelon 72; Worcestershire sauce 72; yams 72
African influences: colonization 124; antipoverty programs 185; Comprehensive Anti-Apartheid Act 196; dance 53; decolonization movements 195; diaspora 196; health care programs 185; heritage 91; leadership (priest) 83–5; organizations 51; religion 83–4; social; South Africans 195; tradition 188; welfare 185
African Descendants Caucus 196
African Methodist Church 76
African Methodist Episcopal Church 138
African National Congress 195–6
Africanness 192

Africanus 96–9
Afro-American League (AAL) 117
Afrocentrism 170, 191–2
agriculture *see* African and African American agricultural contributions
Alabama 25, 159, 164
Alexander, Elizabeth 15
Alexander, Michelle 40
Ali, Muhammad, 86–7, 169, 198
Allen, Richard 12, 76, 83, 100–1, 124
American Anti-Slavery Society 84
American Committee on Africa 195
American Federation of Labor 152
American Negro Academy 107
American Revolution: 1–2, 76, 93, 102, 122; black revolution 162
Americans of color 1, 5–6, 52, 89–90, 94, 96, 117, 161, 173, 178
Ames, Jessie Daniel 156
Ani, Marimba 192
Anderson, Claud 16
Anderson, Marian 68, 194
Anderson, Osborne 131–2
Angelou, Maya 77, 195
Angola 16
antiwar movements 172
apartheid *see* South Africa
Arab Spring 198
Argentinean dissidents 198
Armstrong, Louis 154
Asante, Molefi Kete 192
Asia 172, 199; Asian 199
Association of Black Anthropologists 169
Association of Black Psychologists 169
Atlanta 156
Atlanta University 147
Augusta 24
Azalea, Iggy 67

Baker, Ella 158, 200
Baker, Josephine 78
Baldwin, James 11, 77, 154

Baltimore 24, 40
Banneker, Benjamin 69–70, 98–100, 104
Barber, John 71
Battle Hymn of the Republic 58
Baylor, Elgin 87
Beastie Boys 67
Belfast 197–8
Bell, Derrick 38, 60, 161, 201–2
Bell, Joyce 169
Bennett, Gwendolyn 78
Bernstein, Leonard 59
Bertelsmann 66
Bethune, Mary McLeod 78
Bibb, Henry 76
Birmingham, Alabama 165
blackface see minstrelsy
black American culture 51, 154, 185; cowboy
    culture 74; cultural liberation 192; cultural
    expressions 61
black American impact x, 3, 8, 11–12, 14;
    death penalty 13; endurance 12; family
    185, 188; farms 43; folk tales 80–1;
    household income 178; humanity 186,
    199; language 81–2; morality 12; scholar-
    activists 191–2, 201; survival 12; values
    12–13, 188; West African relationships 181
black American musicality: banjo 56; blues 59,
    61–2, 64; commodification 64, 67; country
    63; dance 67–8; Ethiopian songs 57; fiddle
    playing 63; freedom-fighters 105, 113,
    125, 127–8, 131, 133, 157, 197; gangsta rap
    66; gospel 60, 64; hip hop (rap) 61, 64–7;
    international 67; jazz 60–4, 154; Jazz Age
    62; opera and concert singing 68; ragtime
    61–2; record companies 64; recording
    industry 66–7; rhythm and blues (soul) 64;
    rock and roll 64; socially conscious rappers
    67; square dance calling 63; "Swing Low,
    Sweet Chariot" 58; tambourine 56
black Americans: activism 139; activists
    200; agricultural economies 24–5;
    armed resistance 163–4; Atlantic slave
    trade 16; anti-racism activists 156, 197;
    businesses 37; capital 26, 28; capitalism
    17; church 190; colleges and universities
    26; communists 146; de facto segregation
    35, 160; defense industry 39; economic
    power 21; expanding civil rights 185;
    freedom activists 151; human commodities
    24; identity 167; intellectuals 195, 199;
    internationalists 149, 193; plantation
    products 17; political-economic power
    144; political institutions 30; prisoners
    40–1; resistance 13–14, 54, 77, 167, 185,
    187, 193, 195, 197, 202; resisting nativism
    185; self-defense 144, 163–4; soldiers

and troops 21, 36, 178; spiritual 188;
    transmitted wealth 22; unemployment 165,
    178, 185; wage exploitation 34; vote 153,
    158–9, 182–4; voter registration 153, 164;
    white house 28; workers 17, 175; working-
    class 61; workplace discrimination 39, 157
black anti-slavery advocates 145
black beauty salons 186
Black Caucus of the American Library
    Association 169
black consciousness 144, 158, 163, 165, 168
black counter-frame 46–7, 50, 75, 78, 83, 95–7,
    99, 102, 107, 110, 113, 115, 118–9, 125,
    130, 134, 143, 147, 155, 161–2, 167, 185;
    anti-racist counter-framing 170, 186; anti-
    racist action 189; anti-racist efforts 196;
    agency 144, 165; anti-black stereotyping
    99, 107; anti-slavery counter-framing 106;
    black counter-framing 93, 122, 124, 129,
    131, 149, 159, 168, 171, 186, 190–1, 199;
    black feminist counter-framing 192; black-
    framed 151; black guerilla activity 132;
    "black is beautiful" 167; black beauty 186;
    black resistance framing 104, 144; boycotts
    172; collectivism 181; collective and
    communal sense of freedom and justice
    119; communal 181; full citizenship rights
    159; nonviolent resistance 121, 157–9,
    163, 165–6, 171, 195, 198; poverty 158,
    165; racial change 173; racial equality 117,
    141, 161, 168, 175, 177; sit-in movements
    171–2; sexism 158; we-consciousness 174
black exceptionalism see positive black
    exceptionalism
black feminism 60; African American feminist
    (womanist) 134, 191
black founders 93, 99–100
black inferiority 27, 36, 86, 191
black Jesus 193
black militancy 163
black nationalist (see Martin Delany) 105, 107,
    144, 147, 155, 164, 168, 172–3
black pamphleteers 95, 101–3, 108–9
Black Panthers 146, 168; Black Panther Party,
    The 166, 173–4
black power movement 144, 147, 160, 162,
    165–7, 169, 173, 180; black political-
    economic power 168; black political power
    165; black power activists 167
black pride 78, 107, 145–6, 158, 163, 165,
    167–8; racial pride 124
black prophetic tradition 201
black self-determination 107, 144–6, 164, 166,
    168, 181
black self-reliance 109, 165
Black Student Leadership Network 182

Black Swan Records 64
black Union troops 21, 136; black British troops 122–3; black Canadian troops 123
Bloody Sunday 159, 161
Boeing 41
Bogalusa, Louisiana 164–5
Bonhoeffer, Dietrich 193
Bordewich, Fergus 129
Boston 104–5, 107, 117
Boycott of segregated streetcars (*see* Truth, Sojourner) 139
Bracey, Glenn 12
Brazil 25, 199
Brotherhood of Sleeping Car Porters (*see* Randolph, A. Philip) 78, 152
Brown, Jim 87
Brown, John 109, 112, 131–3; anti-slavery Declaration of Independence and anti-slavery constitution 131
Brown, Morris 100
Brown University 26
Bruce, Blanch 139
Buckingham Palace 200
Buchanan, Patrick 89
Bumbry, Grace 68
Bunche, Ralph 78, 146
Bush, George H.W. 41, 196

Cable, George 80
California 131, 151–3
Cambridge (Maryland) 165
Campanella, Roy 87
Canada 109, 121, 130
Canandaigua (New York) 111
capitalism 22, 26, 37, 140, 151, 163; capitalistic exploitation 90; racism and capitalistic exploitation 155
Carey, Mariah 64
Caribbean 128
Carlos, John 87, 169
Carney, Judith 73
Carnegie Foundation 150
Carter, Herbert 36
Carter, Jimmy 178
Carver, George Washington 71
Caucus of Black Sociologists 169
Chamberlain, Wilt 87
Charleston (dance) 67–8
Chatham (Canada) 131
Chesnutt, Charles W. 82, 114
Chicago 40, 151–2, 160, 168
Chile 90
China 172, 198
Chittenden, Elizabeth 108
Christian *see* religion
Christy, E.P. 54

Clay, Roy 71
Clemons, Michael 197
Clinton, Bill 178, 196
Civil War 20, 30–1, 90, 93, 95, 108, 114, 127, 130, 133–4, 137–41, 144, 153
Civil Rights Act 139, 182–3; civil rights laws 164, 174, 178–9
civil rights activists 95, 144, 147, 158, 185; demonstration 157, 182; pressures 161
civil rights movement 143–6, 151, 153, 155, 157–60, 162, 171–3, 178, 195, 198
Coachmen, Alice 86–7
Coker, Daniel 102, 124
Cold War 87, 155, 161
Coleridge-Taylor, Samuel 75
Colonial Marines 123
colonialism *see* European Americans
colorblind framing *see* white racial frame
Colored National Convention 108
Coltrane, John 64, 154
Collins, Patricia Hill 52, 192
Compaq 41
Committee on Civil Rights 152
communist dictatorships 198
consciousness *see* black consciousness
Condry, Ian 67
Confederacy 20–1, 134
Confederate soldiers 135
Congo (Kongo) 16, 68, 173
Congress 29–30, 99, 155, 159, 178, 184
Congress of Racial Equality (CORE) 157, 164
Congressional Black Caucus (CBC) 169, 183–4
consumerism 174
Constitution *see* U.S. Constitution
Cooper, Anna Julia 77, 114–15
Copland, Aaron 59
Cornish, Samuel 84, 103
cotton gin *see* African and African American agricultural contributions
Covey 125
Cox, Oliver 36, 46, 150
critical race theory 148
Crummell, Alexander 107
Cuba 164, 173, 196
culture *see* black American culture
Curry, Tommy 116
Czechoslovakia 198

Davis, Angela 47, 60, 77, 192
Davis, Miles 154
Davis, Troy 12
Dean, Mark 71
Declaration of Independence 20, 98–9, 101, 104, 110, 113, 118, 123, 126, 138

Declaration of Wrongs and Rights 137
Deacons for Defense and Justice 164–5
Delany, Martin 77, 106–7, 131, 135; "father of black nationalism" 107
Democratic Party 152–3, 155, 183; Democratic convention 158; Democratic presidential administrations 175
democracy 2, 8–9, 13–14, 93–4, 100, 118, 122, 130, 134, 139–41, 149, 152, 155, 158–60, 168, 171–2, 177, 181–2, 184, 189, 191, 201
Derham, Thomas 70
desegregation 143, 145, 154, 157, 164, 166, 174–5; armed forces 152–3
Deslondes. Charles 128
Detroit 35, 39–40, 151–2, 160, 165, 168
disability rights movements 172
discrimination see racial discrimination
Dixon, Thomas 80
Doby, Larry 87
Dodson, Howard 53
"Double V" strategy 194
Douglass, Frederick 10, 15, 31–3, 46, 59, 77, 84, 103, 109–14, 125, 131, 135, 141, 189, 196–7, 199
Drew, Charles 71
drug wars 181
Dudziak, Mary 160
Durban 196
Durban Declaration and Programme of Action 196
Durham 156–7
Dumas, Alexander 75
Dvořák, Antonin 58–9
Dyson, Michael Eric 66

economy see black Americans and slavery system
Egypt 198; Egyptians (Nile River Valley) 69
Einhorn, Robin 29
Eisenhower, Dwight 153
Elliot, Missy 66
Ellis, Clarence 71
Ellison, Ralph 3, 5, 11, 50, 77, 82, 93, 143, 150
Emancipation Proclamation 112–14, 131, 133, 135, 144
Emeagwali, Philip 71
Emerson, Ralph Waldo 80
Eminem 67
environmental movements 172
environmental racism 90, 182
Esch, Elizabeth 35
Essed, Philomena 47, 192
ethnocentrism see systemic racism and the white racial frame
Europe 172, 193, 199; European 196; Eastern European 198

European Americans 150; colonialism 150, 156, 173, 195; colonialism and slavery 196; Western colonialism 155
Evans, Louwanda 179, 186
Evers, Medgar 159
Evers, Myrlie 159
exploitation see Jim Crow, labor exploitation, white oppression and obsession, and unjust impoverishment

fascism 194
Fair Employment Practices Committee 152
farm workers movements 172
Farnam, Dwight Thompson 35
Faulkner, William 80
FBI surveillance 164
Federal homestead acts 43, 46
Federal Housing Administration 143
Federalist Papers 100
Ferguson 182
Fillmore, Millard 55
Fiskhin, Shelley 82
Fitzgerald, Terence 42
Fitzhugh, George 18, 22
Florida 126, 128, 160
food see African and African American agricultural contributions
Ford motor company 35
Forten, James 100, 102
Fortune, T. Thomas 116–17
Foster, Stephen 57, 62
founding fathers 19
Fought, Leigh 197
France 25; French revolution 105
Franklin, Aretha 64
Franklin, John Hope 63
Franklin, Reverend C.L. 64
Franklin, Sekou 182
Freedmen's Bank 31–2, 44; 40 acres and a mule 31; bank panics 31; bank profits 44; U.S. Treasury Bond rates 32
Fulani 74, 81

Gabriel (enslaved blacksmith) 127
Gandhi-King Plaza 199
Gandhi, Mahatma 171–2, 195
Gardner, Ralph 71
Gardner, Newport 100
Garnet, Henry H. 105–6, 138
Garvey, Marcus 117, 146, 191, 194–5
Gay/lesbian movements 172
GDP 21
Geffert, Hannah 132
gendered racism 47, 115, 192–3
General Electric 66
genocide see United Nations

Georgia 24, 155, 159
German Nazi 36, 193
Germany 199
Gershwin, George and Ira 62
Ghana 173
GI Bill 46, 143
Gibson, Althea 87
Graham Du Bois, Shirley 195
Grant, General Ulysses S. 135
Great Britain 17, 20, 104, 115, 122–3, 127;
    United Kingdom 197
Great Depression 34
Great Migration 62, 152, 154–5; large-scale
    migration 151, 182
Great Recession 44
Greensboro 34
Greenwood, Mississippi 167
Grimké, Angelina Weld 78
Grimke, Charlotte Forten 108
Guardian, The (newspaper) 117
Guinea 16

Halls, Prince 124
Haiti 196
Haitian revolution 105, 108, 127–8
Hamer, Fannie Lou 158
Hamilton, Alexander 100
Hamilton, Charles 46, 167, 169
Hamilton, William 100
Hammon, Jupiter 75
Hancock, Gordon 64, 156
Handy, W.C. 56
Hansberry, Lorraine 168
Harlem Renaissance 63–4, 77–80, 117, 154,
    193; international ties 79
Harmony, Mississippi 202
Harper, Frances Ellen Watkins 139
Harper's Ferry (*see* Brown, John) 109, 131–3;
    antislavery fighters 131
Harris, Joel Chandler 80–2
Harris, Roy 59
Harrison, Daphne Duval 60
Harvard 26–27
hate crimes *see* white violence
Hausa 81
Hayes, Roland 68
Haynes, George 147
Haynes, Lemuel 100
Haytian nation 131
Heisenberg, Werner 3
Hemingway, Ernest 80
Henderson 165
Henson, Josiah 129
Hewlett-Packard 41
Higginbotham, Evelyn Brooks 63
Higginson, Thomas Wentworth 80

Hill, Lance 164
Hillbilly music 63
Hindu 194
Holiday, Billie 60; "Strange Fruit" (song) 60
Holloway, Joseph 67
Honeywell 41
Hong Kong 169
Hooks, Bell 188
Horne, Gerald 13
Horatio Alger 31
Horton, James Oliver and Louis E. Horton 105
Howard University 161, 195
Hughes, Langston 78
human trafficking 16
humanistic perspective 200
Hunter, Marcus 31
Hurston, Zora Neale 78

I-consciousness 174
IBM 41
ideology *see* racism
Illinois 152
imperialism 27, 61, 114, 140, 150, 160, 177,
    195–98; white cultural imperialism 191–2;
    racialized imperialism 196; sociocultural
    imperialism 192
Independence Day (fourth of July) 111
India 171, 173, 194–5, 198; Indian immigrants
    194
Indiana 174
individualism 174
institutional racial oppression 15, 125,
    148; institutional racism 47, 115, 165,
    167, 189; institutionally racist 168,
    171; institutional-racism framing 152;
    institutional sexism 115; institutionalized
    system of oppression 150; institutionally
    classist 171
Intel (company) 41
Intergenerational transfer of economic assets
    46
internal slave trade 24
interest convergence 161, 173
intersectionality 155, 192
Iran 90
Ireland 172
Irish 198
Israeli 198

Jackie Robinson Foundation 87
Jackie Robinson Story, The (film) 87
Jackson, Jessie 183
Jackson, Michael 64
Jackson (Miss) Tribune and Sun, The (racist
    newspaper) 116
Jacksonville 165

Jacobs, Harriet 110
James Crow Jr. Esquire 180, 185
Jamestown 2
Japan 67, 194; trans-pacific alliance 194;
    Hiroshima 198
Japanese Americans 90
Jay-Z 65–6
Jay, John 100
Jaynes, Gerald 32
Jazz Singer, The (film) 57
Jefferson County 133
Jefferson, Thomas 13, 20, 49, 70, 89, 98–9, 104,
    122, 124, 126; Monticello 27
Jim Crow 6, 10, 18, 28, 30, 32, 34–8, 41, 43, 46,
    72–5, 77, 82, 94, 101–2, 113–15, 131, 138,
    140–1, 143–7, 149–1, 154, 156–7, 161–2,
    170, 174, 178, 180, 183, 191; convict-
    leasing system 34; "New Charter of Race
    Relations" 156–7; oppression 175; state-
    backed oppression 34; violence 34; white
    economic exploitation 34, 115; workplace
    discrimination 38; *see also* racism and
    segregation
Jitterbug dance 67–8
Johannesburg 199
Johnson, Eddie Bernice 184
Johnson, James Weldon 58, 61, 74, 78, 194
Johnson, John "Jack" 86
Johnson, Lyndon B. 153, 159; "To Fulfill These
    Rights" (speech) 161
Jones, Absalom 76, 101
Jones, Claudia 155–6
Jonesboro, Louisiana 164
Joseph, Peniel 166
Just, Ernest 71

Kansas 160
Karcher, Carolyn 114
Karenga, Maulana 192
Kentucky Derby 86
Keil, Charles 64
Kennedy, John 153, 159, 161, 165, 182
Kern, Jerome 62
Key, Francis Scott 4, 123; *Star Spangled Banner*
    123
King, B.B. 64
King, Coretta Scott 199
King, George 126
King, Martin Luther Jr. 67, 77, 84, 158, 160,
    162–64, 172–3, 178, 194–5, 198–200;
    "Letter from Birmingham City Jail" 198;
    Martin Luther King holiday 184; "Martin
    Luther King and the Montgomery Story"
    (comic book) 198
Kornweibel, Theodore 28
Korean 196

Korean War 36
Ku Klux Klan 57, 113, 140, 163–5
Kwanzaa 192

L'Ouverture, Toussaint 108
labor 15–47, 70; auto industry 39; blue-collar
    workers 39–40; convict 40; enslaved labor
    19–30; exploitation 15, 18, 32, 34, 37,
    40–2, 45, 73; income and wealth lost 43,
    45; infrastructure 26–7; manufacturing 35;
    medical practitioners 70; pilots and flight
    attendants 179; railroads 28; sharecropping
    32; textiles 23; *see also* oppression
Ladner, Joyce 7
Lawson, James 158–9
Lee, Spike 154
legal segregation *see* Jim Crow
Levine, Lawrence 58
Lewis, Carl 86
Lewis, John 159
Lexington 165
Liberia 124
Liberty Medal 196
liberty-and-justice rhetoric 21, 93–4, 112;
    liberty-and-justice frame 94, 162; liberty-
    and-justice framing 84, 104, 177, 196;
    liberty-and-justice ideals 95, 100, 102, 108,
    130, 143, 161, 168, 178; liberty-and-justice
    language 118; liberty-and-justice reforms
    169; real liberty and justice 200
Lincoln, Abraham 21, 55, 112, 114, 131, 133,
    135–6
Lincoln, C. Eric 119
Lipkin, Joan 197
Liston, Sonny 86
literature 74–7
Locke, Alain 78
Logan, Rayford 151
Los Angeles 151–2, 165
Lott, Eric 55, 57
Louis, Joe 86
Louisiana 127, 159, 164
Lowndes County Alabama 163
Lowndes County Freedom Organization
    (LCFO) 163, 166
lynchings 90, 113, 116; anti-lynching crusade
    115–6, 144; anti-lynching society 115

MacDonald, Biona 202
Macon, Dave 63
Macklemore 67
Madison, James 10, 100; Montpelier 28
Mair, Marian 65
Malcolm X 77, 105, 146, 163–4, 167–8, 173,
    191
Mamiya, Lawrence 119

Mandinka 81
Marable, Manning 139, 159, 167, 181
Marcuse, Herbert 58, 60
Marx, Karl 25, 37; Marxist class analysis 146
Mason, Senator James 133
mass incarceration 41, 181; corporations 41;
    criminal-justice reform movements 181;
    manufactures 41; retailers 41
Massachusetts 79, 139
Massachusetts Bay Colony 1, 123
McCarthyism *see* U.S. Communist Party
McComb 165
Medals of Honor 134, 136
Medicare 172
Memphis 162
Memphis (Tenn) Daily Commercial Appeal
    (segregationist newspaper) 116
Michigan 152
Michigan State University 89
Microsoft 41
middle-class 22, 45, 77, 173, 179
Middle Eastern Americans 90, 196; Arabs 172
migrations *see* Great Migration
Milwaukee 40
minstrelsy 54–7, 63; college parties 57; films 57
Mississippi 25, 139, 158–9, 164
Mississippi Freedom Democratic Party 158
Memphis 117
Monk, Thelonious 154
Monroe, North Carolina 163
Montgomery 159
Montgomery bus boycott 157–8, 162; "forces
    of justice" 162
Montgomery's Women's Political Council
    (WPC) 158
Morris, Aldon 172
Morrison, Toni 11, 77, 79, 82, 154
Mueller, Jennifer 45–6, 180
Murray, Paul 36
music *see* black American musicality
Muslims 51, 194 (*see* African Muslims)
Myrdal, Gunnar 7, 49–50, 150; *An American
    Dilemma* 7, 49, 150

N-word 18, 55, 187
Napoleon 127
Nas 66
Nash, Diane 159
Natchez 165
Nation of Islam 167–9
National Afro-American Council (NAAC) 117
National American Women's Suffrage
    Association 145
National Association for the Advancement of
    Colored People (NAACP) 78, 115, 117,
    144–6, 148–9, 157–9, 163–4, 174, 196; "An

Appeal to the World" 148–9; lawsuits 146;
    Crisis (journal) 147
National Association of Black Social Workers
    (NABSW) 169
National Association of Colored Women
    (NACW) 145
National Black Political Agenda 174
National Black Political Convention 174
National Conference on Social Welfare 169
National Convention of Colored Men of the
    United States 137
National Council of Negro Women 174
National Equal Rights League 137
National Negro Convention 106
National Press Club 190
National Rifle Association 163
Native Americans 1, 99–100, 121–2, 126
Nazi *see* German Nazi
Negro Question 141
Nelson, Alice Dunbar 78
Nelson, Mandela 196, 198
neo-slavery 42
neoliberalism 175
New England 23, 100
New Jersey College 26
Newton, Huey P. 168
New Delhi 199
New Haven youth movement 182
New Orleans 24, 70, 79, 128
New Orleans Tribune 93
New York 23, 40, 75, 79, 84, 113, 126–7, 141,
    150, 152, 160, 162, 168, 182
New York's Cooper Institute 112
New York Abyssinian Baptist Church 193
New York Union Theological Seminary 193
Newman, Richard 100
News Corporation 66
Niagara Movement 117
Nixon, Richard 173, 178; "southern strategy"
    173–4
Nordstrom 41
Nortel 41
North (region) 27, 86, 102, 111, 124, 130, 136,
    140, 150, 152–3, 155, 157, 160, 166, 182
North Carolina 135, 137–8, 141, 155

Oakland 182
Obama, Barack 11, 15, 183, 189–90, 199–200
Obama, Michelle 154, 199–200
Oberlin College 144
Ohio 152
Oklahoma City University 89
oppression 94–5, 102, 105, 115, 118, 123–4,
    139, 143, 146, 160, 166, 177, 180, 185, 187,
    189–90; African American identity 11, 125;
    anti-black discrimination 179; anti-black

rallies 163; cognitive and emotional labor 122, 186–7; colonization 121; defamation-of-character laws 11; exploitation of black labor and resources 10; gendered oppression 192; gendered racial oppression 186; genocidal oppression 177; immoral racist foundation 191; organized resistance 121, 144; race and gender oppression 155; racial and class oppression 146, 156; racial oppression 200; racial repression 115; racial subordination 115; racialized other 10; racialized oppression 192; racialized oppression globally 190; U.S. government oppression 190; violent oppression 122; white-on-black oppression 15; white oppression and obsession 10–11, 54–5, 69, 83, 97, 103, 106, 117, 121, 125, 145, 152, 162, 165–6, 171–2, 185, 189, 193, 195, 197, 201–2; white oppressors 121; white racial oppression 99; *see also* racism

Oregon State University 89
Organization of Afro-African Unity 195
Owens, Jessie 86
Owens, Major 184

pacifist 171, 197; Christian pacifism 173
Paine, Tom 100
Palestine 173; Palestinian 198
Pan-African (movement) 107, 146–7, 150, 168; pan-African congress 150; pan-African identity 195; pan-Africanism 146, 150
Paris 79, 169
Parks, Rosa 157–8, 164
Patterson, Floyd 86
Patterson, William 149
Peace Information Center 156
Pennsylvania 70, 102
Petersburg fighting (1864) 136
Philadelphia 40, 76, 83, 101, 108, 138–9, 150, 152; black Philadelphians 123–4
Philips, John 91
Philippines 79, 196
Pickett, Bill 74; bulldogging 74
Pierce, Franklin 55
Pierre Cardin 41
Piersen, William 8, 52, 55
Pittsburgh Courier, The 87, 157
Pleasants, Mary Ellen 131
Poage, George 86
Poland 172, 198
Polk, James 55
positive black exceptionalism iii, x, 7–10, 63; African American labor 9; agents of freedom 10; anti-oppression counter-framing 9; black freedom movements 9, 61, 143–4, 154, 158, 160–3, 169–3, 183,

193; black freedom struggle 166; black liberation movements 9; deficiencies 7; elite white men 7; exaggerations 7; liberty-and-justice framing 9; negative black framing 7; pathologies 7, 50, 55, 73, 150; petitions 99, 123; slavery 10; systemic racism 7, 9–10, 94
post-racial framing 174, 180; postracial society 179, 188
Potomac 160
Presley, Elvis 57, 65
Price, Leontyne 68
Princess Anne 165
prison-industrial complex 38, 40, 42
pro-white government programs 46 (see federal homestead acts and GI Bill)
protest movements: anti-oppression revolts and liberation 13; anti-colonial movements 172; anti-colonialism movements 79, 146, 156, 161, 194; anti-imperialist 61; anti-racist 61; anti-slavery pamphlets 101–4; college protest 170; international anti-nuclear movements 197; protest movements 180; protest oppression 144, 174; violent protests 166
pseudo-science 27
Puerto Rican independence 158
Pushkin, Alexander 75

Queen's College (Cambridge, England) 107

race war 157
racial discrimination 13, 15, 40, 43, 95, 139, 141, 161, 167, 174, 178, 182, 185–9, 191–2; home loans 43–4; *see also* racism, systemic racism
racial hierarchy 27, 73, 148, 178
racist history (US) 1–3, 198; covering up 3–5; oppression 2; plantation tourist sites 29; racial oppression 2, 4, 52; racial inequalities 3, 178, 200; racialized history 4; racialized past 179, 200; slave-labor 29; systemic racism 3, 5; whitewashed history 3
racial inferiority 194; *see also* black inferiority
racial profiling 30
racial realism 60, 190, 202
racial totalitarianism 143–4, 154
racism 39, 61, 67, 79, 87, 118, 125, 140, 147, 149–50, 152–55, 162, 166, 185–6, 187–8, 189, 193, 194–5, 201–2; antiracist movement 155; global racism 196; historically white institutions 170–81, 186–7, 192; racist ideology 186; racist U.S. society 152; racist practices 160;

reverse discrimination 171; white-racist institutions 146; white-racist society 93; *see also* systemic racism
racist epithets 187
Radical Abolitionist Party 131
Rainey, Gertrude "Ma" 60
Rasmussen, Daniel 128
Randolph, A. Philip 78, 151–2
Reagan, Ronald 40–1, 196; war on drugs 40
Reconstruction 30–2, 139–41, 144, 147, 184
Red Ball Express 36
Red Tails 36
religion 83–5; Baptist 85; black ministers 84; Catholic 85; Christian 96, 108, 194; Christian morality 99; Christian religious language 103; Christianity 85, 116, 131; Christians 141; Methodist 85; Pentecostal 85; Southern values 85
reparations 28, 196, 201
Republican party 131, 153, 155
resistance *see* African American, black counter-frame, and white oppression and obsession
Revels, Hiram 139
Revlon 41
Revolutionary Action Movement 166
Rhode Island 139
Richmond armory 127
Rickey, Branch 87–8
Ring Shout 53–4, 59
Robeson, Paul 68, 78, 87, 146, 149, 155–6, 168, 172–3, 194–5
Robinson, Jackie 87–9
Robinson, Jo Ann 158
Robinson, Rachel 87–8
Rock, Dr. John 108
Rockman, Seth 24
Rodgers, Jimmie 63
Roediger, David 18, 35
Rogers, Ibram 170
Rojas, Fabio 170
Romania 198
Roosevelt, Eleanor 149
Roosevelt, Franklin 152–3; New Deal programs 153
Roosevelt, Theodore 117
Rose, Tricia 65–6
Rudolph, Wilma 87
Rush, Dr. Benjamin 70
Russwurm, John 103
Rusticus 96–97
Rustin, Bayard 146–7, 163, 171–2, 194–5, 197
Rutgers University 26

Saint-Domingue (Haiti) 127
San Francisco State University 89

Sanders, Barry 95
Savannah, Georgia 165
Schmeling, Max 86
Schouler, James 121
scientific racism 27, 49
Scott, Dred 107
Seale, Bobby 168
Second American Revolution 93, 109–10, 140
segregation 149–50, 156, 172, 192; anti-segregation activism 173; job segregation 179; racial segregation 158, 166, 173; *see also* Jim Crow
Selma 159
Senegal (*see* Fulani) 16, 74, 199
Sewall, Judge Samuel 79
sexual violence 193; *see also* white violence
Shadd, Mary Ann 108, 129; *A Plea for Emigration* 109
Sierra Leone 16
Silicon Valley 71
Singh, Nikhil 173
Slate, Nico 194
slaveholders 19–22, 24, 26, 54, 70, 102, 104, 121, 125–7, 130, 133–5
slave labor system 21–2
slavery system 14, 24–5, 29–30, 37, 76–7, 94, 102, 110, 124–5, 129, 131, 133, 140, 177–8, 180, 192; banks 23; capitalism 25–6; chattel slavery 148; economy 151; escape 130; economic prosperity 25; fleeing enslavement 122, 126, 134; fugitive slave law 101, 123, 130, 133; general strike 133; industrial revolution 25; labor 29; northern manufacturing 23; plantations 129, 132; private property 30, 130; rebellions and revolts (insurrections) 124, 126–8, 130, 132; slave patrols 24, 30; spirituals 54, 58–9, 62; sugar plantations 128; U.S. companies 23
Smith, Adam 15
Smith, Bessie 56, 60, 154
Smith, Earl 89
Smith, Tommie 87, 169
Smith, Wendell 87
social justice 177, 182, 190–1, 197, 201; social injustice 190
social networks 144
societal transformation 201
sorrow songs 54, 57–8
Soul Man (film) 57
South Africa 90, 172–3, 196, 198; apartheid 158, 195–6, 198; Free South Africa Movement 181–2
South Carolina 68, 84, 126, 130, 160; Third South Carolina regiment 135
Southampton 112, 128

Southeast Asia 198
Soviet Union 155, 160
Spain 25; Spanish 126, 128
Spencer, Peter 100
Springsteen, Bruce 67
sports 85–6; black athletes 86, 169, 182;
    black jockeys 86; college rebellions 89;
    desegregation 86, 88; integration 88; Negro
    professional sport leagues 86, 88
St. Augustine 165
Stanton, Edwin (Secretary of War) 136
Starkey, Mary Ann 137–8
State Department 150
stereotypes see white racial frame (stereotypes)
Stewart, Jeffrey 70
Stewart, Maria 105
Still, William Grant 69
Stokely, Carmichael see Ture, Kwame
Stono Rebellion 126
student movements 172
Student Nonviolent Coordinating Committee
    (SNCC) 157–8, 163–4
South (region) 18, 20, 22, 24, 27, 34, 36, 62,
    72, 85, 104, 116, 130, 133, 136, 139–40,
    152, 154–5, 157, 160, 163, 165, 182, 185;
    secessionists 130, 151
Southern Christian Leadership Conference
    (SCLC) 157–8
Southern Regional Council 157; biracial
    collaboration 157
Stowe, Harriet Beecher 80
Stuckey, Sterling 54, 59, 81
Sudan 74
Sugrue, Thomas 39, 160
Syracuse 137; Syracuse University 89
systemic racism 3, 5–7, 9–10, 26, 38, 46, 76,
    90, 95–96, 102, 119, 147–8, 160, 163,
    171, 179–80, 189, 191–2, 200–1; anti-
    oppression counter-frames 5, 94, 101, 103;
    anti-others sub-frames 5; black counter
    frame 5–6; collective memory 6, 171;
    collective forgetting 6; home-culture frame
    5, 83, 94–5, 119, 125, 185–6; physical
    and psychological costs 45; pro-white 5;
    racial subordination 96; systemic racial
    oppression 26, 94; systemic white racism
    5–6; white racial frame 5–6; white virtue
    55, 63, 99, 140; see also racism, white racial
    frame

Target 41
Taylor, John 86
technology: inventors 70–1, 79; scientific and
    technical knowledge 69
Temple University 192
Tennessee 115

Terrell, Mary Church 144–5, 147
Texas 160
Texas Instruments 41
Tharpe, Sister Rosetta 60
Time/Warner (company) 66
Tourgée, Albion 80, 114, 141
Trading Places (film) 57
TransAfrica 195–6
Tropic Thunder (film) 57
Trotter, William Monroe 117
Truth, Sojourner 84, 139, 197
Truman, Harry 152–3, 155, 182
Tubman, Harriet 84, 129, 181, 197, 199
Tuskegee Airmen 36
Tulsa 37
Turner, Nat 84, 104, 112, 128–9
Ture, Kwame 46, 77, 163, 166–7, 195
Twain, Mark 55, 80
Tyler, John 55

U.S. Communist Party 146–7, 155–6; anti-
    communist faction 156; anti-communist
    repression 155, 160; interracial coalitions
    147; McCarthyist (-ism) 160, 172
U.S. Constitution 30, 94, 99–100, 113, 118,
    139–40, 178; first amendment 155
U.S. Constitutional Convention (1787) 96
U.S. Council on African Affairs 195
U.S. House of Representatives 138
U.S. national anthem 169
U.S. racism see also racism and systemic
    racism
U.S. Supreme Court 29, 107, 178, 180;
    appointments 174; Brown v. Board (1954)
    161; Dred Scott v. Sandford (1857) 29, 107;
    Plessy v. Ferguson (1896) 114
U2 (music band) 67
Umoja, Akinyele 51, 164
Uncle Tom's Cabin (novel) 57
underground railroad 84, 129–30; conductors
    129
UNICOR 42
Union 134, 139; Union army and navy
    134–5; volunteer African American Union
    soldiers 135
Unionization efforts 172, 175
United Nations 147–9; UN General Assembly
    149; UN Genocide Convention 149
Universal Negro Improvement Association
    (UNIA) 146
University of Alabama 26
University of Arizona 89
University of California, Berkeley 89
University of Kansas 89
University of North Carolina 26
University of South Carolina 26

University of Texas at El Paso 89
University of Virginia 26
University of Washington 89
University of Wyoming 89
unjust enrichment 43–4, 103, 107, 115, 118, 148, 180; social inheritance 45
unjust impoverishment 29, 44, 103, 148, 180; racial exploitation 45, 93
urban uprising 165–6 *see also* protest movements and white violence
Utamaru 67

Verrett, Shirley 68
Vesey, Denmark 84
Viacom 66
Victoria's Secret (company) 41
Vietnam 173; Vietnamese 196
Vietnam War 36–7, 158, 163, 169
Virginia 20, 84, 104, 109, 112, 126–7, 131–3, 155, 158
Voting Rights Act 159–60, 183

Wah, Lee Mun 201; *Color of Fear, The* (film) 201
Walker, Alice 82
Walker, David 77, 103–5, 107, 110; *Appeal to the Coloured Citizens of the World* 103, 106
Walker, Madam C.J. 186
Wall Street 23
Walters, Ron 197
War of 1812 122–3
Warfield, William 68
Washington, Booker T. 146, 194–5
Washington, DC 28, 33, 107, 113, 139, 152, 165, 198
Washington DC United Women's Club 145
Washington, Denzel 154
Washington, George 19–20, 122, 127; Mount Vernon 28;
Washington, John 136
Watermelon Man (film) 57
Waters, Ethel 56
Watkins, Mel 81
Watt, James 25
W.E.B. Du Bois 9, 14, 18, 26, 51, 58, 72, 77–80, 83, 93, 105, 114, 117, 134, 140, 146–50, 155–6, 162, 172–3, 189, 191, 194–5, 199; *Darkwater* 189; double consciousness 148; *Souls of Black Folk, The* 83; *Philadelphia Negro, The* 147; U.S. sociology founder 147
"We Charge Genocide: The Crime of Government Against the Negro People" (petition) 149
Weaver, Robert 78
welfare handouts 143; social welfare programs 178

Wells-Barnett, Ida B. 34, 46, 77, 114–7, 144, 147, 193; *Red Record, The* (pamphlet) 115
West, Cornel 53, 61, 163, 167, 199, 201
West Indies 112
Westminster Abbey 198
Westmoreland County 126
Wheatley, Phillis 75, 100
white anti-slavery activists 102
white backlash 157, 171, 174, 178
white elite 22, 100, 161, 177–8
white exploitation 33
white identity 148
white oppression and obsession *see* oppression
white plantation owners 19
white paternalism 140
white privilege 148
white prejudice 150, 167
white racial frame 17, 27, 35, 42, 63, 94, 97, 99, 103, 118, 162, 191; anti-racist counter-frame 78, 95; anti-racist counter-framing 191; anti-racist frame 185; antiracist 109, 118, 162; antiracist framing 106, 191; colorblind framing 171, 189; counter-frame 99, 105; counter-framing 98, 130, 152, 177, 189; capitalistic management 35; meritocratic 180; racially framed 136; racist framing 49–50, 55, 80, 86, 121, 192; stereotypes 56, 72, 74, 97, 101, 103, 105, 121–2; sub-frame 95; white denial 62-3; white frame 104, 107, 117–8, 121; white framing 88, 129, 153, 170; white racial frame of oppression 134; white racial framing 96, 177, 188; white racist framing 55, 57, 67, 73, 89, 99, 110, 122, 128, 140, 156, 194; white virtuousness 63, 98–9, 103, 118, 201; *see also* systemic racism
white racism *see* oppression, racism, systemic racism
white racist images 33, 56; white imaginary 57; Aunt Jemima 72; savages 89; white-racist perspectives 80; white racist behaviors 187; Uncle Ben 74; *see also* white racial frame stereotypes
white "saviors" 89
white slavemasters 18, 19, 22, 24, 128, 132
white supremacist 50, 52, 89, 140, 159, 164–5; global white dominance 197; global white-supremacist order 150; white-racist supremacy 194; *see also* systemic racism
white violence 37, 113, 115, 117, 121, 125–6, 143–4, 148, 159, 161, 163, 168, 182; police brutality 30, 65–66, 143, 159, 164–5, 174, 182; rioters 37; terrorism 140, 164–5
White, Walter 78
whiteness studies 189
Wiggins, David 88

Wilder, Craig 27
Whitman, Walt 80
Wilder, Craig 181
Wilkerson, Isabel 153
Williams College 26
Williams, Robert 163–5; *Negroes with Guns* 164
William and Mary 26
Wilmington (North Carolina) 37
Wilson, Woodrow 117
Windburn, Anna Mae 154
Wingfield, Adia 186
Winthrop, John 1
Wonder, Stevie 64
Wood, Gordon 93

Woodson, Carter 96; *Mind of the Negro, The* 96
World Conference against Racism, Racial Discrimination, Xenophobia and Related Intolerance 196
World War II 36, 62, 71, 90, 143, 151–2, 155–6, 160, 194
Wright, Dr. Jeremiah 189–90
Wright, Richard 77–8, 146, 155, 177, 193–4
Wright, R.R. Jr. 147

Yale 26–7

Zatz, Noah 42
Zirin, Dave 88